THE FLYING NORTH

Alaska has some of the crookedest rivers in the world. It took time, but the best of the pilots eventually learned to use them. "Two streams, when you get the know 'em, don't look no more alike than two people." They learned to follow these baffling courses even in winter, when they were blanketed with white, by following the line of timber along the shore. It was difficult, in winter, to tell a river's direction; twists and turns were so frequent that a compass was useless. The flyers learned to judge by fallen trees—"The tops always lay downstream."

THE AVIATOR'S BOOKSHELF
THE CLASSICS OF FLYING

The books that aviators, test pilots, and astronauts feel tell the most about the skills that launched mankind on the adventure of flight. These books bridge man's amazing progress, from the Wright brothers to the first moonwalk.

THE WRIGHT BROTHERS *by Fred C. Kelly*
(23962-7 * $2.95)
Their inventive genius was enhanced by their ability to learn how to fly their machines.

THE FLYING NORTH *by Jean Potter (23946-5 * $2.95)*
The Alaskan bush pilots flew in impossible weather, frequently landing on sandbars or improvised landing strips, flying the early planes in a largely uninhabited and unexplored land.

THE SKY BEYOND *by Sir Gordon Taylor (23949-X * $2.95)*
Transcontinental flight required new machines piloted by skilled navigators who could pinpoint tiny islands in the vast Pacific— before there were radio beacons and directional flying aids.

THE WORLD ALOFT *by Guy Murchie (23947-3 * $2.95)*
The book recognized as *The Sea Round Us* for the vaster domain—the Air. Mr. Murchie, a flyer, draws from history, mythology, and many sciences. The sky is an ocean, filled with currents and wildlife of its own. A tribute to, and a celebration of, the flyers' environment.

CARRYING THE FIRE *by Michael Collins (23948-1 * $3.50)*
"The best written book yet by any of the astronauts."—*Time Magazine*. Collins, the Gemini 10 and Apollo 11 astronaut, gives us a picture of the joys of flight and the close-in details of the first manned moon landing.

THE LONELY SKY *by William Bridgeman and*
*Jacqueline Hazard (23950-3 * $3.50)*
The test pilot who flew the fastest and the highest. The excitement of going where no one has ever flown before by a pilot whose careful study and preparation was matched by his courage.

Read all of the books in THE AVIATOR'S BOOKSHELF, available wherever Bantam Books are sold, or order directly from Bantam by including $1.25 per order for postage and handling and sending a check or money order to Bantam Books, Inc., Dept. WW3, 414 East Golf Road, Des Plaines, IL 60016. Allow four to six weeks for delivery. This offer expires 3/84.

THE FLYING
NORTH

JEAN POTTER

BANTAM BOOKS
Toronto • New York • London • Sydney

THE FLYING NORTH

A Bantam Book / published by arrangement with
Comstock Editions, Inc.

PRINTING HISTORY
Comstock edition published December 1972
3 printings through March 1977

Bantam edition / November 1983

ABOUT THE COVER ARTIST

ROBERT BROWN has been freelancing as an illustrator for ten years. Most of his work has been for paperbound book covers. Bob is a pilot interested in ultralight aircraft. He has researched backgrounds for a series of paintings of remarkable aviation historical events. He lives in North Babylon, New York.

ISBN 0-553-23946-5

Published simultaneously in the United States
and Canada

PRINTED IN THE UNITED STATES OF AMERICA

H   0 9 8 7 6 5 4 3 2 1

TO
DASHIELL HAMMETT

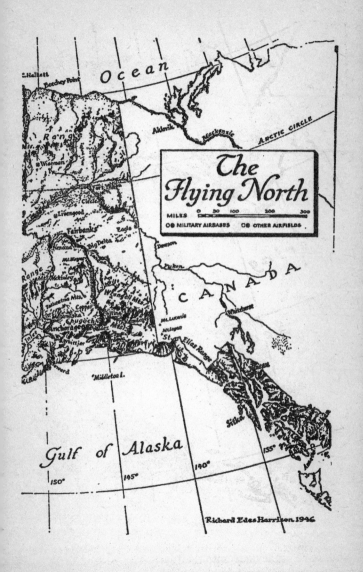

The Flying North

MILES 0 30 100 200 300
○● MILITARY AIRBASES ○● OTHER AIRFIELDS

Richard Edes Harrison 1946

Contents

FORTY YEARS LATER

Preface to the 1983 Edition

This book is based on intensive interviews that I conducted nearly forty years ago with leading pioneer pilots of Alaska, who also read the text for accuracy; in large part, it is their own story. Some of these pilots also helped me prepare the biographies of two fellow pioneers who were no longer alive. Four of the nine pilots to whom I devoted chapters were still flying actively in the mid-1940s, so the book was written partly in the present tense. Today eight of the nine pilots are dead and the survivor (Sig Wien) has stopped flying. I am sobered to realize that the book is now a piece of American history: a unique authentic account of the early development of aviation on our northern last frontier where "trailblazing" to an extraordinary degree was accomplished in the air.

Time, in fact, has made a treasure of these pilots' recollections. Their dream of Alaska's future importance in an air age has since been realized so dramatically that their prophetic words and perilous flights seem even more worth reporting than when this book was written. Expansion of flight within and through Alaska has been tremendous. Today, to quote an airline executive in California, traffic at the vast, modern airport at Anchorage (pop. 173,000) "makes major U.S. airport cities with many times that population look like Podunk." In the past two decades alone, passengers handled at the Anchorage International Airport have increased tenfold to an annual three million, one third of these transiting on major domestic and foreign carriers including Scandinavian Airlines, Varig-Brazilian Airlines, Japan Air Lines, and Air France to name only a few.

I am thankful to have interviewed the pioneer pilots while it was still possible. The late celebrated author, Dashiell Hammett, who was not one to use an exaggerated word, once called the record of early aviation in Alaska "breathtaking." It is a record of awesome courage in humane service, of the most arduous progress, of which Americans everywhere may be proud. I will be glad if it inspires some of my countrymen in pioneer work today, in our era of spectacular technological advance during which real progress—in serving the basic needs of humanity including its need for survival—has fallen distressingly short. This would seem to be the frontier of the future.

JEAN POTTER CHELNOV

Rome
March 1983

Preface

This is a book about the bush pilots of Alaska.

Alaskans are the flyingest people under the American flag and probably the flyingest people in the world. Only certain northerly sections of Canada and the Soviet Union may rival Alaska's aviation record. By 1939 the small airlines of the Territory were hauling twenty-three times as many passengers and a thousand times as much freight, per capita, as the airlines of the United States. The federal government and large corporations had little to do with this. The story of how it happened and what the pilots have meant to the people and what the people have meant to the pilots is one that no statistics can tell. It is a great saga of pioneer history.

I have spent a year and a half in Alaska to learn this history, flying and talking with the men who lived it. Since much of the action described borders on the fantastic, the manuscript was prepared on the scene and checked for authenticity, wherever possible, with those involved. Old documents and newspapers were also used to verify facts, but this account of Alaskan flight is based chiefly on human sources.

Space, and in some cases the impossibility of gathering enough material, has prevented my telling the stories of all the Far North's pioneer pilots. I regret that some who have contributed much are barely mentioned. Of the nine airmen chosen for fullest treatment in this book, three have crashed to death; four of the six who live are still flying. Some of these nine men have flown Alaska daringly. Some have flown it cautiously. Some have flown it skillfully. Some have flown it awkwardly. All are outstanding; and they have been selected because each represents a different facet of the democratic, energetic, curious, ingenious, fearless spirit of the frontier.

During World War II Alaskan aviation changed almost beyond recognition. The Territory became a thundering international skyway. There was the "Red Star line"; more than 7,000 Lend-Lease bombers and fighters were ferried along the top-of-the-world route from the United States to the Soviet Union. Day after day Soviet formations took off from Nome for Siberia and Europe. There was the "White Star line"; day after day bombers of our own Air Forces left bases at the tip of the Aleutian Islands to raid Japan. In support of these military operations the Army and the Civil Aeronautics Administration built a vast system of airports and airways which is nearly as complete as that of the States. Instrument navigation along these airways is now routine and as this book goes to press Northwest Airlines is preparing to operate a regular schedule from the States through Alaska to Asia. The flight frontier in the old sense is gone.

But the work of the bush pilot continues and may be expected to continue a long time in this huge land of small, scattered population. Few of the Far North's settlements are reached by the new airways, and even today the flyer who would serve trapper's shack and mine camp must navigate much of the time "by the seat of his pants," land and take off from crude homemade fields. Operators from the States may speed to and through Alaska, but most of the air traffic in this flyingest land is still handled by local companies, much of it bush-style.

Many pilots generously cooperated to make this book possible. I am much indebted to them for the time they spent and for their loan of pictures, in some cases the only existing copies, to illustrate the work. I am especially grateful to Pilots Noel Wien and Joe Crosson, survivors of the early period of Alaskan flight, who painstakingly told me not only their own stories but also those of fellow pioneers who are dead. I am also much indebted to many mechanics, who remembered things the pilots modestly forgot, and to other Alaskans—passengers and founders of the air services—too numerous to mention by name.

I owe thanks to the Army in Alaska, particularly to the late Lieutenant General Simon Bolivar Buckner, Jr., a great admirer of the bush pilots, who gave me permission to go to

Alaska and travel there during a period of wartime restriction; also, for kind assistance, to Brigadier General Dale V. Gaffney; and to many officers and enlisted men in their commands. I also owe thanks to the Civil Aeronautics Administration in Alaska, to Marshall Hoppin, former Regional Manager, and Walter Plett, present Regional Manager; and particularly to Jack Jefford, Patrol Pilot.

I thank Dr. Charles E. Bunnell, president of the University of Alaska, for making it possible for me to live at his college while writing the book; Miriam Dickey, who first suggested to me that this book be written, for warm hospitality and many favors; the late Charles Brower, Barrow's oldest white resident, for loan of his diary and for interviews on aviation events at America's farthest-north town; Sir Hubert Wilkins, for interviews and for permission to quote from his book *Flying The Arctic* (G. P. Putnam's Sons, New York, 1928); Explorer Vilhjalmur Stefansson for interviews and reading of sections dealing with historic flights above the Arctic Circle; and E. L. Bartlett, Alaska's Delegate in Congress, John Groves of the Air Transport Association, Mary Grace and Alice Weigel for overall reading and suggestion.

Most of all I thank Dashiell Hammett, who served with the armed forces in Alaska, for sharp edition and for his confidence in the concept of this book.

JEAN POTTER

New York City
    July, 1946

1
The Dogs Look Up

THE SUN hung low at noontime and the snow glimmered in a twilight haze. It was February 12, 1924—a short white day in the Far North. Through the Kuskokwim—country shaggy with scrub spruce, rough with drifts and hummocks, slick with frozen lakes and rivers—Fred Milligan was slowly traveling with his dogs. He was the only man on the trail. Since pushing off from the settlement of Telida five hours before, he had not seen a sign of human life.

The harnessed team ran steadily. Mile after mile the snow was cut with twisting tracks. Mile after mile the silence of the winter wilderness was broken by the panting of animals, the crunching and creaking of sleds and Milligan's gruff cries of "gee" and "haw." It was cold that day; vapor rose like smoke from overflowed ponds, and the dogs' breath steamed thick. Balanced on his sled behind the team, Milligan was wrapped in furs with only his eyes and nose showing.

For twenty years Fred Milligan had traveled this way in winter, carrying the United States mail to little towns like Diamond and Roosevelt and Ophir and Iditarod and Flat. He was proud in his trade. He had worked this route so long he could read every rise, every drop, every curve along the way. His eyes were sharp for holes and drifts. Crossing ponds and creeks, he knew how to sound the ice with an axe, to skirt the yellow spots or wisps of steam that warned of overflow. He knew how to load his sleds so they balanced easily. He knew how to take care of himself and his dogs. He teamed them carefully so they would not fight. He spoke to them sometimes roughly, sometimes gently. "If you're kind you can keep 'em going no matter how tired they are." He made them canvas moccasins—"To a dog with sore feet a fresh fall of snow will feel like cut glass." He fed each animal two pounds of dried salmon and a half pound of tallow a day.

It was not an easy trade. Often, breaking trail after blizzards, Milligan had to walk before his team, stomping and beating the way, lifting his snowshoes waist-high in killing labor. There were sudden storms to buck; once, when his outfit was caught in a 60-mile gale, the sleds overturned, the struggling dogs frosted their lungs and one animal froze to death in his harness. There was always peril of thin ice. Many were the drivers who had plunged to the bottom of deep lakes with nothing to mark their tombs but ragged holes. More than once Milligan's sled had started to break through and he and his team had escaped "only by the leader's hair."

But Milligan was not a man who gave thought to disaster. This February day, as he journeyed along, his mind was empty as the land and sky. Slowly, tediously, the outfit made its way. Now and then a dog lost his footing. The rest dragged back. The sled lurched and swayed. In a voice that they knew and understood, Milligan urged the animals on. They had put many miles behind them, but they still had a long, long way to go.

It happened suddenly. All together the dogs turned their heads and looked back. Milligan turned too: perhaps they had had a scent of game. He saw nothing. He shouted impatiently, but now the dogs stopped short and sat stock-still in their tracks, their turned heads all pointing upward. Milligan's eyes followed theirs and he saw it—miles away, hanging in the dimness—a flying machine.

Now he too could hear the sound of the engine. It grew steadily louder, and a strange wooden contraption, with narrow body and thin wings, came roaring toward him along the trail. Milligan is excited even today when he tells about it. "It flew right over us!" he exclaims. "The pilot leaned out and waved at me with his long black bearskin mittens! He couldn't have been much higher than the treetops!"

For a moment the frightened dogs cowered on their haunches. Then they scrambled up and started after the plane—so fast it was all Milligan could do to hold them. "They'll chase anything."

In a few seconds the plane looked like nothing but a big bird, hovering aimlessly. Then, swift as it had come, it was gone.

Milligan knew who it was, all right. Ben Eielson, the fellow who persuaded the government to send him a plane so he could fly the mail. This was his first trip. He was planning to follow the dog trail all the way from Nenana to McGrath. It took twenty days to make the run by dog team. Eielson was aiming to fly it in a few hours.

The dogs trotted slower and slackened down to their usual pace. The plane had meant less to them than a sudden sight of caribou. But Milligan was full of wonder. In winter this country could play a man's eyes strange tricks. Sometimes, gazing at the huge white mass of Mt. McKinley, a hundred miles away, you would swear you could reach out your hand and touch it. Or, looking through the shimmering miles, you would see the roofs and steeple of a town that was not there. If he had not known about Eielson and heard that engine, "louder than a Ford car," he would almost believe he had seen a mirage.

On and on the dog team continued its rough, winding way. The sun sank, and by mid-afternoon a deep dusk fell over the land. The cold bit more sharply into Milligan's lungs. He urged his dogs more often. They were all tired and hungry. It was still another hour to the warm bunks and barns of the East Fork Roadhouse.

Then he heard it again, coming from the other direction— the noise of that engine, swelling into a roar and fading into silence. This time the plane was flying some distance off the trail. Peering into the gloom, Milligan could see nothing. But Ben Eielson was out there "whistling like a spirit through the sky." He must have made it all the way to McGrath—and now, the same day, he was heading home.

"I decided then and there," Milligan says, "that Alaska was no country for dogs."

Other dog-drivers were not so sure. All up and down the trails, huddled around roadhouse stoves, they talked about "The Aviation." Some raised their voices loud and swore and spat. It was just a stunt. You could never depend on a rig like that. Okay, he did it once, but that don't mean he can do it again. The engine will quit. He'll get lost. He'll run into bad air. What will he do when it snows? He'll smash in the brush. And who is going to go out and find him? The people will never get their mail. And what will happen to the roadhouses? and the drivers? and the natives who sell the dog feed? and the dogs?

But as time passed more planes and pilots came to Alaska, and Al Monsen, one of the men who helped pioneer the McGrath air mail route, asked Milligan if he would go along on a trip as guide. Milligan stared curiously at Monsen's "machine," which stood in the snow on skis. Someone told him it was a Fairchild 71. It was bigger than Eielson's, but it looked pretty flimsy, lashed down with rope so it wouldn't blow away. There was a tarp over the engine and a fire pot was burning underneath. After Milligan had inspected everything, he got busy loading the mail, piling it all in back as he would on his sled.

The fur-bundled pilot came down the hill, lugging a can of warm oil. Opening the door of the plane, he began to swear.

"Who loaded this?" he shouted. "You can't fly a ship this way. The mail has to go up front."

Milligan pulled out the sacks and reloaded them. He watched Monsen spread a map on the snow, pull a protractor from his pocket and lay out a course for McGrath. He helped haul off the fire pot, pour in the oil and scrape frost from the wings. Then he climbed inside with the pilot.

"I set on the mail sacks. I begun to get excited when he slammed the door. He started the engine. It made an awful racket, but the take-off was swell. We got up there to 2,000, and he poked me and grabbed hold of the stick and then let go. The ship began to rise. He yelled, "See why you can't load this thing tail-heavy?' I showed him the trail and we flew it, and after twenty minutes we saw Knight's roadhouse. That used to take me a good nine hours.

"I saw the mileposts sliding under me. We landed and took off in the snow. In three hours we made all the places I used to make in twenty days. That's what made a hit with me. When we got back I told him, 'It's too late to get rid of me now. I'm staying. I'm in the aviation business.' "

Milligan, today an airport traffic manager for Pan American World Airways, has been in the aviation business ever since.

It was a natural for Alaska—The Aviation.

Vast, untamed country separated the small inland settlements. There was no way but a slow way to move between them. In summer stern-wheeled steamers, launches and poling boats floated along the rivers, but after the fall freeze-up each town holed in for a long, stark winter alone. Only by tramping and sliding along the dog trails could men move overland with mail and freight, struggling against difficulties which the seasoned sourdough "might laugh at but certainly could not laugh away."

In all Alaska, mammoth sprawl of land more than twice the size of Texas, there was only one railroad of any length. Reaching 470 miles from the port of Seward to the Interior town of Fairbanks, it was so rough over frost-heaved ground that the locomotive regularly jumped the track. In winter the route, through twisting mountain passes, was often shut by snowslides.

In all Alaska there was only one long road, the Richardson Highway. Narrow, crooked pioneer course, it also reached inland to Fairbanks—from the port of Valdez. In summer Fords and Dodges jounced the 360 miles, with good luck, in three days. In winter the way was blocked by deep drifts; the road was closed.

"We are provincials," an Alaskan wrote. "But a new trail is to be broken across the unfurrowed prairie of the northern sky."

It was a natural for Alaska—The Aviation.

2
Flyingest People

TODAY YOU stand at Merrill Field,* just outside Anchorage, Alaska's largest town, and find it hard to believe your ears and eyes. Merrill is still a frontier airport. The modern control tower looks out of place in a row of wooden hangers and tumbledown shacks. But the runway is one of the busiest in America. Parked along the edge is a row of small, bright-painted planes, and all up and down the line pilots are loading freight, passengers are climbing aboard, engines are growling. In swift, noisy parade the ships are pulling out, taxying, turning, and roaring skyward.

In one month of 1945 Merrill Field had 10,000 landings and take-offs—more civilian operations than LaGuardia Field, New York.

You walk along the runway and stop beside a red plane with an open radial motor and narrow, tapening fuselage. The pilot, wearing duck pants and brown leather jacket, is loading a pile of wire cable and groceries into the cabin. "Okay," he is telling his mechanic, "you can slide that over there on top and my passenger can set right here."

"What kind of a ship is that?" you ask.

"A damn good one," the pilot tells you. "Fairchild. Built in 1930."

"How about the engine?"

* Named in honor of Russel Merrill, gallant ex-Navy pilot who arrived in Alaska in 1925 and later pioneered air service out of Anchorage. Merrill left Anchorage on the afternoon of September 16, 1929, in a Whirlwind Travel Air, hauling an urgently needed compressor for a gold mine, and failed to reach his destination. His wreck was never found, but a piece of fabric, washed ashore on Cook Inlet, was identified by mechanics who had worked on his ship.

"Wasp. Best engine made. I flew with that engine in '29."

It is with aircraft like this that Alaska's pilots have made their extraordinary record. They have had no choice: on the crude, short fields of the hinterland low speed has been essential above all else. There are a few large modern ships at Merrill Field, and more are on order, but most of the transports even today are small and of ancient vintage. Boxy Ford Tri-motors, stubby Stinson-A's and a battered Orion, used long ago and discarded by airlines in the States. Pilgrims, Vegas, and a flock of Gullwing Stinsons. Some of these planes have been wrecked and patched, wrecked and patched, many times. "Spare parts flying in formation," one pilot has said of his Bellanca. Another, looking out at a wing during flight, cheerfully remarked: "I hope those goddamn termites keep holding hands."

Merrill Field is one of the busiest, shabbiest airports in America—and one of the most intimate. You watch a green Stinson rush past.

"What airline is that?" you ask.

"Airline?" replies an Alaskan, rather vacantly. "That's Oscar."

"Who is Oscar?"

The Alaskan gives you a curious stare.

"You from Outside?"* he asks. "Everybody knows Oscar."

The Oscar Winchell Flying Service, better known as Oscar, is a fellow with a peaked face, wispy hair and a lazy western drawl. He once worked as a cow hand in Arizona. Arriving in Alaska in 1931, he started operating out of Anchorage in a single-engine Stinson, 211-W. He is using the same ship today.

"You know," he says, "there's lucky and unlucky planes. Old 211-W was one of eight Stinsons that come to Alaska around the same time. She's had her crack-ups, but she's still flyin'. All the rest are smashed up and gone."

Oscar flies from Merrill Field to the scattered settlements of the Kuskokwim region. He gives personal service and he'll

---

* The term "Outside" is commonly used in Alaska to refer to the States.

handle any kind of an order, large or small. "Hairpins and diapers and things like that," he confides, "for good will they can't be beat." He keeps his records in a grocer's order book. That and his logbook are all he has.

"Nothin' to it," he brags. "My God, them big airlines with all them bookeepers and credits, and memos and doublin' up—and then they bill you wrong."

The Christensen Air Service, better known as Chris, is a jolly, ruddy-cheeked man who bases three Wacos at Merrill Field and flies like a carrier pigeon to meet the boats at Seward.

With Chris it's only an hour and ten minutes to Seward; the railroad train, chugging through steep-glaciered mountains, takes at least half a day. Chris likes to look down on the crooked track as his Waco moves swift and high. He laughs. "You know," he says, "that's a famous railroad. It's even mentioned in the Bible. Couldn't tell you where, but somewhere in the Bible it says: 'There shall be things creeping and crawling all over this earth.'"

Chris's route lies over some of the finest game country in the world. Often he'll cruise out of his way to show passengers a bear or a mountain sheep. He'll swoop down on the bears, "make 'em kick up a few blueberries," but he's careful of the sheep.

"I want 'em to show," he says. "I don't scare 'em. I've got 'em so they know me. They won't run away."

Chris works hard—sometimes he'll make five round trips to Seward in one day—but in his spare time he likes to stunt. He'll skim glassy water on skis. Once he landed at a muddy field on floats and taxied all the way down the runway to the hangar.

"Why not have a little fun?" he asks. "You can't take flying too serious."

The rough-clad bush pilots are personages. Everybody knows them. Everybody calls them by their first names. They are the most popular men in all Alaska, and the most distinguished. The people could not get along without them. They haul in their small battered craft everything for Arctic and sub-Arctic life and industry.

You can see what the airplane means in the North each

summer when the sun rises high again and the ice crashes down the big rivers and the salmon-fishing season begins. At straggling seaside villages like Dillingham and Nugashik and Agashik float planes circle over the water and slosh down by the wooden canneries till it seems they're thick as the sea gulls. Pilots wear rubber boots and often carry fishermen and cannery workers piggyback over the mud to shore.

The planes fly day and night hauling the workers over and later, when the season limit is called; they'll fly day and night hauling them away. Then the tides are lower; passengers wade through muck and dead fish-heads up to their knees—everybody in the crowd wants a plane at once, they'll hail the ships like taxis, drop luggage if it's too heavy and fight their way aboard. The sober men make it first, and then come the drunks. A pilot has to watch their cigarettes. They're in the money now, wanting to celebrate, all in a hurry to get back to town.

You can see it every June at a northerly winterlocked town like Nome, when the ice pack drifts offshore and the first boat from Seattle, loaded with gold miners, comes steaming through the open water. First boat in eight months; crowds spill out of the false-front stores and line the boardwalks hour after hour to watch her get bigger. She drops her hook offshore in the shallow sea, and lighters full of Eskimo longshoremen chug back and forth, bringing the miners in. When the first gang hits dock the planes start moving.

Day and night it's light, and day and night the sky is full of racket as the little ships taxi and take off, taxi and take off, hauling load after load back into the hills to mines like the Gold Run and the Ungalik and the North Star and the Kougarok. Pilots get so tired they fall asleep in the cockpits while mechanics are gassing their ships. But they never stop, not till they've taken all the miners and their supplies out to the creeks and dredges for another work season.

Everybody travels by air in Alaska—fishermen, miners, trappers, Congressmen, prostitutes, engineers, salesmen; Indians, Eskimos and whites, all crowded together aloft in the narrow cabins. Everybody and almost everything travels by air. Winter and summer, the plane is more universal in the North than the railroad train or automobile.

Merrill Field at Anchorage and Weeks Field at Fairbanks, the Territory's busiest civilian airports, are like Grand Central Stations, but even in 1946 they are engulfed in wilderness. Soon after take-off from one of these centers there is no sign below of human life; not a house, not a telephone pole, not a road. Outside the windows spreads a dizzying maze of snow or swamp, splotched with lakes and cut with twisting rivers. Hundreds of white peaks, unnamed and unclimbed, gleam beyond. Hour after hour the weird mottle of earth may slide beneath the wings, with never a sign of a city.

"Like another world," you venture.

The pilot laughs. It is Main Street to him. "That's John Foster's place," he tells you, tipping the wing to the speck of a cabin far below. . . . "This is Yankee Creek," he says as you soar among the twisted crags of mine country. "In a few minutes we'll be landing at Ophir."

Ophir is a cluster of log houses, with the Stars and Stripes waving from a wooden pole. It's a proud American town and the homemade mine camp airport, roughed out on tailing piles, is far more important than a traditional New England village green. The whole population—thirty, all told—comes trudging toward your plane as it bumps to earth. Whites and Indians crowd around the pilot.

"Hi, Jimmy. You got my meat? When is Agnes coming over? Ed Nolet's ailing, can you take him to town? You got a package for me from Sears Roebuck? Any eggs today? My radio's on the bum, will you take it now? You need gas? Can you stay for lunch, Jimmy?"

But it is the lone prospector who appreciates an airplane most. Out in the brush he waits—grub almost gone, only a sack of beans left, a little rice and a tin of corned willie. All summer he's been working by himself—three months ago a pilot set him down on pontoons on this lake, spruce-fringed lake without a name, lake where nobody ever was before. All summer panning bars and sinking holes and fighting mosquitoes—sleeping under a tarp tent, cooking over a campfire— all summer by himself, and not much luck.

Now for four days he's been cussing, shivering, waiting to go back to town: September 10th, dates all marked off on the calendar, sure I didn't miss. 20th was the date. Where's that pilot? Maybe he forgot. Maybe he lost the map. Maybe he went Outside and how the hell will anybody else find where I'm at? September 20th, grub for two days, startin' to get cold nights. Take me weeks to walk back. Where's that monkey?

Then he hears it: no noise like it, rattle over the treetops, that's his engine, there's the red ship, there he comes, good boy, low over the woods, droppin' down.

Sometimes a prospector or trapper will cut spruce boughs and build a message in the snow, hoping a pilot will happen to fly overhead and see it:

> HELP
> HUNGRY
> NEED GRUB
> LAND

STOP DAMN IT STOP, one wrote; it took a lot of branches and a lot of work, but it got results.

Once Pilot Joe Crosson, flying a float ship full of passengers, saw a man standing by a lake below flashing a gas can in the sun.

"I circled him a few times and he run and got a boat, and then he flashed the can again. It looked like he might be in bad shape. It was sure a small lake he was on. I couldn't land there with all that load, so I dropped down on a bigger lake near by. I was the only one that had boots, so I had to pack all my passengers out of the plane to shore. I left them waiting there and flew back empty, to land on the little lake where he was. It looked bad, really just a pond; water was choppy, and there was tall timber at the end; but I landed okay and taxied back toward this fellow, shut off the engine and yelled: 'What's the matter?'

"He was setting in his rowboat, had a kind of silly grin on his face.

" 'Oh, nothing,' he said. 'I just wanted to let you know I was here. This sure is a pretty nice lake. Why didn't you never land here before?'"

Often they're "bushwhacky," those men who have been out so long in the hills alone. "They'll come running to you with a wild look in their eye: 'What's the date? What time is it? What's the news?' They'll say they're out of sugar. They'll say they're out of flour. They'll say they have a pain in their belly—but sometimes they're just lonesome, just want somebody to talk to, that's all."

Nevertheless, an Alaska pilot will risk his neck to land when he sees a distress signal. He keeps his wilderness appointments scrupulously, marking the dates on a calendar, the locations on a map. He knows well what true emergency can mean. Once Oscar Winchell was unavoidably delayed a week in calling for a trapper and his wife at Post Lake.

"I got there, buzzed the lake, didn't see nothin' of those people. I come back next day, buzzed the lake again. This time they run out o' their cabin. I dropped a box o' grub with a note tellin' 'em to hike a mile and a half down to Post River. I couldn't land on the lake, the snow was drifted too rough.

"The box lit within 100 feet but they couldn't find it. I circled around, yelled at 'em about where it was at. They couldn't hear me, but they had a great big old Dane dog and he run sniffin' through the drifts and found it for 'em.

"I met 'em over to the river. I come down in the deep snow, taxied up and yelled, 'You wanta go to Anchorage?'

"They stood there with the tears rollin' down their faces.

"They said when the plane didn't show up they'd started walkin' forty miles to Farewell but they'd lost the trail, got scairt and turned back. It was awful tough goin', and on the way he'd had a heart attack. They'd just got back to the lake the second time I flew over. They hadn't had no grub for a week.

"I looked 'em over. They had a good catch o' fur and this big old dog—too much of a load for my plane, she was sunk on her belly, prop touchin' the snow, and we was twenty-five hundred foot above sea level. But I could see they was feelin' low, so I thought I'd make a try. I let 'em git in the cabin, the big dog crawled in too, I tried to taxi but five or six miles an hour was fast as we could go. So I told 'em: 'I can't make it, I can only take half o' you at a time; but I'll come right back for the rest.'

"That big old Dane dog he was eyein' me. I thought a lot

o' that dog for runnin' and pickin' up the grub, and I didn't like to leave him behind. But first I took the lady over to Farewell with the fur and then I come back and got the man and him. We loaded 'em all in at Farewell; the lake there was slick so we took off fine and flew in to town."

Nobody needs an airplane like a fellow out in the hills.

"Carl Dunlap and Joe Shaw was workin' a claim over on Tobin Creek—lonely spot on the other side of a four-thousand-foot mountain from Squaw Creek. They took two big Malamute dogs with 'em from Squaw to haul wood for timberin'. They was goin' to sink a deep shaft.

"Carl was showin' Joe how to handle dynamite. They was standin' in their cabin, and a spark flew out from the fuse in his hand over to a box o' caps on the table. The dynamite exploded. Both men was blinded. Their bodies was riddled with splinters like porcupine quills. They was hurt too bad to go for help, and anyhow neither one of 'em could see.

"They thought of them two borrowed dogs, stumbled around till they found a pencil and paper and wrote two notes: HAD SERIOUS EXPLOSION and PLEASE COME WITH HELP. Awful scrawls, but best they could make. They tied one to the collar of each dog and let 'em loose. One of the dogs was caught in a bear trap. The other played around and chased rabbits a while and finally turned up back home at Squaw Creek.

"The men there took two teams, went through the mountain pass and hauled Carl and Joe back to Squaw. Both of 'em was sufferin' agony. There was no doctor there so the people sent a message for a plane.

"It was 50 below zero when A. A. Bennett flew over from Fairbanks in his open Swallow and picked 'em up. Weather was stormy; on the way back, his ship was forced down. Everybody at Fairbanks was worried, no word, no word—the mayor was goin' to send a message to every wireless station in the Interior. But just before noon of a Sunday came the noise of a motor, and a big crowd run out to the field to meet the plane.

"Carl and Joe was sittin' in the cockpit with Turkish towels wrapped 'round their heads.

"When the engine stopped somebody said 'Hello Carl,' and he asked, 'Where are we?'

"They told him Fairbanks.

" 'Thank God,' he said.

"We took 'em both straight to the hospital."

Sometimes in a roadhouse, when the fog hangs low outside and the planes are grounded and the stove is warm—a few rounds of poker help, too, and a few shots of whiskey— sometimes the pilots will start talking. Their "hangar-flying" yarns are often difficult to believe, but if you check you find that some of the most remarkable ones are true. The folklore of Alaskan aviation is trivial and important, grave and humorous.

"By golly, there was a lady over at Takotna goin' to have a baby. She knew it would have to be a Caesarian; she'd had one that way in Norway twelve years before. There was two part-Indian girls too, expectin' about the same time, and they'd asked me to fly over and get them too.

"Couple of days before I was due there I was on my way out from Anchorage with a radio for the Nixon Fork Mine when I got word to come to Takotna right away. I stopped at the mine on the way to deliver the radio, jumped out in a big hurry and went tearin' up to the cabin. It was cold that mornin', 60 below. When I started back down to the plane I had no breath left, felt all choked up, walked slow, held my mitten over my mouth. I told an old fellow I was feelin' bum. He asked me where I hurt, and when I told him, he said, 'You frosted your lungs. If you can make it you better get back to Anchorage and see a doctor today.'

"I flew on to Takotna, feelin' worse and worse. They brought the three women down to the plane. The one she already had pains sumpin' awful. I put her in the back seat with one o' the half-breed ladies. The other one sat up front with me. I thought, 'By God we got to hurry.'

"I started the plane and took off, but we run into a strong head-wind. As we went through Rainy Pass it was startin' to snow. It was gettin' so dark I could just barely make out the mountains. I thought, 'Well if we don't get there we'll all die anyway, what's the difference? Got to keep on to Anchorage.'

"We made it, and I come overtown but there wasn't a light within two miles of the field—them was the early days—there wasn't nothin' but a couple o' shacks by the airport, and nobody was expectin' me. I circled, and pretty soon my boss come out with a car to shine the headlights—he'd heard us flyin' over town.

"We rushed 'em all to the hospital. She had her Caesarian that night and one o' the other girls had her baby too, the other had hers two days after. The doctor was so busy with the ladies that night he had no time for me, so I went to an old horse doctor who punched my arms full o' iodine and after that I was in bed four weeks."

Joe Crosson had a close one. Five minutes after he landed Mrs. Jack O'Connor at Fairbanks she bore her child. A bystander told him: "You should have circled, Joe. You could have collected two fares instead of one." At least three babies have been born in the air over Alaska. Pilots know when their passengers are expecting, usually fly them to town in plenty of time, but once in a while a woman fools them.

Agnes Clark, wife of the mail driver at Ruby, was in heavy labor when Pilot Jim Dodson arrived, and she was having difficulty. There was a nurse aboard his Stinson, but he opened the engine full throttle as he headed back toward Fairbanks. He was worried.

"There's the stork," he told another passenger, pointing to the ship's speeding shadow far below. "There's the old stork, trying to beat us in. I hope we make it."

As they crossed the Novitna River, at 6,000 feet, the child was born. The nurse worked ten minutes before it breathed, and Dodson heard its first cry. Today Catherine Clark is a husky, four-year-old girl and Dodson is her godfather.

Dodson was all alone in his small plane with Mrs. Hilbert Olsen when she bore her daughter, early in 1945. As the Stinson roared through a night snowfall, Mrs. Olsen kicked the side of the cabin. "The baby's coming!" she cried. Controlling the ship with one hand, Dodson reached back and did his best to help her with the other. He radioed for a doctor, who was waiting at the Fairbanks field when they came down. The doctor had forgotten his scissors; Dodson stepped into the hangar for a pair, which were sterilized and used to cut the umbilical cord.

There's almost nothing an Alaska pilot isn't called upon to do. One cold evening just at dusk Pilot Estol Call landed at Merrill Field and started to unload his plane. A car drove up; the Anchorage Hotel, hearing the ship pass overhead, had dispatched its taxi to the airport.

"You got any passengers?" the driver asked Call.

"You bet," Call answered. "I got one inside."

The taxi man opened the door. "Anchorage Hotel," he shouted, "Anchorage Hotel. You want to go to the Anchorage Hotel?"

The passenger did not answer. Nothing stirred, not even his eyes. The taxi man shook him and he fell over.

"God," said the driver, "this man's dead."

"Yeah," said Call. "He's froze. They found him on the trail that way, setting on a log. I just put him up there beside me in the seat, that was the easiest way to fit him in."

Most of the planes in Alaska have been to small to take coffins. The dead have usually been wrapped in canvas sacks. Pilot Alex Holden, hauling a corpse that had been awaiting transportation a long time, bundled it up and tied it on top of the cabin of his Loening amphibian—outside. Oscar Winchell has a weirder tale. He arrived one summer night at war-crowded Fairbanks in a five-place Stinson with a corpse, the dead man's widow, her aunt and two sacks of platinum.

"I landed at one in the mornin', called everywhere, but the town was so packed I couldn't find no place for the ladies to stay. The widow, she was about wore out, so finally I called the Clerk o' the Court and got 'em taken care of. But I still had no place to sleep myself, and I couldn't locate the undertaker—he was out doin' the town.

"It was three o'clock before he come drivin' up to the field. Him and I loaded the body in his car and drove to the funeral parlor. By that time I was awful tired—I'd flew near a thousand miles that day. Besides, I couldn't go walkin' around the streets with a hundred fifty thousand dollars' worth of platinum, with all them strangers in town. I asked the undertaker if he had a place to put me up.

"He said, 'No place except right here in this room, but you

can stay here if you want.' Son of a gun, I spotted a bear rug, just laid down on it, rolled up in it, used the platinum sacks for a pillow. There was dead bodies layin' all round me, but I was so wore out I went right to sleep.

"In the mornin' I woke up and heard footsteps—*squeak, squeak, squeak*—it was an old building'—here come two men from the FBI. They started toward a corpse and one of 'em says to the other, 'Okay, let's take his fingerprints and get this job over with and get out o' here.' I was feelin' kind o' ornery, so I jest raised up and asked 'em, 'What's your hurry?' They stood petrified in their tracks and stared at me. After a little while I jest took my platinum sacks, got up and walked out; they was still starin'—neither one o' them guys ever moved or said a word."

There's birth, there's death, there's everything in between. Pilot Hermann Lerdahl had a rough surprise.

"I was flying Bishop Bentley on a trip to some of his Missions, and we stopped at Stevens Village. The people said they had a sick little girl to go to town. They brought her down all wrapped in blankets, and we loaded her in and took off.

"Pretty soon she unwound herself and ran up front where we were sitting and began to hit the Bishop with her fists. He said, 'Now, now, little girl,' but she grabbed his hand and started to bite—that kid was sick all right, she was insane. She bit a hole right through his glove, ran back, tore the feathers out of a pillow, grabbed the logbook and bit a piece off that. She even put toothmarks on the metal window frames. The Bishop was a big man but he could hardly hold her down."

The insane, traveling on the airlines of Alaska, are usually bound in makeshift strait jackets and accompanied by attendants. But there has been more than one mishap. Once a deranged woman opened the door of a plane and hurled herself out. Another passenger caught her by the foot just in time.

"There she hung, the ship doing 80 miles an hour, the door open, the weather was freezing cold. The guy who was holding her by the foot told the pilot, 'I can't hold onto this lady no more and I can't pull her back in, the wind is too strong.' The pilot couldn't land, the snow was too deep and he was on wheels. Only one thing he could do; he throttled down slow as he could, swung low over the drifts and let the fellow drop her out. All she got was a few broken bones."

An Alaska pilot knows all about the people's lives.

"One time I picked up a passenger at Anchorage, a nice little girl from the States. She wanted to go to Takotna. Soon as she got in the plane she said, 'Do you know So-and-so over there? I'm going to marry him.'

"Oh gosh, I thought, this is terrible. That old cuss, everybody knows he's half-lit all the time and goin' to pieces and livin' with another woman. I ask her, 'Does he know you're comin'?' 'No,' she says, and she kind o' giggles, 'he thinks I'm comin' next month! I saved up all my money and this is going to be a surprise!'

"Oh God, even worse than I thought. I try to figure how I can keep the kid in the plane till I get him in shape, but soon as we land she hops out and runs up the hill with her little grip into the store. I tie down the ship and follow her up and I ask the fellow in the store, 'Did you tell that little girl where he lived?' and they're all chucklin', holdin' their sides. 'Sure,' they say, 'she's on her way up to his cabin now.'

"I run out, but it's too late; she's just knockin' on the door. I feel sick about it, walk back in the store. Pretty soon I take another look. There she come slowly down the hill with her grip, cryin' and cryin'. I took her aside: 'Don't feel too bad, kid,' I told her, 'we all have our disappointments.' She said she spent all her money to get there, not a dollar left. I told her: 'If you want to go back to Anchorage it won't cost you a nickel.' I told the other passengers she was a writer, just lookin' into the minin' business a little; and she begun to feel better, and I flew her back to town."

There are sad trips—and happy ones.

Jim Dodson got an order from a trapper at Fort Yukon for a wedding ring and a planeload of liquor. He arrived with this gala freight on the appointed day. The trapper met him with a long, sheepish face. "Gosh, Jimmy, I can't use that stuff, looks like I'm not gittin' married after all."

Dodson hesitated. Another trapper spoke up. "You got the

liquor? You got the ring? Okay, Jimmy, you can switch the order to me."

Fort Yukon had its wedding anyway. Dodson was the best man. He kissed the bride, climbed into his Stinson and flew on for a load of beaver.

An Alaska pilot hauls "passengers, freight and a little bit of pretty goddamn near everything." Malamutes and Husky dogs are regular passengers. Roped to the seats, they growl and scramble in windy weather and are more likely to get airsick than human beings. When a Chicago zoo ordered four live walruses Pilot John Cross flew them from Cape Prince of Wales to Nome in a Stinson.

"They were young ones, only walrus in captivity at the time, weighed about a hundred and fifty pounds apiece. Friendly animals, very sensitive—when I'd scratch their heads they'd cry like babies. I wrapped them in canvas sacks and fed them with milk bottles. They were so frightened at first they screamed. But after we took off they lay with their heads together and quieted down."

At Nome Pilot Cross delivered the walruses and picked up a load of pigs for delivery to a mine. They were more difficult cargo.

"I wanted to haul them crated, but the box was too big for the door of my plane so I took the walrus bags and wrapped them one by one. They were vicious, those pigs, squealed and fought so I could hardly get them loaded. In the air they nearly tore the bags to pieces."

The biggest animal ever carried in a plane in Alaska was also one of the easiest, a cow.

"Dave Clough over at McGrath wanted it for fresh milk for his daughter's ailin' baby. Daisy, she was a real big cow, must 'a' weighed eight hundred pounds. Leo Moore took her over from Merrill Field in a Pilgrim.

"Leo tried to git her used to the ship, would coax her up a plank into the cabin 'n' feed her. It sure worked. When the time come for take-off she just walked right in like into a boxcar. Nothin' to it. He didn't even tie her down much, just roped her head 'n' horns so she wouldn't take the windows out, had extry boards on the floor so she wouldn't step through.

"Daisy was a real airplane cow, she seemed to like the trip; 'n' long after, every time a Pilgrim come into McGrath, she'd walk right up 'n' stand there like she wanted another ride."

An Alaska pilot needs ingenuity and strong arms. In 1940 a whole store was hauled by air to Ophir. Timbers for two-story buildings, cement, counters, doors, window frames, sheet-iron tubing, window glasses and all the stock were flown and landed there by Pilots Johnny Moore, Chet Browne, and Ralph Savory in two Pilgrims and a tri-motor Ford.

"If the ship'll take her," the pilots say, "we'll fly her." Bunks and poling boats have often been wedged into small single-engine craft. A dredge shaft was once hauled in a Bellanca; the pilot had to take out the front window to fit it in. A small gas tractor was carried in a Stinson. The pilot removed the doors of the plane and flew with the track frame sticking out two feet on either side. "The tail shook a little," he admits. This was not the worst. "If she's too big to get in," they say, "we'll tie her on outside." Pilot Jack Peck once lashed a big cookstove onto the fuselage of his Ryan B-1. A Michigan sled weighing 260 pounds was hauled by Oscar Winchell underneath his Stinson.

An Alaska pilot needs good aim. He will land wherever he can: on the snow on skis, on water on pontoons, on rough clearings on wheels, but if conditions are too poor he will drop a small load from the sky. Swooping low, he will tip his plane and shove the carefully wrapped packages through the door. Mattresses, frozen meat, cases of canned milk and gasoline, even dynamite go tumbling through the air. The men below set colored flags on the snow or soft tundra for a target. Women stand by their cabin doors and count the bundles as they come down.

Jim Dodson likes to tell about the time he threw out a package of meat to the Midnight Mine and it bounced right up on the chopping block. But once he dropped a load of mail on a windy day, and the string broke; letters fluttered through the woods "like a flock of ptarmigan." The people spent days hunting for them. Oscar Winchell, at Candle Creek, had a sadder hit when he dropped what he thought was a load of meat. "We was in a hurry 'n' not payin' too much attention to the packages." He later learned it was a victrola and 300 records. "Only two of 'em was not broke. The people played them two over and over all summer long."

Winchell took a big load of meat to Julian Creek in a Stinson—"whole froze hindquarter o' beef, gee God that thing must 'a' weighed a hundred and seventy-five pounds. I gets it up to the plane, and I take the door off, rope the meat through the window and fix it so it won't hit the strut. I fly over, circle in gusty air, loosen the rope, wiggle and wobble, and it falls off nice and I keep headin' on down the creek thinkin' I done a good job.

"Next fall I find out I knocked a lot o' logs off the bunkhouse, busted a window and near killed a fellow in his sleep."

Alaska pilots fly scheduled meat runs to the mines, routine as grocers' truck routes, delivering on appointed days. One man, to drum up business, started hovering over remote camps and dropping meat that had not been ordered. "I'd just write C.O.D. on the sack and throw it out and hope they'd pay me next time they come in to town." Most of his customers did pay him. They were pleased. Billy the Finn at Moore Creek was more than pleased:

"A whole month my camp is out of meat. My men all going to quit because no meat. I tell them I walk to Flat, walk for days by shoepac. I stand by my cabin and I say 'Oh Lord, if only I had some meat!' I listen, I hear a noise, a plane come over, it drops a sack. MEAT it falls out of heaven right by my door. I cannot believe it is true. That flyer is the best man I ever seen."

Alaskans today are the flyingest people under the American flag. This did not happen easily.

3

Earliest Birdmen

THE FIRST PLANE in Alaska was built in 1912 at the Gold Rush settlement of Nome.

The big stampede was over. The wind-swept tents were gone—and the violence—and the sickness—and the sudden wealth and poverty.

Nome was settling down to be a good town.

It had wooden houses with bay windows jutting out over narrow streets, fine clocks and barber poles and a handsome hotel, the Golden Gate, of gingerbread architecture. It had several churches, two newspapers, and a man to teach piano to the children.

He, Henry Peterson, gray-haired, proud-walking, loud-talking fellow, sort of an eccentric, had the first plane built.

For months Professor Peterson and his helper hammered and sawed at a funny-looking rig in a shed. School kids flocked around and stared. It had a rotary-type engine and the frame was strung with piano wires. Peterson told the children never to touch it. He said it was a flying machine.

Eskimos named it *Ting Mayuk* (Bird of the Tundra).

White men, before long, were calling it rougher names than that.

Peterson sent for an aviator from the States. One cold spring morning he said the plane was all set. Horses dragged it two miles out of town to Gold Hill. Hundreds of merchants and miners followed through the deep snow. Everybody paid a dollar and got a ribbon badge.

Peterson tied a long rope to the plane and asked for volunteers to get it flying. Everybody wanted to help.

They pushed and pulled it up the slope.

They pushed and pulled it down.

The engine growled, the wings shook, the aviator tried his

best—but the airplane just plowed through the snow like an auto.

Some said they thought it needed a smooth piece of ground. Peterson said maybe it needed a stronger engine.

The next day people were laughing all over town.

The first plane to fly in Alaska took to the air at the log cabin city of Fairbanks on the Fourth of July, 1914.

It was the biggest, rowdiest Fourth Fairbanks had ever known. There were foot, horse and bicycle races, tugs of war, rock-drilling contests, baseball games and—an AERIAL CIRCUS.

Arthur Williams, owner of the Arcade Restaurant, and two other merchants hired Aviator James Martin* from the States and paid his boat fare all the way north; also his wife's; also the freight on his small tractor biplane. It cost them thousands of dollars.

The circus, they advertised, would be held at the ball park. It would be a big show with a high charge: five bucks a head. They slung a rope from the lower bleacher to the race track, so large a mob did they expect when Martin went through his terrifying maneuvers.

They took a bad loss, those sporting backers of Alaska's first airship. When the plane went up, the ball park with its bordering rope was almost empty. Roofs, woodpiles and fances all over town were covered with people. Some even climbed to the belfry of the schoolhouse to watch the show "for free."

Never anything like it; Martin's machine, after one false try, lifted into the air. Round and round it went for nine whole minutes, 400 feet above the baseball diamond, before it settled down.

The birdman said he did not care to fly very far from the

* James Martin, one of the earliest pioneers of aviation in the United States, invented the first successful tractor biplane in 1911 and set a world speed record with it of 70 miles per hour. He was an Army consulting engineer in World War I, and a close friend of General Billy Mitchell's. He subsequently invented numerous other aeronautical products and manufactured both planes and automobiles at a factory at Garden City, Long Island.

park. Chimneys of the wood-burning town were puffing so much smoke he might lose his way.

Still, he sailed the sky.

People saw him do it—four different times.

The Fairbanks *News-Miner* printed a long article. "Regarding the possibility of flying through the atmosphere with heavier-than-air craft," the paper reported, "the minds of many of the sourdoughs of Alaska have been set at rest."

It was not until 1920, when the Army Air Service's Black Wolf Squadron flew from New York to Nome, that Alaskans saw what an airplane could really mean.

General Billy Mitchell sponsored the Black Wolf flight. Mitchell knew Alaska. He had worked once for the Signal Corps, building telephone lines through the North. He said the Territory was important, strategic, right on the sky road to Asia. He wanted to prove that planes could fly to the top of the continent.

Alaskans were glad and proud.

"OUR AIR EXCURSION BIGGEST THING WORLD KNOWS TODAY," boasted "Wrong Font" Thompson, the *News-Miner's* bluff, exuberant editor, "ALL EYES ARE ON US!"

The streets of Fairbanks were bright with banners. Brush was cut from the ball park's edge so the planes could come down safely. Jack Buckley, Fire Chief, laid a white cross to show the Squadron where to land.

"When an airplane is on the ground," the newspaper warned its readers, "do not touch any part of it or you might endanger the life of the pilot. . . . Almost any place in town will be as good a place to see the flyers from as the Park Grandstand, and less dangerous."

Fairbanks waited and waited.

It took the Black Wolf Squadron, in its four open-cockpit De Havillands, nearly six weeks to reach Alaska—twice as long as Captain St. Clair Streett, leader of the expedition, had planned.

"It is purely a mathematical problem when the flyers will arrive," Wrong Font Thompson angrily told his readers. "When the wind blows, they can't fly. When it rains, they

can't fly. When the lightning is flashing, they can't fly. . . .
Judge Griffin of Richardson, who came to town for the
purpose of being here when the airships arrived, has engaged
his room here for the season."

Striking north from Portal, North Dakota, over Canada,
the De Havillands landed on the wheatfields, mud flats, short
clearings in the brush. They suffered broken axles, smashed
wings, busted tires and tail skids, broken oil lines, leaking
tanks. They were grounded by fog, wind and storm.

But they got there.

Bleachers of the Fairbanks ball park were jammed when
the ships came in. Citizens sat silent, their eyes turned to the
sky. A man perched on the peak of the power-company
building gave the first shout. Everybody started cheering.
There they came! Four machines roared in over the spruce-
tops—circled the park and landed—swung their tails around
—smothered the crowd in whirling dust.

Nobody minded the dust. People swarmed around the
olive-green planes, touched them, scribbled names on the
sides shook hands with the pilots.

One old prospector ran toward the Squadron, stumbling and
weeping.

"Broken trail!" he hoarsely shouted. "Oh God, broken
trail!"

They were fine fellows, those aviators in their weird-
looking helmets. "As rough a gang of kids," Thompson ap-
provingly wrote, "as the Northland ever saw. . . . Captain
Streett landed here with most of the seat of his trousers
missing, the trip having been hard." Old-timers at Fairbanks
made them honorary members of the order of Pioneers and
presented each man with a gold nugget watch chain. People
gave them Husky pups, fur parkas and mukluks, ivory animals, everything they could cram into their planes.

The Black Wolf Squadron flew on to Nome, where landing
was made on an old parade ground. The boys were not
satisfied. They were in a mood for more. They wanted to hop
across Bering Strait to Siberia. Captain Streett* wired the

---

* In World War II, Major General St. Clair Streett was in
command of the Thirteenth Air Force in the Pacific.

Army for permission, but the reply was firm: Return to the States. Everybody in Alaska was disappointed. Nobody wanted the Squadron to go home.

"Adventurers of an earlier day take their hats off," Thompson wrote, "to the advance guard of the new generation who are blazing a pioneer trail by a means of locomotion which seems almost superhuman and uncanny in its marvelous accomplishment."

Then came several birdmen on their own.

There was Clarence Prest, a plucky boy from Buffalo, New York, who started for Alaska with a Jenny in 1921. He planned to fly through to Siberia and take pictures for a movie company.

Prest's plane was smashed by storm on the way north.

In 1922, in a Standard, the *Polar Bear*, he tried again. He shipped it, by steamboat, to Juneau, Alaska's capital town, and took it off from the beach heading northeast.

Four times his Curtiss OX-5 engine quit him.

Four times his small ship crash-landed in the brush.

Four times he got her off and flew on.

He made it to Dawson, where he did a few stunts and landed on a river bar. Miners passed the hat. He made it to Eagle, almost out of fuel. Motorboat gas was all the people had, but they poured in some ether to liven it up. A woman gave him a cake in case he got hungry. A man gave him a pistol in case he ran into trouble. He soared on toward Fairbanks, but over the Seventy-mile River his engine bucked again.

The *Polar Bear* crashed for good and all.

No way to pull the plane out; it was stuck, propeller twisted, in the middle of a boggy swamp. Nothing to eat; his cake was soaked with gas. A herd of caribou, wild and curious, milled around him, staring and staring. He took his pistol, shot one through the eye and cut it up for meat. He wandered downriver four days in a pouring rain before search parties found him.

Prest said he would try again in 1923.

"Next time," cracked the *News-Miner*, "his airship will

probably knock the top off Mt. McKinley and create a flat site for a summer hotel."

But he did not return.*

There was an ex-Army flyer named Roy Jones. Jones had once worked the Alaskan coast by boat, and he decided to try it by seaplane. He bought the hull of a Curtiss MF flying boat from the Navy, a 180-h.p. Hispano-Suiza engine from the Army, put them together and called his ship the *Northbird*.

In 1922 the *Northbird*, makeshift underpowered job, was the first plane to fly from Seattle up the foggy, windy Canadian coast to Alaska.

Jones and his mechanic Jerry Smith lost their way in the smoke of forest fires. They struck a hidden rock, tearing a hole in the *Northbird's* hull. Much of the time the ship sat motionless on the water, trapped by mist or storm. The flying time was only nine hours, but it took ten days to reach the salmon-fishing town of Ketchikan, first Alaskan port of call.

As the *Northbird* circled over Ketchikan, docks and wharves blackened with people. As it sloshed to a stop on Tongass Narrows every bell and whistle in town was ringing and blowing, even the fire alarm.

Citizens carried the aviators piggyback up the street, and Pioneers initiated them into their order. Canneries gave all the high-octane gas they could spare and merchants raised a thousand dollars to keep the *Northbird* aloft. Jones flew it all that summer and part of the next—hauling joy-hoppers, cannery men, government agents, fish.

Then, in take-off from a long, wild lake on Revillagigedo Island, the plane, seized by rotten air, stalled and plunged nose-down in the water. Jones lived, but the *Northbird* never flew again.**

* Prest continued to be active in United States aviation, however, and is today a consulting engineer for Lockheed Aircraft at Burbank, California.

**Jones subsequently flew another plane in Alaska and during World War II, serving as an Air Forces officer, he was stationed for a while at Ladd Field, Fairbanks.

There was Ottis Hammontree, an eager garage man who had flown a little in the World War. In 1922 he brought the first plane to Anchorage—an old Boeing amphibian with a Hall-Scott engine.

The Boeing was an underpowered hunk of junk. Hammontree did not fly it much. He sold it to an ex-grocer named Al Jones who loaned it to a railroad worker named Roy Trachel who said he was a pilot. Trachel, first time he tried to take off, plunked the plane into the water of Cook Inlet.

There was C. F. La Jotte, also an ex-Army pilot, who arrived at Nome by boat in the summer of 1923. He was to be Nome's first commercial flyer, working for the Moore gold-mining cooperative.

He hopped off for a spin to Council, lost his way in heavy fog, wrecked his plane on the tundra.

There was Roald Amundsen, the famous explorer. He shipped two planes, a Junker and a Curtiss Oriole, to the Arctic settlement of Wainwright and hired a pilot, Lieutenant Omdal, to fly them. The government of Norway, Amundsen said, wanted them to take the Junker over the North Pole.

Early in 1923 six dog teams with ninety dogs pulled Amundsen and Omdal from Nome toward their base for the Grand Hop. Movie men took shots. People of the Far North coast were prepared to flash news of the take-off by signal fire for hundreds of miles. The whole world was waiting.

The Junker made one trial flight at Wainwright, and landed on rough ice. The left ski was "crumpled like a piece of cardboard."

Amundsen changed his mind.

He returned to Nome on the cutter *Bear*.

The plane, he told reporters, had proved to be lacking in power to lift two persons over the Pole.

There was also Carl Ben Eielson.

4
The Life of Ben Eielson

CARL BEN EIELSON, America's foremost Arctic pilot, holder
of the Harmon Trophy and the Distinguished Flying Cross,
first man in history to take a plane across the top of the
world and first to discover land from the sky, began his
career modestly. He arrived at Fairbanks, Alaska, in 1922 to
teach school.

Eielson had grown up in North Dakota and graduated
from his state university. Slight but broad-shouldered, he had
a lean, strong face and piercing gray eyes. He was only
twenty-five when he arrived in Alaska, but the hair was
already thinning at the edge of his high brow. There was an
intellectual air about him and he had the look, both sober
and determined, of an older man.

Journeying slowly from the States, by boat and rail, Eielson reached Fairbanks late in the year, just as the birch
leaves were turning gold and the first frost of winter hung in
the air. He went to live at the old Alaska Hotel. Mrs. Tom
Foster, proprietress, glanced curiously at him as he entered
her lobby the first evening. She decided he would be a
satisfactory boarder, this polite professor. She showed him a
small room, one of the poorest in the house. "That's fine," he
told her. A few weeks later he went to work teaching
mathematics and general science and coaching basketball at
the red frame high school on Eighth Street.

Eielson was not, Mrs. Foster found, the retiring, bookish
type she had supposed. "He read a lot—but he was a social
fellow. Liked to dress up nice in the evenings, had a way with
the girls, was great on going to all the dances. He lived every
minute to the full." She smiles as she tells of the gay, noisy
parties he sometimes gave in his room. But the gray-haired

Fairbanks lady cannot talk of Eielson very long without wiping tears from her eyes.

She is proud and sad as she opens her frayed box of snapshots. "There he is—Ben." Ben, in breeches, fur parka and helmet, confidently leaning against an open-cockpit Jenny. Ben, in tailored business suit, soberly receiving a gold watch from the mayor. Ben, in winter greatcoat and felt hat, cigarette in hand, casually greeting a crowd at the depot. And there is a darkish photograph of a coffin piled high with flowers. The date is 1930. BEN, reads a banner across one of the wreaths, FAIRBANKS, ALASKA'S GOLDEN HEART—THERE'S A SOFT SPOT IN IT FOR YOU.

Everyone who knew Ben Eielson speaks of him proudly and sadly. No man has been more beloved in the history of the Far North. Alaskans, it is said, took to him instantly. They could tell he was their kind. Like many of the miners and traders of the Territory, he was of Scandinavian descent —"as stubborn a Norwegian as you could find." He was keen and friendly and warm. "Everybody would crowd around him at a party, and kids followed him through the streets like hound-dogs." He was easy-going in most things, but one subject obsessed him. Soft-spoken, he argued earnestly about it. Boyishly confident, he never swaggered. Although he was a scholar his eyes had the look of a man of action.

"I came up here to teach," he told Alaskans, "but what I really want to do is fly."

Children did not whisper or doze in Eielson's classes. Slouched informally before his pupils, he often forgot the day's assignment. They listened bright-eyed as he told them the scientific principles of aviation, the tough things about it, the great things about it, and what it would mean in a vast, roadless land like theirs. Alaska, he also pointed out, lies on the Great Circle route from the States to the Orient. Silks, mail and other light goods would soon speed through the Far North by air, he declared, instead of rocking slowly across the mid-Pacific by boat. Fairbanks had a big future. Before many years it would be a crossroads city of the world.

Now and then Eielson would turn and gaze out the schoolroom window in silence. Sometimes, deep in thought, he seemed to be looking nowhere. Other times he stared over the roofs at the ball park, a few blocks away, where the Black Wolf Squadron had landed two years before. "I want a ship," he told his pupils over and over. "If this town will buy me a ship, I will show what can be done."

Much as they liked Ben Eielson, Fairbanksans were puzzled. There were many speculations. Some said he was a dreamer, the impractical kind. Others disagreed; but everyone wondered what brought him to Alaska and everyone wondered why he wanted to fly. Everyone wondered if he could succeed. He did not fit the current concept of the rough and tough, swashbuckling aviator.

Eielson had had an easy boyhood. His family, one of the first of Hatton, North Dakota, lived comfortably in a big gabled house shaded by elms. The father, "Ole," prospered from his general store and bank holdings and served twelve terms as mayor. Ben, one of nine children, grew up like many another athletic American—playing baseball and basketball in high school, swimming and hunting in the out-of-doors. But he was an unusually serious boy and displayed even then a kind of lonely curiosity and initiative. He spent the evenings of one winter studying the Bible. "You've got to read it if you want to know history," he told his brothers and sisters. Another winter, by himself, he pored over Shakespeare.

Entering the University of North Dakota in 1914, Eielson made an energetic, all-around record. He was a good student, played varsity sports, joined a fraternity and a literary society. A prominent member of the debating team, he was known throughout the state for his cool logic. He was elected editor in chief of the college annual. But he was restless. At the end of his sophomore year, he transferred to the University of Wisconsin and began to study law. Ben Eielson was never satisfied to stay in any one place or do any one thing very long.

In 1917, at a time when the Army had only thirty-five trained pilots, he enlisted in the air service. It was here that he earned his wings and found his life goal. Commissioned second lieutenant, he had just received sailing orders when the Armistice was signed. Prodded by his family, he returned to Dakota's university. It was not long before he had persuaded a group of Hatton businessmen to buy him a Jenny. He organized the town's first flying club, took the plane to college with him, and during his summer vacations barnstormed through the Middle West. In this gypsy life he was for the first time completely at ease.

"TIME FLIES," he advertised in 1920, "WHEN WILL YOU? TAKE A DIP IN THE CLOUDS. AVIATION IS COMING INTO ITS OWN! The men who thought aviation was dangerous a year ago are taking rides today. Many men who think it is dangerous today will own ships in five years. We are approaching an AERIAL AGE!"

Ole Eielson was violently opposed to all this. Certain from the first that his son would be killed, he threatened, more than once, to burn the ship. It was not necessary. One day, in take-off from a short pasture near Climax, Minnesota, the Jenny tangled with a telephone wire and crashed. The plane was wrecked beyond repair. Eielson, uninjured, reluctantly agreed to resume his study of law.

He went to Washington, D.C. this time and entered Georgetown University, working as a Congressional guard to help pay the tuition. One day he struck up a conversation with Alaska's Delegate in Congress, Dan Sutherland, and they became good friends. Sutherland told him about the teaching job at Fairbanks. Eielson's father encouraged him to take it. "At least," Ole reassured the rest of the family, "there are no airplanes up there." The appeal of a far land was, in any case, too much for Ben Eielson to resist.

Slamming his law books shut, he headed for Alaska. But almost as soon as he arrived he was restless once more—wanting to leave the classroom, living for the day when he could climb into a cockpit and soar away somewhere, anywhere, through the sky. "The City Council," he wrote one of his brothers late that autumn, "has offered to put up a thousand dollars toward getting a plane. Do not mention this to Dad as I am not sure yet, anyhow, and it would worry him."

It was Wrong Font Thompson, the *News-Miner* editor, who took Eielson's hopes most seriously. The two, in the company of reporters and young merchants, often sat in the dingy newspaper office drinking home-brew and talking aviation till long past midnight. That winter they persuaded Fairbanksans to buy an airship. The late Dick Wood, pioneer banker, gave most of the money. A Jenny was ordered, with an OX-5 engine, and the following summer Eielson had an opportunity to try his wings in the North.

Townsfolk who had wondered about Eielson's ambition were now to wonder more. Despite his easygoing manner, there seemed to be a peculiar tension in his make-up. He admitted to a friend that he lay wakeful at night before almost every important flight he made. When he did sleep he rose from his bed and prowled. Once he wandered through the streets to the airfield and woke to find himself banging against the side of his plane. Another time a friend found him wrestling with the foot of his bed. "I'm trying to set the tail," he shouted, "but the darn wind keeps changing." On another occasion he tried to jump from the hotel window and resisted rescuers so violently they had to knock him out. After this episode Mrs. Foster moved him to the ground floor. "But we were still worried," she says. "Before a big trip the boys were always watching him close."

There was more than this to worry about. "When Ben come here," asserts one Alaskan aviator, "he didn't know no more about flyin' than a hog's hip pocket." Others are less dogmatic but according to some of the Territory's foremost air pioneers, close and loyal friends of Eielson, he could not be called a natural-born pilot. Flying, they maintain, did not come easy to him. He was a sweet stunter, they say, but his sense of direction in cross-country trips was not impressive nor, in those early days, were his landings and take-offs. Despite all this he, more than any other man, is considered to have been the founder of aviation in the Far North.

Eielson's Jenny arrived in a crate at the Fairbanks depot on July 1, 1923. He towed it to the ball park and three days later climbed into the wicker seat of the open cockpit ship for the first commercial flight in Interior Alaska. Banker Dick Wood, well fortified with "Alaska Mule," climbed dubiously in behind him. "Somebody HAD to go," Thompson wrote, "so Dick decided it might as well be him." The crowd looked on with mixed feelings. It was disturbing to see "two of the best men in town, everybody's friends, settin' one behind the other in a rig not much wider than a canoe," preparing to plunge skyward. But the Jenny rose neatly aloft, circled town and disappeared.

Eielson's destination was Nenana, a settlement only fifty miles from Fairbanks on the railroad. It should have been an easy course, following the track the whole distance, but somehow he lost his way. To make a short cut, he left the railroad—and could not find it again. Wooded hills swam below him in bewildering sameness. He headed for a wisp of smoke; it turned out to be an Indian village. He circled and circled. It was an hour and a half before he got his bearings, found the "speck in the brush" that was Nenana and landed his plane on the local ball park.

But the Nenana trip was a signal one. The following day he put his Jenny through its paces. He did whip stalls, Immelmann turns, tail spins, loops, power spirals, grass-cutting—and, at the end, dived low. Nenana paid well for its first air circus. When the Flying Professor returned to Fairbanks he had earned more than half the price of his new ship.

Soon after this, President Warren Harding arrived at Fairbanks. "We must show the Presidential Party that OUR TOWN is in the Big Time aerially," Thompson urged. Eielson obliged so skillfully that several of the eminent visitors said it was the best stunting exhibition they had ever seen. "Prof. Eielson has tricks up his sleeve," Thompson boasted, "that will show you you never saw flying till you saw him in action."

Eielson made several more cross-country trips that summer, hauling passengers and light freight to near-by towns. Thompson was jubilant. "He has demonstrated what aerial traffic could do for this country," the *News-Miner* announced. But Eielson himself was discontented again: he considered the Jenny, with its range of only a hundred and fifty miles, too small for effective work in Alaska. New plans were stirring in his mind. "He was shooting over our heads," says Hjalmar Nordale, Fairbanks' mayor. "He was born to something bigger than we realized."

The Flying Professor argued that aviation should not be pioneered by individuals. Alaska's place on future world air routes was too important; the federal government should provide larger planes and funds to develop northern flight on a systematic basis. He wrote many letters to Washington setting forth these ideas. Alaskans smiled at his optimism but he continued his efforts and late that November the *News-Miner* ran a historic headline: "MAIL SERVICE FOR KUSKOKWIM THROUGH AIR."

The United States Post Office Department gave Eielson a contract for ten twice-monthly mail trips from Fairbanks to the town of McGrath, more than three hundred miles distant. It agreed to ship him a Liberty-powered De Havilland for the flights and to pay him two dollars a mile—less than half the cost by sled and Husky. Eielson was elated and prepared confidently for this venture into the unknown.

No flights had been made in Alaska in wintertime. Nothing was known of the performance of airplane engines under such conditions, of icing hazards, of the effect of extreme low temperatures on fuel. Eilson, who had lost his way on more than one short summer trip, must now navigate alone above hundreds of miles of winter wilderness. Only a few scattered roadhouses and Indian camps broke the forbidding frozen expanse over which he must fly. In clear skies he could follow the dog trail. But his sole weather report, relayed by telegram from McGrath, would be out of date long before he landed, and gave no clue of conditions en route. Storm and forced descent off-route could mean death even if he made a successful landing. It might be weeks before ground parties could locate him—if they could locate him at all.

Charles Schiek, Fairbanks carpenter, whittled a pair of 300-pound flat-bottomed hickory skis—"ungodly things"—far heavier than those since found practical in the North. Workers in the local machine shop, with many arguments, assembled the Liberty engine. The ship was warmed by stoves in a shed hangar. On the sub-zero morning of February 21, helpers pushed the plane out on the ball park and loaded 500 pounds of McGrath mail. The Flying Professor, heavily bundled in furs, climbed into the open cockpit and the De Havilland took off in a trail of snow, heading southwest.

The trip to McGrath was made without difficulty, but the return journey was perilous enough. Eielson had planned to stop at McGrath only to exchange the mails and refuel his ship, but citizens had prepared a banquet in his honor and the festivities continued till half past two in the afternoon. He knew the sub-Arctic winter daylight would not last long. To save time, he left the dog trail, flying a compass course. He had been in the air an hour and a half when he realized he was lost. He followed a large twisting river a while, but had no idea which one it was nor where it was leading him. The gas drained in the De Havilland's tank, the dusk deepened to night. He did not know how close he was to the mountains, but landing was out of the question. He could only fly blindly on.

As he later wrote in a report to the Post Office Department: "The country looked flat in the pitch darkness. The sky was entirely overcast; not a star showing. I wandered around completely lost for almost an hour. . . . I saw a light so I cut my altitude and went down to it. It must have been a trapper's cabin. . . . I was tempted to set the ship down there and have a nice place to sleep but knew I would wreck it if I did. I went back to the big river I had left and after following it for some time I saw a red light in the distance. I hit for it and it turned out to be my home field."

A crowd at the Fairbanks ball park had virtually given up hope, but several bonfires had been lit. "The sound of the motor," the *News-Miner* relates, "distant and faint at six-thirty, brought a cheer from everyone. . . . Although a circle was made above town, the ship could not be seen till it hit the rays of the bonfires." The De Havilland sheared through treetops and rocked over on its back. The landing gear and one ski were broken. The prop was smashed. Eielson was not hurt but he was dazed; he had had no idea where he was landing. He wanted to inspect his plane but excited friends lifted him to their shoulders and carried him into the hangar where the mayor, on behalf of the people of Fairbanks, presented him with an engraved watch.

The De Havilland was repaired and seven more mail trips were made. Eielson missed no occasion to dramatize the superiority of his craft over the dog team. Once he rushed a bale of wire to the telegraph station at Takotna. He often hauled copies of the *News-Miner*, just off the press. They were so welcome wherever he landed that he dropped small bright-colored parachutes with copies of the paper over other roadhouses and camps.

These were days of glad accomplishment. "We have the pioneer flyer of the world," Thompson lyricized. "He can leave Fairbanks Monday morning, circle the North Pole and be back in Fairbanks Saturday night for his bath, and will do it this year while other people are still talking about it." The town of McGrath gave a "potlach" celebration in Eielson's honor. Indians presented him with a deerskin parka and initiated him into their tribe with the title of "Moose Ptarmigan Ben." But they were trying days. Sudden fog or snow plagued Eielson on many of the trips and the spring thaw brought new trouble. Landing on the river at McGrath, the mail plane's skis tore through the shell ice and were broken off. Eielson changed the ship to wheels and made the rest of his McGrath landings on a gravel bar without mishap. At his home base, however, he had repeated difficulty.

The Fairbanks ball park, only fourteen hundred feet long, with stumps and a high woodpile at one end, was a poor place even for landing on skis in winter. In springtime it was downright treacherous. The thawing earth was soggy and a trench of water bordered the runway. The wheeled De Havilland boomed down at sixty miles an hour, much faster than the Jenny, and Eielson cracked up his plane, in these Fairbanks landings, three out of eight times.

On one trip he brought in a passenger, a sick Swede named Hosie Hummell, to the hospital. As the De Havilland settled on its back, Eielson leaped out to Hummell's aid and released his safety belt. Hummell fell on his head with a heavy thud.

"Yeezus, Ben," he complained. "You always land like this?"

Eielson grinned sheepishly.

"Well, not *always!*"

The last of these crackups was major. As the De Havilland landed its wheels sank deep in a boggy spot and the plane crashed sideways. Propeller, rudder and—most serious—two of the wing struts were smashed. Local mechanics could not repair this damage without new parts. The Post Office Department, notified of the accident, refused to supply them or to finance the wing work. Although Eielson had two more flights to make under his contract, the Department ordered the plane returned to the States.

"Your experiment," the Assistant Postmaster General wrote, "has been successful to a marked degree. . . . [But] there are many things which must be done before we can continue on a permanent basis our use of the airplane in mail-carrying in Alaska. . . . The Department, after it has had an opportunity to carefully study every angle of the situation, will ask for legislation to permit permanent airlift in Alaska, but just what form of legislation will be thought proper is something to be taken up in detail in the future."

Disheartened by this double-talk, Eielson soon left for Washington, determined to secure another mail contract or to promote some larger scheme. He told friends that if he could get the proper equipment he was certain that he could fly across the Arctic Ocean. "Easy," he said. Impatiently he had read of Amundsen's 1923 attempt to cross the polar sea in a Junker. He had talked of buying Amundsen's plane. Enviously, he watched progress of the Army's 1924 flight around the globe, and sent greetings to its leader. "Never satisfied to take it slow," Alaskans say. "Always aiming higher and higher. He had a world view. That was the key to Ben."

October, 1924, found him in the States proposing to Army air chiefs that they inaugurate service from the United States to China with stops at Reno, Nevada; Nome, Alaska; a city somewhere in Manchuria, and Peking. He was told that the Army did not have adequate planes. He then argued for military planes for Alaska itself. Rebuffed by lesser officers, he persisted until he was granted an interview with General Billy Mitchell. A letter to Wrong Font Thompson, written from McCook Field, Ohio, shortly after this interview, was full of hope.

Mitchell is a good friend to Alaska. I suggested to him and other officers in the Chief's office what could be done in the way of mapping, photography, gathering data and carrying government agents in Alaska. He was very much impressed and sent me here to give suggestions. I have been doing nothing else but explaining why Alaska needs government planes and I have received the best encouragement. . . . I emphasized that practically nothing has been done about Alaska where the airplane is needed as badly as anywhere else in the world. They all admit this is true. . . . My very best regards to yourself and everyone in Fairbanks. I shall never be satisfied until I get back there.

The year 1925 went badly for Eielson. There was no action from the War Department. He bid against the dog teams for Alaskan mail transport—and lost. Discouraged by government indifference, he put his case before officials of a large aviation company in New York; they declined to invest any money in the Far North. His family persuaded him to return to law school. Three weeks later they received a wire: "HAVE JOINED THE ARMY AIR SERVICE. SEND UNIFORM AND SAM BROWNE BELT."

He spent several months at Langley Field, Virginia, studying navigation and night-flying techniques and helping to perfect a new type of ski for heavy planes. When this temporary assignment expired he returned to Washington to renew his fight for an Alaskan mail contract. Again he failed. Finally he returned to Hatton and went into business with his brother Oliver as a bond salesman. "He didn't like it at all," Oliver recalls. "He was depressed as the dickens. But we persuaded him he should make some steady money for a while."

Vilhjalmur Stefansson, the distinguished Arctic explorer, rescued him from this fate. That fall, on a business tour of their state, the Eielson brothers stopped at the small town of Langdon. Ben, moodily sitting in a barbershop, was summoned to a long distance phone call. His apprehensive father told him that Stefansson was helping the Australian explorer-flyer Captain George Wilkins organize an expedition to fly over the Arctic Ocean. Knowing of Eielson's pioneer flights in Alaska, Stefansson had wired to ask if he would accept a job as pilot. Eielson left for New York the next night and promptly signed at a nominal salary for the extreme peril of transpolar work.

In the spring of 1926 the Flying Professor returned to Alaska with the most pretentious air expedition Fairbanksans had ever seen. There were several pilots, including Major Thomas G. Lanphier, commandant of the Army's First Pursuit Squadron, and several technicians to service the two Fokker planes. One ship, the *Detroiter*, was powered with three Wright Whirlwind engines. The other, the *Alaskan*, was dual-control and powered with a Liberty. Reporters and news-cameramen accompanied the expedition, which was financed by the Detroit Aviation Society, the American Geographic Society and the North American Newspaper Alliance.

No project could have pleased Eielson more. Captain Wilkins, who had spent many years of ground exploration in the Arctic, shared Eielson's vision of Arctic air routes. Wilkins' purpose was scientific and practical: "to explore that area of the polar ice pack never before seen by man ... to discover whether north of Barrow there is any land on which to establish a meteorological station." Such a station would mean much to aviation, military and civilian, and to weather-reporting generally. Finally, to demonstrate the shortness and practicability of international routes across the Arctic, Wilkins hoped to make a flight from Barrow, farthest-north town under the American flag, to Europe.

Fairbanksans, remembering Eielson's mishaps on shorter trips with slower-landing planes, shook their heads. Barrow, a small fog-and-wind-swept village at the edge of the Arctic Ocean, lay more than 500 miles to the north of their town and seemed as inaccessible as the Pole. No flight had ever been made from Fairbanks to Barrow. There was no telegraphic communication with Barrow and the hop would be little safer than one across the ice pack itself. The route lay over the least known part of Alaska. There were no accurate maps. The menacing Endicott Mountains, "jaggedest range on the continent," must be crossed and beyond them lay a vastness of Arctic prairie which few white men had ever penetrated by foot or dog team. "Many of Eielson's friends tried to dissuade him," Wilkins recalls. "They told him he was headed for his doom."

Eielson laughed. The planes were christened with wine at a crowded ceremony. But the expedition seemed to have been launched under an evil star. As Major Lanphier taxied the *Detroiter* for its first Fairbanks take-off, it swerved into a high drift; a newspaperman stepped into the whirring prop and was decapitated. The next day, as Eielson flight-tested the *Alaskan,* he misjudged his landing; the ship stalled and plowed through a fence. The undercarriage was broken and the propeller "twisted like a ram's horn." Remarks were made that Eielson did not have much experience with large planes. However, when Major Lanphier took the *Detroiter* up for its first hop he too misjudged; it stalled and crashed with greater damage.

Despite these setbacks and many more, Wilkins continued his Arctic project that year and returned, in the face of much public ridicule, in 1927 and 1928. He staked his own money for more planes and secured other sponsors when some of the original ones withdrew. He hired other pilots, notably Alger Graham of Detroit who did excellent work. But it was Eielson who was Wilkins' firmest supporter on the three expeditions. Eielson did the great bulk of the flying and he and Wilkins, developing rare teamwork, together made history which neither would have been able to make alone.

Wilkins, who knew Arctic conditions intimately, served as the navigator. Although he was a pilot in his own right, he gave Eielson full responsibility for handling the controls of the plane. They spent a total of some 500 hours aloft together, each doing his own work and trusting the other completely. "Eielson was a ready, deliberate, reasoning pilot," Wilkins testifies. "He met emergencies calmly.... He summed up every situation and looked at it from all angles and then, whenever there was a chance, he went ahead."

The first year, after the initial crack-ups, an old Club propeller was fitted to the *Alaskan*: there was not time for another to be shipped from the States. Eielson and Wilkins, in this makeshift job, made the first flight to Barrow late in March with a load of fuel and supplies. They barely missed disaster when peaks shown on the map at 5,000 feet proved to be twice that high. But they found a way through the mountains, reached the snow-covered tundra and continued north hour after hour. When they reached the top of America they did not know it; white earth and ocean looked the same. Wilkins suddenly realized from the character of the ice ridges that they had missed Barrow, passed the coast and were heading out over the ocean.

He let Eielson continue unknowing for more than an hour.

Then he passed him a note: "If you look ahead you will see 100 miles farther north in this area than any other man has seen from the air until today. We are 100 miles out over the Arctic Sea. What do you say to going on half an hour longer, just to make it good measure?"

"Whatever you think best," Eielson replied.

After the half-hour had passed Wilkins signaled for return. A sudden blizzard blew up and the two men, navigating by dead reckoning, searched for Barrow until it seemed hopeless. "I found I could see houses and villages everywhere," Wilkins has written. "If I had followed my inclination and every impulse at the moment we would soon have been flying in circles." At last they sighted a bluff and followed it around till a real village dimly appeared through the snow and Eielson landed the *Alaskan* smoothly on the frozen Barrow lagoon.

Slowed by mechanical trouble and fog, the expedition was unable to make any more flights over the ice pack in 1926. Arctic publicity of the year went to Richard Byrd's *Josephine Ford*, which flew from Spitsbergen to the Pole and back, and to the dirigible *Norge*, which flew from Spitsbergen to Alaska. But Wilkins made five more freighting trips from Fairbanks to Barrow, four of them with Eielson. Each time they took a heavier load, until they were hauling 4,750 pounds in a ship designed to carry less than half this amount. They delivered enough fuel for extensive Arctic work and returned in 1927 with two Wright powered Stinson biplanes.

It was 30 below zero on the morning of March 29 when Wilkins and Eielson left Barrow on their first long flight over the Arctic Ocean. For five and a half hours they soared to the northwest. Then came a dread sound; the engine began to miss. Eielson put the wheeled plane into a long slow glide and brought it down on the moving pack ice at 77 degrees North and 175 degrees West, some 500 miles from Alaska's northern shore.

Wilkins was triumphant in this accident. It proved what he had long contended and most other explorers had denied: that safe wheel-landings are feasible far out on the polar sea. He chopped holes and took echo soundings. The roar of the Wright prevented him from judging the intervals between the detonated charges, so he asked Eielson to snap the engine off. Eielson complied, but later he told Wilkins what his thoughts had been: "Go ahead and take the sounding. If we stop the engine we will never get it started again and nobody but you and me will ever know what the sounding is." The depth of the ocean was found to be more than three miles— the greatest registered to date in the Arctic Ocean.

It was two hours before they had the engine running again. It then gave only 1,400 revolutions, but they decided to attempt take off, for by this time an ugly storm was brewing. Five attempts were made before they were airborne. They headed back toward land but had been aloft only ten minutes when the Wright missed again. Again Eielson landed. By this time the blizzard was upon them. Eielson worked for an hour over the engine. The Stinson rose on the second try, narrowly missing an ice ridge, and continued its course through the whirling snow.

It was seven o'clock in the evening. The two landings and many tries at take off had taken much fuel and a forty-mile side-wind meant still less gas margin. As the plane "crabbed" in the direction of Barrow darkness prevented Eielson from reading the turn-and-bank indicator and the compass. Wilkins leaned over the gas tank with the help of a guarded torchlight and guided him by touching him on the arm. At two minutes past nine, by Wilkins' description,* "The engine cut out suddenly. . . . There was no sputter . . . but a sudden silence, except for the hum of the wind in the wires.

"Eielson snapped the switch right and left: there was no response from the engine. We could feel the sag of the falling plane. With great coolness and skill Eielson steadied the machine, righting her to an even keel and an easy glide. . . . As we came within a few hundred feet of the ground . . . we could dimly see it serrated with ice ridges, but they gave us no idea of height or distance.

"Near the ground the air was rough. The plane swerved and pitched but Eielson, still calm and cool, corrected the

* A number of the Wilkins quotations in this chapter are taken from his book *Flying in the Arctic*, courtesy of G. P. Putnam's Sons, New York.

controls for each unsteady move. In a moment we were in the snowdrift. We could not see beyond the windows of the plane. I felt Ben brace himself against the empty gas tank. I leaned with my back against the partition wall of the cabin and waited.

"The left wing and the skis struck simultaneously. . . . I gripped Eielson's shoulder and slipped through the door of the machine. Wind and driving snow filled my eyes. Dimly about us I saw pressure ridges as high as the machine. We had undoubtedly struck one as we came down. Along the extreme edge of the lower wing the fabric was torn. The machine still rested on the skis, but they had turned on their sides, the stanchions twisted and broken."

When morning broke, still stormy, the two men found they had been lucky almost beyond belief: they had landed on an island of ice, on a smooth stretch which measured less than thirty by fifteen yards with towering ridges on all sides. They were some sixty-five miles northwest of Barrow, Wilkins estimated, and the floating isle was drifting in the wind at a speed of several miles an hour. They sent a message announcing their plight but because the wireless machine had been damanged they had little hope that it would be received. For the next five days the gale continued and they were driven along parallel to the coast to a point about a hundred miles east and north of the farthest-north town.

On the sixth day cold, clear weather came. Ice formed across the leads of open water. Eielson and Wilkins took swift advantage of this change. They drained what little fuel they could from the tank and improvised an oil-burner from a gallon can. They built sleds—one from the lower part of the plane cowling, the other from the tail ski. Loading them with concentrated foods and a few other essentials, they left the shelter of their plane and set out across the frozen sea toward land.

For thirteen days the aviators struggled across the pack ice, sinking to their waists in soft drifts, crawling on their hands and knees across broken pressure ridges. They used the snow to live by—melting it for drinking water and building houses of it each night to sleep in. During Eielson's work on the engine he had frozen several fingers. Blistered and blackened, they pained him so that he could not use them; he was forced to carry supplies by means of his armpits. He and Wilkins moved for the most part in dogged silence. "A little ruminating now and then, short discussions as to the accuracy of navigation ... solicitious inquiry as to the condition after strains and falls that brought uncontrollable cries of pain from one or the other as we tumbled or pinched our feet and ankles between the steel-like ice—that was the extent of our conversation," Wilkins has written.

On the morning of April 16 they stumbled up to the fur-trading station of Beechey Point, 180 miles east of Barrow. Word was sent by dog team of their arrival and Pilot Alger Graham flew to their rescue. At Barrow the little finger of Eielson's right hand had to be amputated. In the absence of a doctor the local missionary performed the operation.

Eielson sent his family a snapshot of his haggard arrival at the top of the continent. It shows him standing in a fur parka, his good hand grasping the frozen one, his face, darkened from exposure, alight with a keen smile. "After a walk on the Arctic Ocean last year—taken at Beechey Point," he scribbled on the back. Scientists and geographers had fuller comment. Once more he and Wilkins had made history. They had proved that men marooned far out on the ice pack can walk with safety to land.

The next year Wilkins and Eielson returned to Barrow for the first airplane hop across the top of the world. They came in a Lockheed Vega, second one of its kind ever built. The bright painted monoplane, powered with a Wright J-5 engine, had been specially equipped for the long Arctic journey. There were two extra gas tanks in each wing and the ship carried an imposing array of instruments including altimeters, fore-and-aft and lateral inclinometers, drift indicators and five compasses. Perhaps its most novel feature, one which many Alaska pilots have since envied, was a window built into the floor for vertical vision.

Several weeks were spent at Barrow in preparation. Eielson prowled in his sleep at night; during the days, while his partner worked over the navigational calculations, he sat in a big leather armchair in the late Charles Brower's whaling station, reading or staring into space. "I don't know what he was thinking about," Brower told me.* "He wouldn't talk much. But once when I mentioned another pilot's fatal crash he said when his time came he hoped he'd go the same way." Shortly before departure Eielson wrote a letter to his brother Oliver:

We are again at Point Barrow, as far north as we can get on the American continent. We flew over here in 40 below weather making an average speed of 120 miles an hour. This plane certainly steps out when you give her the gas—makes 145 full out.

In a few days we are going to cross the unexplored territory to the northeast. We hope to land at Kings Bay, Spitsbergen (2,200 miles away) but we may not be able to get any farther than Etah, Greenland (1,900 miles by the route we take) depending upon conditions. We have to take off with 3,500 pounds of gasoline, etc. If we smash on the take-off, and there is always a good chance of it, I will not be able to get home till September —the first boat.

The next mail does not leave here till August, but I am sending this letter with a fellow who leaves here tomorrow by dog team for Nome. . . . Best regards to all. . . .

Your brother

BEN

P.S.—Expect to see you before you receive this letter.

He did. Some two weeks after he wrote this he and Wilkins in their small practically untried monoplane crossed the top of the world in twenty hours and twenty minutes. It was a unique flight, one of the most amazing in all air history.

The 1928 Wilkins-Eielson hop caused less popular excitement than the 1927 New York-to-Paris dash of Charles Lindbergh—but aviation experts consider it more of a feat. Nor had the trans-Atlantic flights of 1926 involved the same problem. Byrd, striking from Spitsbergen to the Pole and back, had paralleled a meridian. It was thus necessary for

* Brower, "King of the Arctic," Barrow's oldest white resident, author of *Fifty Years Below Zero*, 1863–1944. It was Brower that Will Rogers had intended to interview when he and Wiley Post crashed to death near Barrow in 1935. I visited Brower for a few days at Barrow in the summer of 1944.

him to change direction only once: at the Pole itself. The crew of the dirigible *Norge* had likewise followed a direct line—in their case first straight north and then straight south. Eielson and Wilkins, to explore new regions, flew a curved path around the polar regions. This lengthened their trip, and, since they must cross meridians, it was necessary for them to change direction some fifty times to maintain their course. During a part of the journey direction changes were required every few minutes.*

It was a flight for and by science. Only men of broad scientific vision would have conceived it. Only men of firm scientific confidence would have tried it. Still it required much plain gambling courage. The compass, in the Arctic region of maximum declination, could not be entirely relied on; its use must be supplemented by solar navigation. Sight of the sun could mean the difference between life or death, but there was no way of telling what weather might be met across this "blind spot of the globe." Since Barrow in that year had no radio station** it was not even possible to have a report from Spitsbergen. Leaving the top of the continent in silence, in a ship carrying barely enough gas to reach their destination, they must use the elements where they could, defy them where they had to, and trust to luck.

Take-off of the heavily laden Vega was made on the morning of April 15 from a homemade strip of glare ice. Snowbanks towered on both sides. The strip was only fourteen feet wide; because of weather conditions Wilkins dared not wait till it could be broadened. The slick surface, deliberately cleared of snow for utmost momentum, made Eielson's task extremely difficult. There was a light cross-wind. As Wilkins has described it: "From the cabin window I could

---

    * Wilkins' brilliant navigation was based on a method and map prepared by O. M. Miller of the American Geographic Society.
    ** Only radio communication for the flight was provided by a small set taken to Barrow by Wilkins and Eielson. They left the receiver there and took along a hand-driven generator to broadcast reports during the long hop. The Barrow schoolteacher received many of these reports; however because of Barrow's ice-locked isolation months passed before the world learned that they had been received.

see the tail planes swaying and missing by no more than a foot first one bank and then another.... An error of a few pounds' pressure on the rudder, a swing of a few inches one way or the other, and . . . disaster would surely have followed. Eielson kept his nerve. ... We lifted, swung sickeningly, touched the ice again—then soared smoothly into free air!"

The first eleven hours aloft passed well. As the Vega moved steadily above the ridged and gleaming pack no land was sighted but Wilkins made frequent notes of ice conditions. At midnight local time the sun was still visible: "From an altitude of 3,000 feet we observed with the naked eye the dull red orb dance and skip like the masthead of a distant ship rising and falling with the waves." But the gas consumption had been higher than anticipated; fog banks lay directly ahead and "far, far away in the very distant eastern sky, pillars of high storm clouds hung like wraiths under the pale blue zenith."

After they had continued two more hours, part of this time through mists, Eielson gave a shout and pointed out the window. Piercing the fog were rugged mountains: Grant Land. The aviators had come more than half way and were accurately on course. Jubilantly, Wilkins opened a thermos of coffee and they had a meal of biscuits and pemmican. There was cause for celebration. But the breakfast was an uneasy one. Skies ahead, in the neighborhood of Greenland, looked dark and threatening. Ice-landing conditions there were known to be treacherous and by this time Wilkins was almost certain, from all signs of wind and temperature, that a gale raged beyond at Spitsbergen.

"There are two courses open," he told Eielson in a note. "Down there we can land. ... Can we get off again? If we go on we will meet storm at Spitsbergen and perhaps never find the land. Do you wish to land now?"

Eielson hesitated. He wriggled in his seat. Then he wrote his reply: "I'm willing to go on and chance it."

The extreme cold (48 below zero) caused the engine to falter; time and again it was necessary to advance the throttle full and climb steeply. Unable to top the thick cloud layers, Eielson skillfully made his way between them, compensating for his deviation from the course without Wilkins' aid. Toward the end of the journey the air, as expected, became violent. In Wilkins' words: "Our now almost empty plane was tossed like a cork on a stormy sea." The Vega flew into one of the fiercest storms Spitsbergen had experienced in the month of March in many years.

Two needle-pointed peaks were sighted through the murk—but only dimly; surface wind was furious and blowing snow and salt spray filled the air. As the approach was made "a patch of smooth, snow-covered land was passed in an instant's flash and dead ahead loomed a mountain. . . . Eielson avoided it by a narrow margin. . . . We swung broadside to the wind and crabbed our way out to sea. . . . Back we turned toward the land, only to be warned again by the steep mountains. We were like an imprisoned bird beating against a window pane."

Knowing that they were running short of fuel, the men looked for the smooth snow-covered land they had passed. By this time the windshield before Eielson was covered with snow and frozen oil. Wilkins, looking out the side window, passed him notes as fast as he could. "Turn right . . . Now to the left . . . A bit more . . . Turn back . . . Turn back . . . Keep as close to the land as possible . . . THERE IT IS ON OUR RIGHT!"

Eielson made a narrow circle to sea and "heading into the wind came low into the teeth of the snowdrift. . . . My face was hard against the windowpane as I tried to learn if the surface was smooth or covered with broken ice. It was impossible for Eielson to see, but with steady nerve he braced for all eventualities and leveled the ship and lowered her gently until lost in the swirling snow. . . . We came smoothly to rest. . . . Once on the ground we could see no more than a few feet to each side of the machine. . . ."

Hurrying out into the storm, Eielson and Wilkins drained the oil, stamped snow about the skis, tied on the engine covers. Twenty gallons of gas were left—enough for an hour and a half of flight—but storm grounded the Vega for five days. On the sixth the men laboriously tramped a runway and, after several failures, took off. Almost immediately they sighted two tall radio masts and a group of houses, and came down to land at Green Harbour, Spitsbergen.

A group of Scandinavians came skiing toward them. "Who are you?" they cried.

Eielson answered them in "Old Norse," the language of his grandparents. "This is Captain Wilkins," he said. "We have come across from Alaska."

"Impossible!" the men replied. "The plane is too small and anyway you're speaking Norwegian."

It was not long before wine was flowing freely at the Green Harbour radio station, and messages of the arrival were flashing out to an astonished world. "No foxes seen," Wilkins wirelessed the American Geographic Society according to a prearranged code, signifying that he had sighted no land. "Arrived safely," Eielson notified his father, who had had no word of him for many weeks. "Will be home soon."

"Never," declared Colonel Leopold Amery, Colonial Minister of Great Britain, "since Balboa stood on a peak in Darien and saw for the first time the broad Pacific, has so significant a new vision of the world been spread before human eyes in one day as when Wilkins flew in twenty-two hours from America to Europe by way of the Arctic." Acclaim came from many nations. Eielson and Wilkins were feted and honored by the rulers of Norway, Denmark, Sweden, Belgium, Holland, Germany, France and England. In Scandinavia the Leiv Eiriksson Memorial Medal was awarded to Eielson, "Transpolar Flier of Norwegian Ancestry, for Viking Deed and Daring." In England, Wilkins was knighted by King George V.

Returning to the States, the aviators received an ovation in New York and proceeded west, amid great fanfare, to Eielson's home town. As he landed the celebrated Arctic craft on the hayfield where he had once landed his first Jenny, 5,000 North Dakotans, including the Governor, were waiting to greet him. Brass bands blared. Local barnstormers in helmets stood importantly among the crowd. Eielson, clad in a summer suit and straw hat, climbed out of the cockpit and was surrounded by reporters.

He scarcely answered their questions. "Twenty and a half

hours and two meals," he told them. "I guess that's all there was to it." Quizzed about his Arctic hardships, he appeared annoyed. "It seems like a mockery," he said, "to compare our trips in a well warmed cabin airplane with the hardships other explorers have endured." A neighbor asked what his greatest thrill had been. He replied that it was when the French Air Minister's wife, "a charming girl," had asked him for the privilege of a kiss.

Eielson and Wilkins did not rest long on their laurels, but soon set out on another exploring expedition, this time to the Far South. Striking out from Deception Island in the South Shetlands a few days before Christmas, they covered an air distance of 1,200 miles and sighted six hitherto unknown islands. They were the first men to fly into the Antarctic and the first to discover land from the sky.

Eielson was by this time recognized as one of the foremost pilots in America. Early in 1929 he received the Distinguished Flying Cross for "one of the most extraordinary accomplishments in all time." President Hoover presented him with the Harmon Trophy, highest aviation award of the United States Government, for the outstanding air contribution of 1928. Eielson had planned to accompany Wilkins on another Antarctic expedition that year but after some debate he decided not to do so. He was contemplating marriage, and he had earned less on the exploration flights than he would have earned teaching high school. Further, the young hero was now able to draw upon his new prestige to put across an old project.

He had not forgotten his dream of a network of airlines through Alaska to Asia and Europe. Visiting New York, he persuaded officials of the giant Aviation Corporation to invest money in the Far North. Alaska by this time had a number of small competing air services. The Aviation Corporation agreed to buy several of these pioneer firms and merge them into a strong, stable organization with the ultimate aim of launching a route to the Orient. Eielson was to be vice president and general manager of the new subsidiary, which was called Alaskan Airways.

The contract specified that he was to concern himself with executive problems, hiring other pilots to do the flying. His father, nonetheless, was anxious and begged him to stay on the ground. His brother Oliver, planning a business trip to South America, threatened to cancel it unless Ben gave his promise. "I'd just have to come home to bury you," he bluntly said. Eielson assured them his flying days were over. "I guess," he remarked, almost as if he meant it, "it's time for me to settle down."

He returned to Fairbanks that summer full of enthusiasm. At last, the Flying Professor announced, money would be available to develop northern flight on an international scale. "Mrs. Foster," he told his old friend at the Alaska Hotel, "now we'll really be able to put Fairbanks on the map!" The Aviation Corporation had tremendous funds which it could invest in the Arctic. Some of the New York executives were still skeptical of the commercial possibilities, but they needed only to be shown.

He looked for new business—and found more than he had hoped. An American trading motor ship, the *Nanuk*, was ice-bound off the village of North Cape, Siberia. Aboard her were fifteen passengers and $1,000,000 worth of fur. Officials of the Swenson Fur and Trading Corporation in Seattle feared a market collapse and wanted the fur removed immediately for shipment to London and New York. They offered Eielson's company $50,000 to rescue cargo and passengers and ferry them to Alaska.

Eielson knew the dangers. The flights to Siberia would be long and hazardous ones over a little-known region of brewing storms. Only one Alaskan, Noel Wien, had flown a round trip between America and Asia and he had made his trip in the month of March in fair weather. By the time Eielson had settled his terms with the Swenson interests it was October. Winter darkness would soon shroud the Far North. But this was the biggest transportation contract of any kind ever offered in Alaska. It would give the New York management full proof. He determined the trips must be made and decided to fly some of them himself.

A game young Fairbanks mechanic named Earl Borland agreed to accompany him. Borland was moody as the time for the journey approached. "I have a feeling," he said, "we'll never come home." Eielson was in high spirits. "He ate lots of ptarmigan and waffles . . . ," Alaskans recall. "He talked about polar flying. . . . 'We'll have a real party,' he said, 'as soon as we return.' "

Late in October Eielson and Borland flew to Teller, tiny Bering Coast settlement which was to serve as the jump-off point to Asia. They made one successful trip to the *Nanuk* in an all-metal cabin Hamilton. A trip was also made by a pilot named Frank Dorbandt with Mechanic Bud Bassett in a Stinson. As they headed back toward Alaska with the first loads of fur, the two planes were caught in a blizzard, forced down on the Siberian coast and grounded there for several days. They returned safely to Teller when the weather cleared and the pilots planned to make a second trip at once but stormy skies bound them to earth on the Alaskan side for nearly a week.

On the gloomy morning of November 9 Eielson and Dorbandt, according to an eyewitness account, waited together after breakfast in the Teller roadhouse. Eielson sat with his feet propped on the counter, reading a magazine. Dorbandt restlessly paced the floor. The two men were temperamental opposites and had clashed on several occasions since Eielson had returned to Alaska with his new title and power. Dorbandt, an Anchorage pioneer, was big of heart, hot of temper, loud of mouth. He was one of the ablest pilots in the North, but also one of the most reckless and impulsive. A few weeks later, when Eielson had postponed a local trip because of bad weather, Dorbandt had accused his new boss of cowardice.

"When are we going to take off?" Dorbandt asked on this fateful morning.

"We'll wait for the next weather report from the *Nanuk,*" Eielson tersely told him.

Dorbandt tore a piece of wrapping paper from the counter and scrawled a rough diagram of Bering Strait and the two continents.

"You know," he shouted, "all we have to do is hit right across here!"

Eielson did not reply.

"Well," Dorbandt told him, "you can sit here if you want. I'm leaving."

At 10:45 people in the roadhouse heard the roar of the Stinson's engine and saw Dorbandt's ship lift into the air, heading toward Asia.

Eielson went silently upstairs and returned in his parka. He and Borland walked to their ship. At 11:15 the Hamilton bumped off the sea and disappeared into the unsettled sky to the west.

Some time later, Dorbandt and Bassett, foiled by dense fog in Bering Strait, returned.

Eielson and Borland did not return. Nor did they reach the *Nanuk*. Days passed. Weeks passed. There was only silence.

5
The Death of Ben Eielson

SOON AFTER Eielson and Borland disappeared the sun dropped below the horizon, not to rise until the following year. Only a few dim hours around noontime each day gave light enough for flying in the sub-Arctic region, and this only in favorable weather. The winter of 1929–30 was exceptionally stormy. The temperature dropped to 40 below zero and repeated seventy-mile gales swept between the two continents. "Never," says Jack Warren, old-timer and manager of the Teller roadhouse, "have I seen so much ice, snow, wind and fog."

Joe Crosson, a close friend of Eielson's, was the first pilot to arrive at Teller for search work. Others were delayed by storm or accident. It was not till late December that the little group, representing most of the pilots* and flyable planes in the Territory, had gathered there poised for take-off to Siberia. Even young Harold Gillam, who had previously made only one cross-country flight, was present. "Give me a ship, give me a ship," he had begged Alaskan Airways officials in Fairbanks. "I want to look for Ben." They had hesitated, but in the end he had his way.

The search planes, anchored to the ice before the roadhouse, were a sad spectacle. None had adequate range to reach the *Nanuk*, which was to be the base of operations on the Siberian side. None had any but the crudest of instruments. All but one, a small Stinson biplane, were open-cockpit. For comfort and safety none of these ships could

*Pilots Crosson, Dorbandt, Matt Nieminen, Harvey Barnhill, Ed Young, and Harold Gillam, with Fred Moller and Alonzo Cope acting as mechanics. The last four of these men have since crashed to death in the North.

compare with those in which Eielson and Wilkins had made their Arctic flights, or with the all-metal cabin Hamilton in which Eielson and Borland had been lost.

Jack Warren, the roadhouse manager who was host to the Eielson Relief Expedition at Teller, experienced such strain that he cannot discuss the search calmly even today. "Those pilots," he says, "were all a bunch of nerves." As time passed, Dorbandt was reported to be verging on a breakdown. Crowded together in the bleak frame building, the men looked out past high snowbanks to whirling gloom. Weather at North Cape was reported no better. "Ceiling and visibility nil," the *Nanuk* flashed day after day. "High winds." The universal edginess of weatherbound airmen was sharpened by a driving sense of urgency and a brooding sense of hopelessness.

It was the mechanics who had the hardest physical lot at Teller. Each morning they stumbled to work through pitch-darkness: at least three hours were required to warm the engines with fire pots and they must be ready by daylight in case of a weather change. Crawling inside flimsy tent nose-hangars, the shivering men kept watch, but accidents were inevitable in the high wind. Sudden blazes required long hours of cruel exposure in the out-of-doors to rewire the planes. Most of their servicing was futile. Time after time a fur-bundled pilot took off from the frozen runway to scout the sky, only to return with bad news: Bering Strait was impassable. Often, landing on the rough ice, the planes were damaged. Pilot Dorbandt broke an axle on one try, a ski on another, and a landing gear on a third.

An appeal was made to Washington for help from the Army Air Corps. The reply was flat: the Army had no properly equipped planes and no men experienced in Arctic winter flight. It was unable to assist. Had another pilot been lost in these latitudes in winter, officers would have known only one Army flyer well qualified to go to his rescue: Ben Eielson.

In New York Stefansson proposed that help be sought from the Soviet Union, which was known to have done considerable Arctic air work with government planes. But since no official relations existed between the United States of America and the Union of Soviet Socialist Republics, State

Department officials declined to act. It would be impossible, they declared, to seek favor from a government which had not been accorded diplomatic recognition. Stefansson, aided by former Assistant Attorney General Mabel Walker Willebrandt, continued his efforts. As a result two cables were dispatched to Moscow—one by Senator William E. Borah, Chairman of the Foreign Relations Committee, and one by Secretary of Interior Ray Lyman Wilbur.

"The fact that we Americans do not recognize the Soviet Union," the Soviet newspaper *Chudak* said in a cartoon, "that is nothing. But if they do not recognize our planes on account of the fog—that will be bad." The Union of Soviet Socialist Republics, however, moved to generous action on behalf of a man whom it counted a great Arctic pioneer. Dog teams were dispatched from Wrangel Island and mainland points across the ice pack and overland and a $1,000 reward for news of Eielson was offered by Moscow to Siberians. Soviet planes were ordered to proceed to North Cape as soon as possible for search work.

The Aviation Corporation meanwhile prepared to give all possible support to the hunt for its lost executive; a total of more than $500,000 was to be expended by the company before it was through. Alfred Lomen, prominent Nome merchant who had outfitted many Arctic explorers, was placed in charge of the Teller operation and instructed to outfit the men with the best of winter gear. The corporation contracted in Canada for three Wasp-powered ski-equipped cabin planes—Fairchild 71's—also hiring a group of Canadian pilots and mechanics to fly and service them. Against the advice of Stefansson, who maintained that swift, safe flight to Alaska could be made by following the Mackenzie River, the company decided to crate these Fairchilds and ship them as far north as possible by boat. They would leave Seattle, it was announced, as soon as they could be assembled.

For Eielson's fellow flyers this was not soon enough. Forty days had passed. He and Borland had carried provisions for only thirty. On the stormy morning of December 19 Crosson and Gillam loaded a Stearman and a Waco with extra gas and provisions to last several weeks. "This time we'll make it through," Gillam confidently declared. The others looked on morosely. "No one in his right mind," says Jack Warren, "would have started out to Siberia in that weather." Since the two pilots had no radio contact, it was agreed that Gillam would follow his more experienced partner and land wherever he did. Heavily bundled, they climbed into their open cockpits, waved goodbye, and flew into the gloom.

"We made it that time," Crosson told me. "We managed to sneak across the Strait." Heavy fog boiled up from the broken ice. Winds funneling through the international channel, he says, "seemed to blow in 23 directions at once." He and Gillam flew low, fighting for control. Visibility was almost zero but they managed, by following the black streaks of open leads, to continue their course. They proceeded in this near-blind fashion for two hours, till they sighted a snow-covered bluff: Siberia. The fog was thinner here, but darkness was nearly upon them. They followed the winding, white, treeless banks in search of a place to land. After some time Crosson sighted a village in the dusk and brought his Waco safely down upon the ice before it. Gillam landed in his ski tracks close behind.

Through the snow came a group of Soviet Eskimos dressed in skin clothing with "strange-looking separate hoods like helmets and mittens made of the foreheads of reindeer." Matter-of-fact, they helped drain the oil, cover the motors and pull the sleeping bags from the planes. They led the flyers to an oval-shaped hut where they were greeted by "Kacherb," the broad-smiling village Chief. Almost all night Siberians and Americans conversed with sketches and gestures. The Chief told Crosson and Gillam they were near the south mouth of Kolyuchin Bay (roughly halfway to their destination). He had heard of the lost plane. Some of his people had seen it fly overhead. He sketched the direction in which it had been going—toward North Cape and the *Nanuk*.

Next morning the pilots refueled from gas carried in the cabins and took off once more, heading toward North Cape. They soon flew into a blizzard so violent that Crosson decided to turn back. He rocked the wings, signaling Gillam to follow. A few moments later "everything blotted out"; he lost sight of Gillam's ship and of the earth. It was some time before he saw a pressure ridge, found the dim line of shore and followed it back to the village. His goggles froze over as he approached. He was forced to push them back to make a landing and as a result "frosted" his eyes, which was to add to his danger and difficulty in the weeks to come.

Gillam did not arrive. After an anxious night Crosson struck out once more to the west. He scanned the bleak shores constantly but saw no sign of either of his comrades. For three hours he flew through the dimness. Then he saw a scattering of specks, like flecks of black pepper on a white tablecloth. Some made a thin line along the shore: the trading village of North Cape. Two others lay out on the ice: the *Nanuk* and an icelocked Soviet vessel, the *Stavropol*. There was a fourth speck on the snow nearby: Gillam's Stearman.

It was difficult to believe. Gillam, the plucky novice who was later to become one of Alaska's greatest pilots, had managed to reach North Cape on schedule. Separated from Crosson in the blizzard, he had taken a course away from the bluffs, flying blind with only a crude compass to guide him till he found a break in the storm. Fighting his way into clear sky, he had continued on to the *Nanuk* all alone.

Crosson and Gillam were lodged aboard the motor ship and hoped, with the use of fuel offered by the Soviet Union, to search for Eielson without delay and without let-up. But the most ferocious storm of the winter struck the day after their arrival and continued for more than a month. Snow and wind. Wind and snow. Thick, blowing fog. Men traveling by dog team lost their way in this angry blizzard. Crosson and Gillam were hopelessly grounded. On only eight days out of a five-week period was flight conceivable.

"It is the tradition of exploration," Stefansson has written, "not to give up rescue work so long as there is any reasonable chance." Never has this tradition been more gallantly honored than by Gillam and Crosson in their small open-cockpit planes. Whenever take-off was possible they dug out the drifted ships, warmed the engines in snow-block hangars, and struck out into the murk. One flying north, the other south, they scouted the coastline and penetrated far inland. Even when visibility was at its best, hazy sky and frozen earth were almost indistinguishable. "It was," in Crosson's words, "like flying inside a milk bottle." Flurries of storm were frequent. The two pilots returned from some of these hunts, *Nanuk* passengers reported, declaring they would try no more till the weather finally cleared. But they were unable to stick to this resolve. They would set out the next time under even more ominous conditions.

They searched most often in a region near the mouth of the Amguyema River, some sixty miles from the *Nanuk*, where a trapper named Brokhanov insisted that he had seen a strange plane. It had circled his hut, he said, and flown inland. Both Crosson and Gillam returned to this area several times. Each told the other that he felt drawn toward it by a strong and persistent hunch. But they saw no sign there or anywhere else of Eielson's Hamilton.

Meanwhile, back on the Alaskan side of the Strait, the relief expedition was frustrated by foul weather and bad luck. When the eagerly awaited Canadian Fairchilds reached Alaska, one was damaged in take-off from the Fairbanks field. A second, piloted by Captain Pat Reid of Winnipeg, was forced down in a blizzard. It was not until mid-January, more than two months after Eielson's disappearance, that two of the Fairchilds dropped down to join the rest of the expedition's planes, which were still grounded by fog and storm at Teller.

"Everyone experienced a feeling of vast relief," Jack Warren wrote in a summary of the search, "when these two beautiful birds circled the village and the steady drone of their powerful 420 h.p. Pratt & Whitney Wasps was heard. . . . For such a hazardous expedition no better equipment could be mustered." Spirits on both sides of the Strait further improved with the news that Soviet search planes were now also approaching North Cape.

Two Arctic pilots, Maurice Slepnev and V. L. Galyshev, who had been officially attached to the icebreaker *Litke* with two Junkers, were proceeding toward the *Nanuk*. Six other planes, piloted by some of the foremost airmen of the Soviet Union, were also moving northeast toward the *Nanuk*. Two, of the "Land of the Soviets" type, were commanded by Pilot Semyon A. Shestakov, who had flown to the United States in

1928. Two more, Dornier-Wasps, were under the command of B. G. Chuknovsky. Pilot Mikhail Gromov, hero of a 1925 Moscow-Peking flight, who was later to cross the polar sea en route from Moscow to California, was also on the way in a Fokker.

From Nome the Associated Press flashed:

A big aerial drive for Eielson is under way. . . . Airplanes manned by American, Russian and Canadian aviators are today either moving toward North Cape, Siberia or poised at various places in Alaska and Siberia awaiting favorable weather for massed attack to solve the mystery of his fate.

From the *Nanuk*, passenger Marion Swenson wirelessed the New York *Times*:

Airplanes in three groups were headed today toward our ice-locked ship with fliers of three nations in final attempt to solve the mystery hiding the whereabouts of Carl Ben Eielson and Earl Borland. The combined Soviet Union, Canadian and American groups represent the greatest rescue armada ever assembled in the Arctic.

Continued storm, however, prevented this array of international aircraft from reaching the *Nanuk* in time to aid in the search.

Not until January 25 was there a day of clear weather at North Cape. On that morning the sun rose low and red on the horizon, returning to the Arctic for another year. Crosson and Gillam, who had nearly exhausted the local stock of fuel, decided to return to Alaska for a fresh supply. "We'll be back," they told their friends at the *Nanuk*. They shook hands all around and flew away to the east.

A few hours later, the two planes returned. A startled crowd hurried toward them as they taxied to a stop.

"Well," Crosson slowly announced, "the search is over."

He reached back and pulled out a mass of crumpled metal. "From Ben's plane," he said, and turned abruptly toward the *Nanuk*.

Supper aboard the boat that night was an awkward meal. Crosson and Gillam were hardly able to tell their story. They had been flying low, five miles apart, following the coastline.

As they neared the Amguyema trapper's hut which they had circled so many times in the winter dusk, a dark streak was sighted on the sunlit snow. At first they thought it was a dog team. But in Crosson's words it "seemed to lay at a peculiar angle." They dropped to look closer. Not until they got down to 300 feet did they see that it was a shadow cast by the wing of a snow-covered plane. They landed and ran to the wreck of the Hamilton.

The aircraft lay on a sloping mound, deep in drifts, pointing southeast toward Alaska. One side of the fuselage was sheared away and the tail was torn off just aft of the cabin. Shoveling carefully into the cockpit, they had found the sides crushed in, the seats mashed, the safety belts hanging empty. There was no sign of Eielson or Borland. It was probable that they had been hurled out of the wreckage to instant death. By all indications the crash had been violent and uncontrolled.

Eielson must have been circling the trapper's hut in search of a place to land. The weather, by the trapper's report, had not been stormy, but the hands of the plane's clock confirmed the fact that night was falling. As the Hamilton banked in the dimness, a wing must have struck the snowy rise. It was impossible to be sure; but this, Crosson and Gillam believed, was the way the disaster had happened.

Now that the storm had broken, Soviet, Canadian and American planes were able to reach the *Nanuk*. They hauled men and supplies to the scene of disaster and a group of Siberians under the leadership of Pilot Slepnev began the slow, grim work of digging for the dead. Camping in tents beneath the Hamilton's wing, the Soviet crew labored steadily for weeks in the sub-zero weather, hacking trenches through deep drifts packed "hard as cement."

On February 5, according to the log of a Soviet worker named Kalinin, the Hamilton's motor base, stained with blood, was located some fifty feet from the plane. On February 6, a broken pair of pilot's glasses was uncovered. On February 9, scattered parts—ailerons, ventilators and other sections. On February 12, Borland's mittens. The following day, Borland's body was found. Work was then interrupted by storm which capsized the tents and formed new drifts over the area. Not until February 18 did a Siberian named T. Yakobsen, digging a hundred and twenty feet from the Hamilton, come upon the body of Eielson.

"It was a great relief that this wearisome and nerve-straining search was concluded," Kalinin wrote in his log, "but it was a mournful day for us all." The aviators' bodies were loaded into Slepnev's Junker and flown to the Soviet ship *Stavropol* where Dr. U. U. Kreszanev prepared them for burial. Siberian women at North Cape sewed American flags, improvised from red and blue muslin and white ship canvas, to wrap them in.

Even in death, Ben Eielson was a pioneer. To the men who participated in the Eielson Relief Expedition, Soviet-American friendship is an experience dating back forty-three years. Men like Crosson have a personal feeling about it. "Those Russians did everything in their power for us," he says, "and they wouldn't take a cent in pay. They were swell people." One of his proudest possessions is a Soviet air medal later presented to him, Gillam and Pilot Ed Young by Pilot Slepnev. They, in a gesture of appreciation, had given Slepnev a gun. Deeply touched, he told them: "I will make you a gift of the most precious thing I own." The shining red medal, which he had received from his government for Arctic accomplishment, shows an airplane silhouetted against a snowy peak. He had a message engraved on the back: ED JOE AND HAROLD—MY BROTHERS AND FRIENDS.

The exchange of messages between Moscow and Washington at the time of the search was probably the first official communication involving friendly cooperation between the U.S.A. and the U.S.S.R., and as the expedition prepared to disband at North Cape,* Crosson and Young sent wires to both governments asking that Slepnev and his mechanic Bruno Fahrig be granted permission to accompany them back to America. It was given. The two pilots, on special

---

* The relief expedition was terminated late in February but Canadian and American pilots worked many weeks after this, hauling fur and passengers to complete Eielson's contract and returning fuel which had been made available for the search on the Soviet side. Pilot S. E. Robbins is among those who deserve credit for these flights.

invitation from the United States, were to travel to Alaska as representatives of the Soviet Union's aviation commission.*

Late in February, on the wind-swept ice before the *Nanuk* and the *Stavropol*, Americans formally took custody of their own. Both vessels' flags hung at half-mast on that foggy morning. The Chairman of the Chukotsk area, who had traveled more than 400 miles by dog team to be present at the ceremony, expressed his sorrow that the tragic loss had occurred on Soviet soil. Pilot Young gave America's thanks for Soviet aid. Slowly the bodies were hauled by sled to the Canadian Fairchild that was to carry them home. They were lifted inside and the windows of the plane were shrouded with black. Storm delayed the return trip; not for two weeks was the funeral plane, accompanied by the honoring Soviet ship, able to fly to Alaska.

Violent weather and solemn pomp attended the body of the thirty-two-year-old aviator all the way on its long, slow journey back to North Dakota. Rough wind and water tossed the steamer on its voyage to Seattle. Crowds thronged the water front when she docked, and the city observed a moment of silence. Thousands later filed past the coffin, which was draped with Soviet and American banners. Army caissons rumbled and planes circled overhead as it was escorted to the railroad station in a driving rainstorm. As a black-draped locomotive drew the body through the West to North Dakota many thousands stood at stations to watch it pass. Thousands more stood bareheaded at the Hatton graveyard in a sudden blizzard as the coffin was lowered into the Eielson family plot.

Proposals had been made that Eielson be interred with full

---

* This was the first but not the last time that American and Soviet pilots worked together in the Far North. In 1934, when the Chelyuskin expedition of Soviet scientists was marooned on an Arctic ice floe, the Soviet Union purchased two planes in Alaska for rescue work and hired two Alaska mechanics, Bill Lavery and Clyde Armistead, to service them. Lavery and Armistead were later invited to Moscow, where they received the Order of Lenin and life-long pensions. Lavery, son of a pioneer Alaskan airplane company manager, later pioneered service between Fairbanks and Anchorage and is today one of the leading young flyers of the Territory.

military honor at Arlington. His father declined. "So many people are buried there," he told reporters. "After all, what is fame?"

History has paid living tribute to the name of Ben Eielson. Not only has Alaska surpassed the States in per capita volume of flight; during World War II Eielson's vision of international air traffic through the Far North was sensationally realized. Not far from the site of the Fairbanks ball park, two large Army airdromes were built. The sky thundered as flight after flight of Soviet Lend-Lease bombers and fighters arrived from the States and headed on toward Siberia and Europe. Old-timers who once watched anxiously for the speck of Eielson's Jenny seldom looked up as these large formations passed. More than 7,000 red-starred planes took this short, safe, northerly route around the top of the world to war.

The earnest young flyer had not known it would happen so violently. Still, he was sure it would come. It was certain as the power of his Liberty engine to lift him over a mountain. He figured on it and, in the way of the pioneer, cheerfully worked for it to the end.

6
Spilling Dollars

IT TOOK MANY KINDS of men to build aviation in Alaska.

Cross the big bridge at Fairbanks, turn left by the depot, stop at the first white house on Pioneer Avenue and you will meet a railroad conductor named Jimmy Rodebaugh.

Rodebaugh, a stocky, baldish, energetic man, works with switch engines and bells and twisting track. He has to get up at six in the morning. But he will sit in his parlor half the night talking about airplanes. He is rather bitter, rather proud. Rodebaugh is no pilot. But it was he, in 1924, who promoted the first honest-to-goodness flying business in the North.

To Jimmy Rodebaugh, The Aviation was strictly a dollar-and-cents proposition. He was a railroad conductor by profession but he had tried his luck at many things—started a sawmill, owned part of a mine, made a lot of money trading in furs. Rodebaugh had lived fourteen years on the frontier. He knew the meaning of a mile. He also knew, he thought, how to cash in on a good deal.

Fairbanks, when Ben Eielson made his first flights there, was a ghost town, "in bad shape, sure needed something." Once, after the gold strike of 1902, 8,000 people had lived at Fairbanks and it boasted it was the "bigegst log cabin city in the world." In 1924 less than 1,500 were left.

"OUR TOWN," Wrong Font Thompson defiantly wrote in the *News-Miner*, "OUR TOWN IS THE HEART OF THE TOP OF THE WORLD. THERE IS NOTHING WRONG WITH OUR TOWN. We do not blame you for living in the States. Someone has to live there and we would rather it be you than us."

Smith's Hardware and Gun Store still offered gold pans,

picks, skis, toboggans, sleeping bags, fur mitts, fur parkas, fur pants.

The Golden Grocery still featured "Miners' and Prospectors' Orders Shipped with Care."

But most of the mining was done by armchair prospectors slouched under mooseheads in hotel lobbies. The era of the giant mechanical dredge had not yet come. The era of the boiler and sluice box was gone. All the bonanza gold had been dug from nearby ground.

Out beyond Fairbanks, everybody knew, out in the thousand and one untouched hills, lay rich pay dirt. Miners toiling overland to these far sites could not haul supplies enough to last a season. But a plane, Eielson had shown, could lift a man with his outfit "fast and easy," set them down right by his claim. Planes could do the trick. Rodebaugh decided to buy some ships, bring the log-cabin city back to life and make himself a fortune doing it.

Eielson told him big planes and big money should come from the government but Rodebaugh did not believe any money would come from the government. Besides, he did not want to wait. His palm itched for The Aviation. No business like it—it would be a sure-fire deal, a rip-roaring, fast-growing business, the smartest kind of business a man could be in.

He made a trip to the States to look for planes. He found two ships—not at all what he wanted—Standards—old war trainers, so small they could haul only 400 pounds, so slow with their little Curtiss OX-5 engines they cruised little faster than autos, had to come down for gas every 100 miles. But he paid $5,000 for the two because they were the best aircraft he could find. He had a tinner build some extra gas tanks and replaced the engines with more powerful 150-h.p. water-cooled "Hisso's"—Hispano-Suizas.

Next he looked for pilots. Through a Minneapolis garage man who owned a cracked-up Jenny, he located two men; not what he wanted either—young farm boys—Noel Wien had only 500 hours in the air, Arthur Sampson less. But they were aviators so he offered them $300 a month and paid their boat fares north.

In the spring of 1924 Rodebaugh ordered a stock of

aviation gas in five-gallon cans and launched the Alaska Aerial Transportation Company. "The men," he told Fairbanks, "will be able to take at least three passengers. If you will travel with them they will land you at your workings in minutes whereas otherwise it would take days."

Bustling eagerly about the ball park, Rodebaugh planned a regular operation—eight hours a day, seven days a week. But the air, he learned, is not the same as a steel track. "It was a terrible disappointment," he angrily told me. "Sampson made a world of friends and took them over town for joy rides. But he didn't like cross-country trips. Said he was afraid of bears. Both the men were temperamental. Always balking at the weather. Seemed like they wouldn't go up if there was a cloud in the sky."

Still, the Standards earned a third of their cost that first summer. Wien hauled meat and Malamutes and gold dust. Once he took in $1,500 in a single day. Alaskans were crazy to fly. Joy-hoppers would pay $10 apiece, twice as much as they'd pay in the States. Miners would give more than a dollar a mile to ride in the airships. The Aviation looked like such a good deal that everybody wanted to get in on it. Early in 1925 citizens decided to start a bigger outfit—the Fairbanks Airplane Company.

Rodebaugh turned in his Standards and became the largest stockholder. All up and down the main street—in the bank, the hardware store, the meat market and the grocery—merchants and clerks dug into their pockets. Mining men invested and traders from outlying settlements chipped in. The grand total was $28,000.

The Fairbanks Airplane Company took out incorporation papers. It abandoned the ball park and smoothed a real field from a vacant lot at the edge of town. A hangar was built with boards from an abandoned railroad roundhouse. The managers looked for new pilots and they voted to get another plane—a large plane with a cabin; that, everyone agreed, was what the company should buy.

Pilot Wien went Outside to find one. He wired bad news. Alaska, it seemed, was ahead of the nation. No cabin planes were for sale in the States. There was a Waco model, but he did not trust it; it had not yet been tested for stress. There was a Bellanca under construction which promised to be a good ship but it would not be ready for six months. That was too long, the managers wired back. The Fairbanks Airplane Company could not wait.

Finally, at Curtiss Field, Long Island, Wien found a second-hand Fokker—big monoplane built in Holland—just what the company hoped for—fifty-four foot wingspread—large and spacious—156 cubic feet in the cabin—fancy upholstery like a car—heavy 180 h.p. B.M.W. German engine—cruised at ninety miles an hour—quite a ship.

He warned that it was rather large for a land without airfields but the company paid $9,500 for it and another $400 to have it shipped by boat through the Panama Canal.

Rodebaugh and his associates made big plans. Now the new airline could fly heavy loads of passengers and bulky freight, winter and summer, all over the northland. The great ship, Thompson wrote, would "annihilate space and protect all Interior Alaska against railroad washouts, strikes and delays in transmission of humans and freight, render first aid to the injured . . . and make Fairbanks the center of Aviation. . . ." "At last," he rapturously announced, "the Friendly North has passed from the Dog Team Stage into the Airship Class!"

But the Fokker was a dud when it arrived in Alaska.

Wien was the only pilot who would ever fly it, and he would not fly it much. Other men refused to take the controls. Haywire foreign rig, they said, dangerous cockpit arrangement, landed too fast. How could a plane like that come down on a river bar? Even the new Fairbanks field was too short.

The big Dutch transport was eventually stored in a shed. It gathered dust. The wings warped. Children broke in and tore up the fuselage for souvenirs.

Early in 1926 the Fairbanks Airline Company hired two new pilots—Joe Crosson and A. A. Bennett, from San Diego, California—but business was slow. Manager Bob Lavery was too busy in his grocery to attend to the airline. The water-cooled Hisso engines were always out of whack. Customers grumbled. Stockholders began calling each other names. Rodebaugh was impatient. So was Pilot Bennett. The two decided to pull out of the Fairbanks Airplane Company and start a new outfit of their own.

Bennett was a tall, gangling fellow, used to be a logger and a salesman. He was a live wire, a go-getter, he'd go up in any weather, flew more than anyone else, really did things in a slambang way. He and Rodebaugh bought three planes—brand-new Waco 9's, just out, with Curtiss OXX-6 water-cooled engines. The Wacos were open-cockpit jobs but they flew faster, hauled half again as much load, used less than half as much gas as the Fairbanks Airplane Company's Standards.

That spring, when the dirigible *Norge* landed at Teller after its trans-Arctic flight, pilots of the two rival companies raced north from Fairbanks to get news shots for Pathe and INS. Bennett flew his pictures down to Whitehorse, Canada. This, and a batch of mining trips, grossed $10,000 that month. Rodebaugh was elated. It was just what he'd figured. Fairbanks was electrified. The Aviation really was a bonanza business. "There was never a mine in the community could pay off like that."

Then it happened.

"Crack! Crack! Crack!" Rodebaugh says, ruefully shaking his head. "Some aviation sucker had to put up the money."

His brand-new Wacos were wrecked in six weeks.

One smashed onto a bar in the Koyukuk region. Another "slid off like a dart" and crashed by the Fairbanks field. The third nosed over in the Kantishna. He and Bennett had not one flyable plane left.

They decided to make another try, and sent for new parts by express. In two months they had the Wacos in the air again. They hired a second pilot, Ed Young, local trapper and roadhouse keeper who had flown in the war, and they borrowed money for a fourth plane—a Swallow—with two air-cooled Wright Whirlwind engines.

The Fairbanks Airplane Company, not to be outdone, bought a Swallow too.

That fall some 200 miners, having finished their summer work in the Iditarod, clamored for airplane passage to town. This was big business, more than $75,000 worth. "Somebody was in line to make a bunch of money." The two competing companies prepared to fight to the death.

Then, "Crack! Crack! Crack!—it happened all over again."

One of the Standards crashed on a bar in the Toklat.

One of the Wacos spun to earth near Medfra, "rolled up in a ball."

One of the new Swallows nosed over on slush ice.

The other plunged into the Kuskokwim River.

This, late in 1926, was aviation in the Far North—four ships smashed, down on river bars, down in the brush—all the pilots out on dog trails, mushing, hobbling home.

The Fairbanks Airplane Company went temporarily out of business, $12,000 in debt. Rodebaugh and Bennett couldn't pay their bills either. People snickered when they saw Rodebaugh on the street. They told him he was the champion lemon-picker of the world.

But he shipped a new prop to his Swallow by dog team and got the ship flying again. Early in 1927 the "Black Bear," well-known frontierswoman in the Iditarod, was charged with stealing $30,000. Her trial, held in Fairbanks, was one of the most crowded Alaska had ever known. Everybody wanted to see the Black Bear in court. Bennett hauled so many witnesses and spectators in one month that he and Rodebaugh were out of the red.

They bought a second Swallow, another Waco and a Zenith.

The Fairbanks Airplane Company decided to buy another Swallow too.

Both outfits tried again.

* * *

Fairbanks was the first—but all over the northland it was much the same story, the founding of the first flying companies.

Not until 1931, seven years after Eielson made his trips to McGrath, did the federal government sign another mail contract for Alaska. Even today the Post Office Department requires the local airlines to bid against the dog teams.

Not until 1939 were any federal funds provided for safe fields and airways.

Nor, for all the aid it has granted to railroads, steamship companies and airlines in the States, has the federal government ever directly subsidized development of the air services of Alaska.

The Territory has done the best it could.

The history has been tangled; small outfits founded all over the land—cutthroat competition, rate-slashing, passenger-stealing, excessive credit, ruination for some, survival for others.

The history has been rough; according to official records the average plane, until airports and airways were built by the Civil Aeronautics Administration and the Army in World War II, had two or three crack-ups a year.

But all down the years merchants and miners kept on shoving out money, pilots and people kept on risking their necks. By 1945 more than 500 planes had been shipped from the States to the Far North.

Some United States capital has entered Alaskan aviation. Pan American, hoping for an eventual route to Asia, bought Eielson's old company in 1932 and has been operating in the North ever since. Northwest Airlines, which flew Alaskan routes for the Air Transport Command during the war, was preparing in mid-1946 to fly commercially to Alaska and through Alaska to the Orient. Inside the Territory several of the local outfits have been merged into a large company called Alaska Airlines, controlled in New York. Art Woodley, pioneer bush pilot, has recently launched an expanded operation—Pacific Northern—with backing from Seattle interests. There have been other such cases.

But most of the air traffic in this flyingest land has been handled by small, Alaskan-owned companies. It is the people and pilots of the Territory themselves who have brought wings to the wilderness.

Flying North and No.1 175

into the sky. Even today, is the Matter and son see result

7
Noel Wien

PILOT NOEL WIEN is one of the few "old originals" of Alaskan aviation who have escaped death in flight. His name is little known in the States, but he is the dean of this rugged school. Arriving at Fairbanks two years after Eielson, he went to work and continued down the years, logging a total of more than 8,000 hours above mountains, tundra and sea.

Wien also brought three of his family into the flying North. Each time he made a trip to the States in the early period he returned with a brother. First it was Ralph, who soloed in 1928 and did some remarkable piloting until he was killed in an Arctic crash. Next it was Fritz, who is one of the ablest mechanics on the Fairbanks field. Then it was Sig, today one of the most active flyers in the North. These transplanted Minnesota farm boys are among the most eminent citizens of the Territory. The Cabots of Boston, the Stuyvesants of New York, the Pennypackers of Philadelphia enjoy no such universal prestige as men, women and children throughout Alaska accord the name of Wien.

Noel Wien, like Eielson, is of Scandinavian descent. He is a tall, conservative-looking man with a ring of graying hair, a tight-drawn mouth and a soft, close-clipped way of speaking. He gives an impression of gentle patience, as if he were talking to a child. He is reserved, friendly. One feels he would do almost anything to help other people. Except for a kind of weathered look, he has the appearance of a small-town preacher.

The first time I met Wien he drove me in a Studebaker to his home near the Fairbanks field. In contrast to many pilots, who handle autos like race cars, he drove slowly and cautiously through the snow-banked streets. We turned into a driveway before a large white frame house with pale yellow shutters. There was a greenhouse beside it. "We grow toma-toes in there," he volunteered, "and cucumbers." A model plane was tilted in the snow near by. "That's my son's," he said, with a hint of a smile. "He builds many planes. We're afraid one day he'll make one that will fly." He led me up the steps, past a stack of sleds and skis, inside.

Mrs. Wien, a striking-looking woman with pale skin and black hair, was baking cookies in a modern fluffy-curtained kitchen. Rows of homemade currant jam lined the shelves. There was a length of fuzzy tweed spread on the table. "I'm making a skirt," she explained, "for my daughter Jean." She set us a tray of coffee and we sat down in a living room bright with flowered chintz, old-fashioned knit throw-overs and full bookshelves. Only paintings of Eskimos and snow-caps suggested that this was Alaska.

As we talked about Arctic aviation the children came home from school. Merrill,* who is named for Anchorage's pioneer flyer, put on his Boy Scout uniform and hurried away. Jean started practicing on a violin. Richard pounded in the cellar. "How about your homework?" Mrs. Wien shouted down the stairs. . . . "Noel," she called a few minutes later, "don't forget, the storm window needs fixing."

Noel Wien is a family man, a Mason and a Presbyterian. He does not drink. He does not smoke. He does not swear. He is frugal with words. "Poor weather," he will say of a howling blizzard. Of a long journey across unmapped tundra he will remark: "A good trip." The forbidding terrain of Alaska takes on a gentle cast as he speaks of it. "I landed on a small dome. . . . I spotted a fair-looking sandbar." He speaks of a historic flight as if it were a small bicycle excursion.

Wien learned to fly in Minnesota in 1921. He did not have enough money to solo; the local school in that year required a deposit of $2,800, the price of the ship. One day, riding with a barnstormer in a dual-control plane, he watched him make two passes at a short cornfield and overshoot each time. On the third try Wien opened the throttle, took the plane around and landed it. This gave him his start. The

* Merrill Wien soloed on his sixteenth birthday in 1945.

barnstormer let him fly the plane alone and carry half his passengers.

In those days Wien was a lanky blond boy who would try almost anything to make a living in the air. He took a job with Federated Flyers, one of the largest stunt circuses of the time. "I'd loop with the wing-walkers," he recalls. "People would scream and faint. The only trouble was I had to ride a motorcycle and play auto polo part of the time." When the circus season ended he signed for still more violent work. In the fall of 1922 two Mexican factions, the Rebels and the Federals, were at war. A man named Hinck, agent of the Rebels, hired Wien at $500 a month to fly to Veracruz and drop home-made dynamite bombs on the opposing force.

Wien took the train to New Orleans and waited for final instructions. No word came from his new employer, nor any money. The plane he was to fly, shipped collect, sat in a crate at the depot; since he had sent most of his earnings to his family he had no way of claiming it. He stayed in the Louisiana city two months, living much of this time on bananas. Then, learning that the Rebels had been crushed, he returned to his Minnesota home.

Pilots in those days "weren't considered much. People thought you might be all right or you might be crazy. They'd put up big picture-posters of you at the county fairs, but nobody would give you a steady job." Wien was flabbergasted in 1924 by Jimmy Rodebaugh's offer of employment at Fairbanks—$300 a month guaranteed. He suspected it would prove, like the Mexican job, to be a fiasco. But he accepted at once and traveled north by steamer along with one of the Hisso-powered Standards which Rodebaugh had bought.

Debarking at Seward, he took the plane by rail to Anchorage, where he and Mechanic William Yunker assembled it. Wien was surprised by Anchorage's dusty, home-made field; there was a road running right through it. "The autos," he says, "were really no trouble at all. There was only my plane, and people were on the lookout for me." For several weeks the young circus ace was in his element, stunting and joy-hopping. "Air conditions in Alaska," he told reporters, "are apparently the same as in the States." Late in June Rode-baugh sent instructions for him to fly the Standard from

Anchorage to its Fairbanks base—a distance of more than 300 miles.

It was the first flight to be made between Alaska's two major towns. There were no landing fields in the jumble of mountains and tundra that lay between them. The extra gas tank built into the center section of the small war trainer gave it just enough range for a one-way journey. Wien planned to navigate by following the railroad track. Depot agents were requested by telegraph to step out and take a look at the sky. On the warm bright evening of July 6, favorable reports clicked back: clear all the way. Wien and Mechanic Yunker took off.

For two hours they followed the steel through the land. Their plane climbed high among the lofty snowcaps of the Alaska range, till the twisting track in the canyon far below was only a thread of silver. Presently the peaks sank behind and the railroad led out across a wide, mottled prairie. The worst of the trip should have been passed. But trouble lay ahead, the kind of trouble the young cheechako would least have expected. It was not ice that imperiled Wien's first long sub-Arctic flight, not snow, not extreme cold—but fire.

Flames, doubtless started by a locomotive spark, swept uncontrolled across the tundra. The billowing smoke rolled up so thick that Wien could see no more than a quarter of a mile—fifteen seconds' flying—ahead. He had not enough gas to turn back to Anchorage. He dared not leave the railroad in this strange, empty land. Lower and lower he was forced, till he was speeding just over the winding track with dark slopes flashing past the wing tips. "It was rather scary," he comments with one of his faint smiles. But he managed to reach Fairbanks and land safely on the ball park.

Shaking hands with his new employer, he told him about the smoky journey.

"I just hugged the track," he explained.

"But what did you do," Rodebaugh asked, "when you came to that sixty-foot overhead bridge at Dead Man's Slough?"

Wien paled. "Bridge? Was there a bridge?"

He thinks he must have flown under it.

Noel Wien's flying record in Alaska is something of a

paradox. He has had his full share of luck. But it is more than this that saved him from the untimely death of fellow pilots. From the start he exhibited a remarkable faculty for doing daring things in a cautious way.

He had none of the driving eagerness of Ben Eielson, none of the devil-may-care rashness of A. A. Bennett. He declined to fly in winter the year he arrived. Most of the time he shunned storm clouds as he shunned whiskey. Rodebaugh called him temperamental; others branded him timid. Today, among the younger pilots, Wien has a reputation for conservatism. "Take 'em out and bring 'em back," they say, "that's always been his motto. There's never been much fireworks to Noel."

But in the early years all cross-country trips were bold ones. Striking out alone above Alaska was like striking out above a strange planet, and a man had nothing to depend on but his compass, his single engine and his own wits. To "take 'em out and bring 'em back" under those primitive conditions was to incur constant risk. Wien made dozens of first flights over hills that had never echoed to an engine. He made countless first landings on rough terrain that had never known human footprints. Suspiciously but steadily he pioneered.

"I was able," he relates of one of the first trips ever made into the Mt. McKinley district, "to land my passengers within sixteen miles of where they wanted to go. The sand bar was 300 feet long with uneven gravel at the end. This made me put first one wing on the gravel, then another, tearing off a little of the trailing edge of the wing but at the same time saving me from running into a log and some bushes."

This kind of thing was routine, and when Wien learned that a miner named Charles Opdyke was dying of pneumonia at Nome Creek he flew out from Fairbanks and took more than a routine chance to save him. After circling a while over the deep-ridged, forested terrain he decided to land on the only possible runway—a small, boulder-strewn hilltop. The Standard bumped to a jarring stop with three inches broken off the propeller. But Wien had come prepared with an extra prop lashed to the fuselage. He installed it, loaded the sick man aboard, and took off down the rocky hillside, barely gathering enough momentum to clear the tops of spruce trees.

Wien's logbook, surprisingly, is more vivid than most.

There were good days:
    "Made trip to Livengood OK 1st one"
    "Beef, meat, freight, Brooks"
    "Brooks, 1 passenger over, $1,000 gold dust back"
There were bad days:
    "Joe Meherin salesman passenger, nosed over in mud"
    "Low ceiling, landed on small sand bar"
    "Caribou Creek 1 pssgr over, made landing, nosed over, broke prop"
Times of tension:
    "Fairbanks-Brooks, 400 lb. beef, air release came out, Hand Pump saved day"
    "Field still soft but made takeoff OK"
    "McGrath 1 over 2 back, a corpse, close shave landing"
And episodes of sport in a new land:
    "Dove on caribou Wickersham dome"
    "Circle Springs—FB passenger back. Shot at bear"

Wien, not Eielson, was the first pilot in Alaska to cross the Arctic Circle and land on the north side. In the spring of 1925 he took two mining operators from Fairbanks, 120 miles south of the line, to the mountain-cradled village of Wiseman, eighty miles above it. Pioneers there made him an honorary member of their frontier Order. On the way home he had a ruder kind of initiation into the ranks of the trail-blazers. His plane met sudden wind over the Sawtooth Range and was swept sideways far off course. The gas ran out. He landed on a sand bar in the dark with only a couple of dried buns for food.

"Forced down, gas and oil out, walked 40 miles back," his logbook reports. He set out on foot the next day, following a compass course toward the nearest town. He ate snow for water, becoming thirstier and thirstier. He shot a few rabbits and toasted them over fires. For the first time he learned something of the shaggy land that had slid so swiftly beneath

the Standard's wings. Spring break-up time had come to the
Interior, with all its soggy treachery to surface transport. He
waded through slush, stumbled over "niggerheads," bent trees
as he fought his way through junglelike swamp. Three rivers
lay across his path. One was frozen solid enough for wary
footsteps. The two others were swollen torrents. He built
small rafts, wrapped around with willow boughs, and floated
across. It took him three days to move the forty miles.

When the Fairbanks Airplane Company's Dutch Fokker
arrived at Fairbanks that spring, other pilots were surprised
that Wien dared to take the controls. He agreed that the big,
fast-landing brakeless ship was dangerous to operate from
Alaska's short fields. Even at his Fairbanks base he had to
"pull it into a near stall at treetop level and then give it a
little drop for three-point landing." He flew it sparingly
before it was stored away—only some 140 hours. Yet the
fact remains that he flew it, and he seems to have had a
curious fondness for the bizarre craft. He says he "rather
appreciated" the reliability of the six-cylinder B.M.W. engine,
"so heavily built, no trouble at all." He still keeps the Fokker's propeller as a souvenir.

In the Fokker, Wien made another trail-blazing trip—the
first commercial flight between Fairbanks and Nome. The
540-mile journey was portentous in mining as well as aviation. His passenger, an engineer named Norman Stines, had
arrived in Alaska to conduct exploratory surveys for the
United States Smelting Refining & Mining Company of Boston. As a result of his reports huge gold-dredges were later to
be built about Fairbanks and Nome, revolutionizing mining
methods and restoring some measure of prosperity to the two
towns. Stines, in June of 1925, wanted to fly from Fairbanks
to Nome for a meeting with company directors who were
arriving there from the States by boat. He was glad to pay
$1,000 for a seven-hour charter. The circuitous journey by
surface transportation might take as many as six weeks.

It was the longest flight Wien had attempted. His employ-
ers assured him that it would be a safe one: he could follow
the Tanana and Yukon Rivers, they said, and there were
"lots and lots of flat sand bars—dandy places to land." There
was a telegraph station en route, almost half way, at the

town of Ruby. It would flash a report to Fairbanks as the Fokker passed.

Accompanied by his brother Ralph as mechanic, Wien left Fairbanks at seven in the evening. "I liked to make those summer trips at night," he says, "the air was so smooth." As the Fokker ploughed westward into a radiant sky, Stines and two women secretaries enjoyed a game of cards, looking up now and then to admire the huge white mass of Mt. McKinley—"pink like a giant scoop of strawberry ice cream." The Wiens peered anxiously earthward. The Yukon River was running high. All the "dandy sand bars" were submerged. For this elephantine ship, loaded with three passengers and 500 pounds of mining papers and books, there would be no safe landing place anywhere in case of emergency.

They continued their course. On schedule, they passed the cluster of riverbank log cabins that was Ruby. Soon after this the two brothers began to worry about the sky. Streaks of gray murk filled the air above the Yukon. Drops of water slid down the windshield as the Fokker entered the edge of a rain squall. It was not a bad storm, but Wien decided to turn back. There was no longer enough gas, however, for safe return to Fairbanks. He decided to attempt landing at Ruby, although it had no airfield. If worse came to worst, crack-up beside a town would be better than crack-up in the wilds.

The passengers forgot their card game as several low passes were made above the village. Stines, a seasoned air traveler in many countries, could scarcely believe his eyes. The only possible runway was a short hillside which sloped up at a thirty-degree angle, levelling out onto a small baseball diamond. It looked like suicide.

Slowly as possible Wien eased the $9,500 airliner onto the upslope. Hurtling over the hilltop, the Fokker ran part way down the other side, where the wheels broke through a patch of soft ground. The big plane nosed up and rocked clumsily over on its back. The propeller was split in two. It was a sad wreck but a safe one. "He turned us up so slowly," Stines relates, "that none of us even lost our position. It was like rolling in a barrel."

"Awfully glad no one hurt," the Fairbanks Airplane Company wired Wien next day on receipt of his news. "Congratulate you on good judgment turning back. Sending propeller first boat, probably Wednesday. Will arrange weather reports Ruby Nome. Best regards Stines and party. Tell if anything we can do." But Stines and his secretaries, to the company's dismay, decided to continue their journey by boat.

Wien, nonetheless, was determined to complete his trip. When the new prop arrived a few days later he installed it and pointed the Fokker downhill toward a drop of only 400 feet. His take-off was close; the Fokker ploughed into brush and dropped almost to the river before it gained flying speed. The German motor, ill-timed to the new prop, vibrated badly as he flew on. But he continued more than three hours, "juggling between strange peaks." The weather was fair and he reached Nome safely, well in advance of Stines.

Early in 1927 Noel and Ralph Wien founded an airline of their own. They borrowed money to buy one of Rodebaugh's old Standards and based at Nome, giving the Bering Sea town its first steady plane service. In the first two months of operation they took in $4,000 and, with the aid of a local bank loan, paid $10,000 for a second plane—the Wilkins expedition Stinson *Detroiter*. "A cordon of police may be necessary," said the Nome *Nugget*, "when Wien takes off in his Stinson. There are six persons anxious to fly to Fairbanks and the plane will not hold that many. There are two passengers for Candle and possibly a flight will be made to Kotzebue with diphtheria antitoxin." Business continued to boom.

Wien nearly lost his Stinson in a freakish accident the first winter. Landing at Lake Minchumina late in December, he left the plane on the snow beside the roadhouse and went to bed. He woke during the night to the wail of high wind. Hurrying outdoors to check on his ship, he saw nothing where it had stood but whirling snowflakes. The Stinson was gone.

Storm and wind continued for three days, sweeping drifts from Minchumina till the surface was sheer ice. On the second day the plane's dim shape appeared briefly far out on the lake. The third day it was gone once more. When the weather cleared, Wien found his $10,000 craft two miles away on the opposite shore—its "flippers" and prop blades bent, its control rods and skis broken. He spent two days repairing it with a monkey wrench and a blowtorch, and continued his journey. The people of Nome suffered more than he from the mishap. It delayed his arrival till after Christmas, and he had all their Yuletide gifts and mail aboard.

The following year he made up for this, arriving at Nome on Christmas Eve with a full load of letters and presents. Children scampered around his plane and jumped up and down. Old women wept; in their memory, Nome had never received any packages at holiday time. No town in Alaska appreciated air service more keenly than Nome appreciated the Wiens', especially in winter; from the icelocked settlement it was a journey of several weeks to Fairbanks by dog team.

It was in March, 1929, half a year before Eielson's journey to death, that Wien successfully made the first round trip by air between America and Asia. Accompanied by Mechanic Calvin Cripe, he used the all-metal Hamilton in which Eielson was later killed. The route, too, was the same, likewise the purpose. He had signed a contract to haul fur from a vessel which was caught in the ice off North Cape, Siberia.

"Sincere congratulations," William MacCracken, Assistant Secretary of Commerce, wired Wien from Washington on completion of the first round-trip flight between the continents. "This is a most worthy pioneering effort." By Wien's account, the trip was uneventful. The spring sun was bright. "We just simply waited for clear and unlimited weather," he comments, "and if we'd run into a storm we would have turned back awfully fast."

They did have "a little trouble," he adds, on the return trip. Cripe, he says, is the one who had a rugged journey and deserves credit. The oil tank of the Hamilton, built into the leading edge of the wing, received no heat from the engine, and as they soared above forbidding, rough drifts—higher than any Wien had ever seen in Alaska—the cap froze. Pressure rose dangerously. Although it was 50 below zero that day, Mechanic Cripe opened the window and stretched out into the icy blast. Just able to reach the vent, he punched it open with a knife, but it soon froze shut again. He repeated his almost insufferable task every ten or fifteen minutes during the six-hour flight.

Soon after his journey to Asia, Wien married Ada Bering Arthurs, daughter of the Nome postmaster. Later that year he sold his company to Alaskan Airways and he and his wife made an extended trip to the States, where they were at the time of the Eielson disaster. When he returned he organized another family outfit, operating out of Fairbanks. He has had many offers of work in the States and Canada, but has chosen to continue his work in Alaska.

Wien no longer flies actively. A few years ago he sold control of the family company to his brother Sig and today he is distributor for the Cessna Aircraft Company in northern Alaska. He plans to spend the rest of his life in the Far North.

"Alaska," he explained, "keeps a fellow guessing.... It tugs at you all the time.... The States are too tame."

Master of understatement, Wien hardly does justice to "The Great Land" of Alaska in words, but he has taken hundreds of photographs of its austere magnificence. He has also taken many pictures of the North's aviation industry. Many of Alaska's pilots have become amateur photographers. None of their albums rivals Wien's for artistic composition and discerning choice of subject. Some of the shots, of crude flying fields and little hamlets, are precise and detailed: the ragged wind sock, the grassy turf, the piled oilcans—all are shown for what they mean. Others, taken from the cockpit, far aloft, give the most overwhelming impressions of forbidding wilderness and sky.

Wien stood in his library one day, looking up to such a photo: the lone wing tip of his plane silhouetted against jagged, cloud-wreathed peaks.

"I remember when I took that," he softly told me. "I always liked Alaska.... I rather liked to fly over the mountains.... This country is intriguing in a way."

8
Over My Station Right Now

ALASKANS HAVE DONE many things for airplanes.

Not only their own planes—all planes.

The late Wiley Post could not have made his round-the-world record in the *Winnie Mae* in 1933 without the help of the people of Alaska.

Post crossed safely from Asia to America on his global solo flight, but over the wilds of Alaska he lost his way. He studied his map, peered down, tried to find the Yukon River but saw a dozen Yukons. He milled around, following first one stream, then another. He fell asleep a while at the controls, woke to stare dazed at the crags of huge mountains. Exhausted and befuddled, he circled above Alaska for more than eight hours.

Then he decided to land by some radio towers at the mining camp of Flat.

"Frenchie," the Flat radio operator, was preparing to sign off for the night, just exchanging his last messages and gossip with the relay station at Takotna. *I-hear-Wiley-Post-is-missing,* the Takotna man told him. The same moment Frenchie heard the roar of an engine.

Hold-on! he flashed.

He looked out, saw a white, streamlined, high-powered ship zooming low over the towers. It was an odd-looking job; no plane like it in Alaska.

Don't-sign-off! he advised. *Looks-like-the-Winnie-Mae-is-over-my-station-right-now!*

The airfield at Flat was a 700-foot clearing, so rough and short you might say it was no airfield at all. But Post squared away and came roaring down in his hot, fast-landing Vega.

It bounced over the dirt, ran into a mound of gravel and

nosed up—breaking one of the landing-gear struts, knocking a hole in the fuselage and, worst of all, bending the Smith controllable-pitch prop.

Mining stopped at Flat the way a light goes out. Everybody ran to the field. Wiley Post was not hurt but everybody could see that he was rumdum. Sixteen hours he had been alone in the air—ever since he left Khabarovsk, Siberia. "He acted like a man half drunk. The way he was he couldn't find his hip-pocket with both hands."

"I'm all done, I guess," he told the crowd.

Everybody felt sorry the field was so poor. Everybody said if the town of Flat had anything to do with it Wiley Post would still make his record.

"Don't worry, Wiley," Harry Donnelley, storekeeper, told him. "You take it easy, better get some sleep. We'll fix your ship."

Frenchie put Post to bed in the wireless station. Miners fetched their welding outfits, but it was no use: they wouldn't work on an alloy drag strut. The people couldn't even figure out how to take Wiley's fancy prop, first one they'd seen like it, off the front of the plane.

Frenchie sent a message through the Takotna relay station to Fairbanks. Joe Crosson, soon as he got it, flew over in a Fairchild 71 on floats, landed at a nearby river town and drove in a truck to Flat with two mechanics and an old fixed-pitch prop. They worked all night installing it and repairing the damage.

Then the people argued.

"He needs more sleep."

"He'd better git goin'."

"Let him take a nap in Fairbanks."

"Better wake him now."

Finally they decided to rouse him. "I'll follow you," Post told Crosson. "You lead me—or I'll get lost again." The *Winnie Mae* was twice as fast as the Fairchild but he "held her back like a wild horse," flew right on Crosson's wing over the hills to Fairbanks. There he got a shave and a bite to eat while mechanics checked the engine and built a stronger strut.

He waved goodbye and flew on to New York, breaking the world record by twenty-one hours and two minutes.

Two years later, when Wiley Post and Will Rogers crashed to death near Barrow, it was Joe Crosson who flew their bodies to the States.

9
Joe Crosson

JOE CROSSON, the dynamic, black-haired "mercy pilot" with the rugged build and winning smile, has received more publicity in the United States than all the rest of Alaska's airmen combined. He has not enjoyed it.

Crosson's work on the Eielson search was headlined throughout America. In 1935, when he rushed the bodies of Wiley Post and Will Rogers to the States after their Barrow disaster, his name was again proclaimed from coast to coast and a move was made in Washington to award him the Congressional Medal of Honor and the Distinguished Flying Cross.

He refused these decorations. Hearing of the proposed honors, he informed Alaska's Delegate in Congress that he would not accept them. "The whole idea of medals was unwarranted," he comments today. "Not at all in keeping with what I did."

Crosson, accompanied by Flight Mechanic Bob Gleason, flew from Fairbanks to Barrow as soon as he learned of the Post-Rogers crash. Fog hung low over the Barrow lagoon as he left at midnight with his death-load on the return trip. His small float plane, heavily weighted with extra gas for emergency, plowed up on a sand bar the first time he attempted take-off. During the journey bad weather drove him off course, and he was forced down on an Arctic lake to refuel. Crosson flew a total of thirteen hours in a nineteen-hour period. But his action, he felt, had been essentially no more than that of Claire Oakpeha, the unheralded Eskimo who ran twelve miles across the tundra to take the first news of the calamity to Barrow and the world.

The Post-Rogers crash was the first fatal air accident Barrow had ever known. "Red plane—she blow up!"

Oakpeha cried as he stumbled into the wireless station. As told in the diary of Charles Brower: "Claire reported that Post, coming out of fog, saw him on the bank and settled in lagoon. He asked where they were and distance to Barrow, stayed a few minutes before taking off, started engine and took off toward ocean. He banked to come in over land. While on the turn, engine sputtered and stopped. They tried to straighten out for landing and crashed in lagoon about thirty feet from the sandspit. The plane was turned over with the pontoons straight on top. . . . Three Eskimo went immediately to the wreck, and one waded out to plane, found both men dead."

The broken bodies of Post and Rogers, wrapped in sleeping bags, were taken to the Barrow hospital. Eskimos superstitiously refused to pose for pictures beside the wreck and chanted a dirge as they moved back to town in their skin boats. The awestruck local doctor was unable to complete the work of preparing the bodies for shipment and Brower had to help him. No one at Barrow was so shaken as Joe Crosson. He was haggard with grief as he loaded his plane for the homeward trip.

Crosson had been one of the last to see Post and Rogers alive. It was he who had driven them to the slough near Fairbanks for the take-off the morning before. He had helped Post arrange for rental of a house, near his own, where the round-the-world flyer and his wife had intended to live. Crosson and Post had been friends for many years. Once, in a Stearman, they had made a "high-powered hunting trip" all over Alaska, killing two bear and sighting so many moose and caribou that Post had talked ever since of repeating the excursion. Rogers had said he wanted to go along too. Crosson remembered well how Rogers had looked, grinning bashfully, hair tousled under a slouch hat, just before the Fairbanks take-off. He could still hear the last wisecrack of America's popular humorist: "Well, boys, I hope we have a forced landing. I won't be a sourdough till I learn to siwash it."

Crosson wanted no medals for his funereal trip. Nor has he ever sought publicity for any of his Arctic work. In the best Alaskan flying tradition, Crosson is matter-of-fact. The term "mercy pilot" visibly annoys him. Until he told me his story, his wife complains, their three young sons had never heard it. Like Wien, he talks in the sparsest of sentences about his hard-fought career. Only by adding to his account the recollections of mechanics, passengers and friends may the record be seen whole.

Crosson grew up on a Kansas farm. He was eleven years old when he saw his first plane, at a county fair. He and his sister Marvel did not have the price of admission, but watched the barnstormer's stunts from behind the fence. He made his decision then. "Joe grabbed my shoulders and jumped up and down," Marvel has written. "I'm going to be an aviator!" he shouted. "I'm going to be an aviator!"

Marvel, three years older than her brother, looked much like him, with the same coal-black hair and flashing smile. She also shared his ambition. A few years later they persuaded their family to move to San Diego, which had a busy airfield. There he worked in a garage, she in a camera store, until they had saved $150—enough to buy the motorless wreck of a Curtiss N-9 seaplane. They installed it behind their house and Crosson ransacked junk yards for parts to make a landplane of it.

Selling the family Ford, they bought a Curtiss OX-5 engine, telling the skeptical owner they wanted it for a motorboat. They tried it out in the yard and blew their mother's chickens against a high board fence. Then they carted their ship out to the airfield and persuaded an ex-Army pilot to take it aloft. The first hop was a success. "It flies! It flies!" they shouted, by Marvel's account. "It's ours! It's ours!"

They both soloed, and barnstormed together for several years. Crosson declares he enjoyed no flight as much as one in which his sister participated. But in 1926, when he received the offer from the Fairbanks Airplane Company, their rare partnership was interrupted. Three years later, flying a Travel Air in the Women's Air Derby, Marvel crashed to death in Arizona.

Alaskans first knew Crosson as a "big kid" with an embarrassed grin and only 500 hours in the air. His first flight in Alaska was brief and ignominious. Hired by telegram to serve as pilot and mechanic, he discovered on arrival at

Fairbanks that the company had only one flyable plane and that Pilot Bennett, who had arrived before him, had no intention of relinquishing it. Crosson went disconsolately to work in a garage, repairing the wreck of another. One morning he lost patience, climbed aboard Bennett's plane, took off and circled over town. Bennett hurried out to the field and was waiting when Crosson came down. "Who the hell do you think you are?" he shouted. "Get back to work and stay out of that ship."

But it was not long before Crosson had a chance to make a trip in Ben Eielson's old Jenny. He flew a miner named Van Curler seventy-five miles to his claim in the Upper Chena. There was a good field there, the old-timer told him. As they glided down Crosson saw it was "nothing but a potato patch, maybe 350 foot long, right in the middle of the river." Van Curler insisted that Eielson had once landed there "just fine." Crosson decided he must meet this challenge. "I came down a little too short," he says, "and hit the niggerheads. Wham! The ship turned over on its back." Van Curler and his groceries spilled out, and Mrs. Van Curler came hurrying in a boat to the scene of the accident.

"Don't you worry," the couple told Crosson, "we'll have her fixed in a jiffy. Did you ever see a Spanish windlass?" Mrs. Van Curler fetched two poles and some cable. They tied one end to the tail, wound the other around a stump, and began winding. They had the ship one-third over when the cable broke. On the next try they succeeded. But the fuel, Crosson found, had all spilled out. "Okay," said Van Curler, "we can fix that too." He brought ten gallons of lamp gas from the shed.

The steel propeller was bent, but this too was solved. Mrs. Van Curler fetched a log from the woodpile. "She held it behind the blade of the prop," Crosson relates, "and we pounded the thing out to where it cleared the radiator of the engine. The top of the rudder was broken but I figured she'd still handle. The cabane struts were mashed clear over but the air was smooth and I thought the flying wires would hold okay. I got in and tried the engine. She was rough, but I let her wind up and took off. Oh boy, that old engine was really jumping around, but I wheeled in to Fairbanks careful as I could, landed, put the ship in a hangar, shut the doors and never told anyone."

He soon learned to mistrust his passengers' concept of an airport. "Those old boys would say they had a fine field but I'd like to see a helicopter that could light on some of the places." Flying a miner named Joe Quigley to his cabin at Moose Creek, in a Waco, he and Pilot Ed Young had an even more violent meeting with the earth. The "runway" to which Quigley eagerly pointed was out of the question. "It was just a little knob. The only thing that could land there would be an eagle." The pilots decided it would be safer to use a river bar.

In Crosson's words: "We sailed over a bunch of stumps and hit. The gravel was hard as pavement. I no more than touched than I saw I was going to run in the river, so I poured on the coal. But the Waco slowed up and rapidly ended in the water, stuck on its nose just slightly upside down at a forty-five-degree angle—in those days a favorite position."

Quigley was hurt. His nose, torn against a strut, was bleeding badly and the river was running red. This was disturbing enough and now, down the hill came Fanny, Quigley's hard-working, hard-drinking, hard-swearing pioneer wife. "Christ," she screamed, "what are you trying to do, kill my man," She hastened to examine his wounds. "By gosh," she told the pilots, "he's got to be sewed up." Fetching a crude doctor's outfit, she began without further ado to mend her husband's nose. "First she tried a baseball stitch, but she couldn't get the skin to pull even, so she finally decided to sew it up just straight. Then by golly she poured on a lot of iodine. Poor Joe was in torture. His nose looked like a pan of hamburger, but it healed okay."

There was, however, no way of mending the plane. Crankcase and prop were badly damaged, and new parts were needed to repair them. The pilots set out on a long hike to the Savage River camp—eighty-five miles away. "You may think the trail is tough," Fanny told them," but don't leave it or you'll be goners. Stick to the trail."

It was not much of a trail. For four days they plowed through soggy mud, sometimes knee-deep. They met an old prospector, "Bull" Shannon, on the way, hobbling along with fifty-four pounds of rock on his back. Shannon declared that his ankle was injured, so each of the pilots took part of his load. Slipping and stumbling, they carried their heavy packs up hill and down, through the muck, and forded swollen rivers. They, too, were hobbling by the time they reached Savage River, a road and an automobile.

Later they returned to the Quigleys in another plane, landed safely on a larger bar six miles from the wreck, hauled the repair parts through the brush, repaired the Waco and flew both ships home. "That," says Crosson, "was the end of that little trip." The Quigley mishap, incidentally, is the only occasion in 8,000 hours of flight on which he has caused a passenger injury.

The pioneer pilots of Alaska, it is said, spent more time "walking out" than they did flying. This is more than a jest. Crosson's first year in the North was a constant contest with dubious runways and with fickle engines. The small water-cooled Hissos which powered the early Fairbanks Airplane Company fleet were such that the pilots find it hard to discuss them in polite language today. "Every time we made a trip," Crosson says, "we'd have to pull the bank and grind the valves." Despite constant overhaul, the engines often boiled over and "conked out" in the air. They were unreliable enough in summer. Later in 1926 Crosson learned what it meant to trust this crude equipment in freeze-up time and winter. He flew thirty hours, crashed three times and spent twenty days awaiting rescue or hiking home.

This chain of misadventures began one bleak November morning as he cruised in a Hisso-Standard 6,000 feet above the Toklat River. One of the engine's wrist pins broke. "Clank, clank, clank, she kept turning over but she sounded like she would fall to pieces." Crosson hastily descended on a gravel bar and came to a jarring stop among boulders. Clad in his bearskin flying suit, he spent the rest of the day trying to repair the engine. It was impossible. The connecting-rod was broken; new parts were needed.

As dusk fell, he built a fire of driftwood, drank some soup, wrapped himself in a blanket and lay down under the wing. But he could not sleep. Wild animals prowled along the river bank. A circle of flashing eyes formed around him in the dark. Since his arrival in Alaska Crosson had heard too many stories about wolves. Terrified, he bounded into his plane and spent the rest of the night cramped in the cabin. Later he learned his wolves had been foxes.

He woke the next morning to the first snowfall of the year. The air was thick with swirling flakes, the ground already blanketed with white. Crosson had food for only a few days. His company, he knew, would not miss him for some time—there was no telegraph station at his destination. He remembered seeing a roadhouse from the air a few flying minutes—some twelve miles—away. He decided it should be a simple matter to walk to it.

His round-soled flying boots slipped in the soft snow, the blizzard blinded him and before long he fell down a bank, painfully wrenching his knee. He lay there a while, afraid to move: "I thought I had broke my leg, couldn't get up, there I was in the snowstorm all alone and nobody knew where I was at." Finally he cagily twisted the leg, stood up, and found that it worked. Bracing himself with a stick he limped along, feeling his way like a blind man. The twelve miles, he says, seemed like a hundred. All day he plodded, and much of the night, breaking trail through dense undergrowth of willow and spruce, climbing over logs and detouring around wide sloughs and beaver ponds as he followed the main bank of the stream to Knight's roadhouse.

His journey home had only begun. The next morning he started along a rough trail toward Kobe, the nearest station on the railroad. Old-timers at Knight's roadhouse warned him to avoid all lakes at this time of year, no matter how sound the ice appeared. But when he came to a large frozen expanse—"nice, smooth, easy walking"—he could not resist. This venture did not last long; he drew back just in time before a gaping, half-hidden hole. "A sled must have broke through. That cured me of walking on lakes." He hurried back to shore and toiled along the bumpy trail till his blistered feet pained him with every step. He spent that night at an Indian settlement.

The Indians told him that the Nenana River, eight miles ahead on his route, had not yet frozen over. He hired one of them to take him across by boat. The native led out his dog team—"nine nice strong big Huskies." Delighted, Crosson stepped aboard the sled. But the driver motioned him off. "No! My dogs too green. You follow." He yelped to his animals and rode swiftly away down the trail. Crosson stumbled along behind, mile after mile, to the river.

He heard the roar of the Nenana long before he reached it. Nor was the sight reassuring; the torrent was full of crashing cakes of ice. The Indian, crouched beside a moose-skin boat, was energetically rubbing a piece of tallow into the seams. The flimsy vessel was no more than nine feet long and ribbed only with willow branches. "Can we both ride in that thing?" Crosson asked. His guide did not reply, but lowered the boat down a steep bank and motioned Crosson into it. Deftly working a double-ended paddle, the Indian steered among the ice cakes and pushed the Arctic airman safely across. "I couldn't take one breath all the way over," Crosson admits. "I was never so terrified as in that wobbly little gadget."

Aching in every bone, he limped the rest of the way to Kobe where he put in a telephone call to the Fairbanks Airplane Company. Manager Bob Lavery was very gruff. "How is the airplane?" he barked. "What was the delay? Where the devil have you been?"

There was a rush job to be done, Lavery added, over in the Iditarod. As soon as Crosson reached Fairbanks he departed in the company's new Swallow on another ill-starred trip. Only luck saved him from the fate of Rogers and Post as he took off with two passengers from a river bar near McGrath. "We had just passed the end of the bar when the motor began to spit. Then she quit cold. The Swallow crashed. The water rushed all around us and for a minute I thought we were floating down the river. Then I saw that the ship was on her back; everything but the cockpit and the leading edge of the wing was under water, but we were high and dry. The Swallow had flopped onto a little sand bar right in the middle of the stream."

Ice cakes were smashing against the plane. At any moment, one might knock it from its precarious perch into the torrent. Crosson and his passengers climbed out and stood helplessly beside the plane as villagers hurried toward them in a boat. Meanwhile an old-timer named Vanderpool came charging along the bank with a team of horses. "We will use a rope," he yelled, "and pull your plane to shore."

The rope was stretched across the river and tied to the Swallow's landing gear. Vanderpool shouted at his horses and they moved ahead. A cry of disappointment came from the crowd as the gear broke away. Crosson and his helpers tried again, pushing the plane over on its belly and tying the rope to the tail. The horses struggled forward once more but the Swallow would not budge. A third try was made, with a pole under each wing serving as a lever. "We got the cockeyed thing into the water and waded in clear up to our necks. We heaved. The horses heaved. Suddenly the plane hopped up onto the bank. Her tail was off. Her wings were all in pieces. All that was left of our new Swallow was the motor."

Officials of the Fairbanks Airplane Company, informed by telegraph of this new disaster, gathered in sullen confab. There was only one way to stay in business. They must repair the old Standard which Crosson had left on the Toklat river bar. They asked the Bennett-Rodebaugh company to land him there with a mechanic and a load of parts. The rival firm magnanimously agreed. Pilot Young made the trip in a Waco and delivered Crosson and Mechanic Ernie Fransen beside the snow-covered wreck.

Crosson and Fransen worked four days installing a new connecting-rod and mending the elevators, which had been damaged in the interim by wind. They made a successful take-off but ten minutes later the oil pressure dropped to zero. The Standard sailed down on a snowy pond. The two men removed the oil screen, cleaned it and took off again. Once more they were forced to earth. Once more they tried the air. Five times in all, this trouble forced them to crash-land. On the sixth try the engine began to miss. They came down on another lake and worked several hours overhauling the plane. They also cut a hole through the fire wall so that Fransen could pour oil from the cabin into the tank. They took off again.

The Standard had just gained flying speed when flames blazed in the cockpit. Crosson sideslipped the ship skillfully down onto the snow and helped Fransen to safety just in the nick of time. The tanks exploded. "We stood and watched her blaze and smoke. There was nothing we could do. That was the end of that ship."

This time Crosson had no river to guide him. He and Fransen were deep in the woods. Although they knew the dog trail was not far away, they floundered for hours and could not find it. "Everywhere, scraggly spruce and soft snow, with not a sign of life." Crosson decided to climb a tree. Clambering up, he discovered to his disgust that they were only 100 feet from the trail, paralleling it, in the wrong direction. By this time it was too dark to proceed so they made a bonfire, built a lean-to of branches and huddled in it till dawn.

When they started along the trail once more it led them straight to the edge of a sheer bank of the Kuskokwim River. There was no bridge. There was no boat. The freeze-up, by this time, had plugged the big stream with slush. After some discussion, Crosson felled a large tree which reached halfway across. One at a time they crawled out along it and, leaning their weight on long poles, stepped gingerly over the mushy surface to the opposite shore. Continuing several more hours, they reached the Medfra roadhouse.

Medfra had no telegraph station, and the nearest railroad stop, Nenana, was 250 miles away. As they sat by the stove discussing their plight they heard a sound "sweeter than music"—the roar of an airplane engine. They ran outdoors just in time to see the new Bennett-Rodebaugh Swallow gliding down to land. The ship descended through spitting flakes toward a snow-covered river bar and crashed.

Pilot Bennett climbed out as Crosson and Fransen hurried toward the wreck. "Why didn't you wave me off?" he snarled. "This is no place to land." His two passengers, a miner and a man with a paralytic stroke, listened uneasily as the flyers took stock. The last time Bennett had landed at Medfra the snow had been firm. Now the freezing river had risen and formed a soft layer under the surface and the Swallow had nosed through. One side of the wooden propeller was broken off.

"Oh, well," said Bennett, "Ed Young has a trip through

here. He'll fly back to Fairbanks and drop us a new prop."
They marked off a safer landing place and proceeded to wait
for the last functioning plane and pilot in Interior Alaska.
One day passed, another and another. A week was gone, and
Young had not appeared. "By gosh," Crosson told Bennett,
"maybe you could use the metal prop off my burnt-up Standard." Fransen went back by dog team to fetch it. He found
it badly twisted. The flyers tried, without success, to straight-
en it against a log. They decided to take it to the local
blacksmith's shop. Hopefully, they turned it over a hot flame.
The blade, made of duralumin, melted and dropped off.
"That," says Crosson, "was the end of that noble experiment.
We continued to wait for Ed."

Ten more days passed and the fidgety flyers decided to wait
no longer. By this time the winter was setting in for good;
the temperature had dropped to 40 below zero. Bennett and
his passengers set out with the only available dog team for
McGrath. Crosson and Fransen started on foot over the long
trail toward Nenana. They had not walked far when a
dog-musher told them the news. Ed Young, too, had crashed.
His Hisso engine had failed en route, his ship had spun down
on a frozen lake and he had caught the mail team back to
Nenana. Crosson and Fransen followed along the trail and
eventually reached Fairbanks after an absence of nearly
three weeks.

A few months later, in another Hisso-powered Swallow,
Crosson flew all the way from Fairbanks to Barrow. It was
the first commercial flight ever made to the farthest-north
town. He started out on only three hours' notice. The Wilkins
expedition had arrived at Fairbanks and was preparing to
proceed north for its second year of work. One of its planes
had been wrecked and Wilkins and Eielson had not enough
room aboard their heavily loaded ship for A. M. Smith, the
reporter attached to the party. Smith decided to charter one
of the Fairbanks Airplane Company planes and Crosson
agreed to haul him in the Swallow. It was planned that
Crosson would fly ahead 200 miles to the Arctic town of
Wiseman, land and refuel. Since he did not know the route to
Barrow (Wilkins and Eielson were the only men who had

flown it), he would wait there until they came over in their larger ship and follow them north.

Crosson arrived at Wiseman on schedule but not without difficulty: his engine was up to its old tricks. In the bitter sub-zero weather the radiator had frozen and broken. As he worked on the snow runway, trying to repair it, the Wilkins plane appeared and circled overhead. Not wishing to delay the expedition, Crosson motioned Eielson and Wilkins on. He took his engine to the Wiseman roadhouse and spent most of the day mending it with a soldering iron. The next morning he told Smith he was ready to proceed.

It was hardly a route for the Swallow. The winter trip from Fairbanks to Barrow is one of the most forbidding in the world. From Wiseman north the mountains rise steeply and for 150 miles you follow a maze of big dizzy canyons past a jumble of savage, giant peaks. This little known, little climbed range is much more formidable than the Rockies. Crossing the Endicotts is as lonely as a flight over water, and much more awesome. There is a fearful splendor to this Arctic ertravagance of the earth. The jagged ridges and slopes, extending as far as eye can see, look like the breakers of a violent ocean suddenly transfixed into thousands of menacing forms for all time. Even the pilots of modern transports say it gives them a feeling of gloom.

You cross the Arctic divide and the timber line of the continent sinks behind you and you head north over tundra with hundreds of miles still between you and your destination. "Weird and uncanny," Wilkins wrote of a trip in his larger plane. "The monotony and uncertainty of it would drive any man crazy if endured for long." And when you reach the top of the continent, finding Barrow is a challenge. Many flyers have failed. During World War II an Army captain in a long-range plane flew more than 500 purposeful miles north from Fairbanks, turned and flew more than 500 frustrated miles back. His plane came so close to Barrow, the Weather Officer reports, that villagers could hear the roar of the engines. There was a fair ceiling that day, too, and the pilot had radio communication. "Somebody must be crazy," he told superiors on return to his base, "there's no damn town up there. Nothing but snow and ice."

There was much of bravado in Crosson's 1927 journey. Knowing that his small open-cockpit plane had the most temperamental of engines and a perilously low fuel range for the trip, he took along a rag doll for a good luck mascot. With only an old ship's compass and a crude map to guide him, he found the way. He trusted his Hisso through the mountains. He followed the icy reel of the Anaktuvuk River to its confluence with the Colville and then struck over the snowy flats toward the coast. By this time his compass was of little use; it had shaken loose from its mounting and dropped to one side. He navigated by the light of the dim sun, judging his position by the shadow of the struts on the Swallow's wing. Reaching the shore line fifty miles east of Barrow he followed it around, through flurries of snow, to the town. It was nearly dark and there were only a few gallons of gas left in the tank when he landed on the lagoon. The ground temperature was 40 below zero.

Crosson was not content to return to Fairbanks by the same course. He wanted to see more country, try another new route. Two days later, in a calm between snow squalls, he left Barrow alone and headed south along the Arctic coast, where no aircraft except the dirigible *Norge* had previously flown. For three hours the Swallow soared steadily above drifted banks and rough pressure ridges. Then the Hisso began to boil. He put his plane in a long glide and just reached the smooth ice of a lagoon. Steam rushed out as he removed the cap. He filled a can with fine ice chips and poured them into the leader tank. During this time he left the Hisso running, fearing he could not start it again alone. Climbing back into the cockpit he barely touched the throttle and the ship startled him by shooting ahead "like a torpedo" on the slick runway, crossing most of the lagoon before he could make his take-off.

Snow filled the air as he continued his lonely course. He skirted the edge of a blizzard and arrived in the nick of time at the Eskimo village of Kotzebue. The natives, who had never seen a plane, "crowded around the Swallow and laughed and laughed." When the storm cleared, four days later, he started out again, heading inland toward Fairbanks, and followed the Kobuk River to the town of Noorvik.

There, as he landed on rough river ice, the right landing gear strut was broken. Repairs were made with local help and he proceeded, dodging more storms. He flew into a bad blizzard as he neared Fairbanks but managed, by following a river and a railroad track, to land safely at his home base.

In the smallest ship ever to penetrate far into the Alaskan Arctic, Crosson had made, in all, a 1,580-mile circuit over strange territory. This trip lifted him from the ranks of the barnstormers into the world's small, select group of flying explorers. His caliber was promptly recognized by Wilkins and Eielson, who took him on their Antarctic expedition the following year. When Eielson returned to Alaska in 1929 to form his new company, Crosson went to work for him—and after Eielson's death and the Pan American purchase Crosson, more than any other man, took his place and worked to realize his vision of large-scale air service in the North.

Pan American, merging Eielson's company with local outfits, formed a subsidiary called Pacific Alaska Airways. Pacific Alaska, in the years that followed, spent many millions of dollars and brought the Territory its first fleet of radio-equipped multi-engine transports, its first flight communications system—its first airline in the usual sense of the word. "Big silver ships" came to Alaska and the pilots wore trim Pan American uniforms. Headquartered at Fairbanks, Pacific Alaska established a winter mail route to Nome, launched service over the mountains to the capital town of Juneau. First with Clippers, then with landplanes, it also inaugurated in 1940 the first regularly scheduled airlines service between Alaska and the States.*

It was a new venture for Pan American, which had hitherto specialized in warm-weather routes. The New York officials made Crosson chief pilot and soon promoted him to a management post. By 1937 he was head of the Alaskan subsidiary. With his aid, Pan American tapped a pool of technical skills that could not have been hired in the States at any price. Bush

---

* First service between the Territory and the States was launched in 1929 by a company called Alaska Washington Airways. Pilot Anscel Eckmann, in a Wasp-powered Lockheed Vega, made the first non-stop flight. But operations of this company were on more of a charter than a scheduled airline basis.

flyers, with Crosson actively participating, cannily selected the best field and station sites for the system's northern routes. Pan American's Alaska fleet was winterized with the help of veteran local mechanics: frontiersmen who had engineered coldweather flight in the early days, developing the first skis and fire pots. Here, too, Crosson knew the problems: in 1932, weary of scraping frost from aircraft wings, he had made what is believed to have been the first wing cover in the North— from a length of bed-sheeting.

With time not only Pan American, but also the American armed forces, gained much from the organization that Crosson built. When the first squadron of Army planes flew north in World War II, Pacific Alaska's operations manual served as a kind of Bible for the pilots. Air Forces officers, when they entered the Alaska theater, sought much advice from Crosson. The Eleventh Air Force borrowed him as late as 1943 for technical trouble-shooting in the Aleutians.

Crosson had less and less opportunity to fly in his Pan American post—most of his 8,000 hours were logged before 1935. By 1941 his headquarters had been moved to Seattle. In this time "big kid with the embarrassed smile" had developed into an executive of hardy poise. He forsook his fur parka for tailored suits, drove to his downtown office in a Chrysler, carried on daily telephone consultations with New York. His head was not turned. Youngest Division Manager in Pan American's far-flung system, he was also, without doubt, the most forthright and unassuming. He continued to speak the ungrammatical talk of the frontier. Secretaries could not break him of the habit of answering his own phone. He was never too busy to see an old trapper or a new pilot.

Crosson built a very loyal organization. The pilots would do anything for this pioneer who knew their problems backward and forward and faced them as his own. The entire staff worked hard for him, respecting him as men respect the employer who has earned his title the hard way. But he paid a personal price for his promotion. As the years passed his famous smile came more slowly. His black hair was streaked with gray. All the way, the building of Pacific Alaska was a trouble-shooting job. There were many times when he sincerely wished he were back in the cockpit. The humors of his old Hisso engine had been no less predictable than those of the New York and Washington officials to whom he must now report.

Crosson struggled, as Eielson before him had struggled, against the federal government's indifference to the Far North. For years Pacific Alaska was obliged to bid on a point-to-point basis against the dog-drivers for mail contracts. The result was a disconnected series of routes without rhyme, reason or possibility of profitable operation. Not until 1938 did Washington grant Pacific Alaska a regular foreign air mail subsidy, and its terms were much less favorable than those granted to Pan American elsewhere.

Beyond this, it was no easy job to operate a modern airline on the frontier. When Pacific Alaska announced that it would concentrate on scheduled main-line service between major towns, curtailing service to roadhouse and creek, Alaskans were not pleased. They did not take kindly to suspension of charter work nor, easygoing customers that they were, did they appreciate the stiffness of the printed timetable. Revenues, for a period, declined. And by the time Alaskans had begun to accept the notion, Pacific Alaska's "scheduled service" had become something of a Territorial joke.

Pacific Alaska's operating procedures, laid down in New York, were conservative; to Pan American, a safety record was paramount. Also, since it operated from a United States terminal, Pacific Alaska was subjected to federal safety regulation from which local companies were relatively free. Bush pilots were able to fly rings around Pacific Alaska's crews, especially at the fog-shrouded terminal of Juneau. Day after day the silver Lodestars and Electras of "American's Merchant Marine of the Air" stood weatherbound on the PAA airport while pioneer float pilots in small ships landed and took off from the water just beyond. Alaskans, somewhat unfairly, nicknamed Crosson's operation "The Blue-Sky Outfit."

Crosson had many disappointments. Pacific Alaska lost money and, for all its accomplishment, did not progress as he believed it might with fuller support from New York. As early as 1937, on the Fairbanks-Juneau run, the company was obliged to turn away passengers for lack of space. The most modern ships provided by the New York management at the time were two twin-engine ten-passenger Electras. From this year on, Crosson states, traffic demands exceeded available seats. He argued for superior equipment but it was not until 1940 that more adequate planes were provided for regular service. (PAA's terminal airports, he maintained, could have accommodated larger craft considerably before this year.)

In cold fact Pan American had no great interest in its Alaska operation as such. Pan American had entered the North chiefly to gain a foothold for future operation to Asia. Formation of Pacific Alaska, a company attorney told Congressmen, was "motivated more by experimental considerations looking to long-range developmental objectives than by the immediate commercial possibilities of the investment." The board of directors, discussing System policy in New York City's Chrysler Building, were far more concerned with Pan American's more lucrative, subsidized routes to the west and south. The northern company was considered something of a stepchild.

Crosson's policy conflict with the New York management sharpened as time passed. In 1944, in a shake-up which he declines to discuss, he left his Pan American post. He has since been managing an aircraft and parts supply business at Boeing Field, Seattle, specializing chiefly in serving the Far North. As World War II closed, two-thirds of Alaska's planes, by C.A.A. records, were more than six years old, a number more than eleven years old: some more ancient than these. With the peace has come a rush of orders for planes and parts. No man knows better than Crosson the equipment needs and problems of the North's operators—large and small.

Aged eleven, Crosson told his sister: "I'm going to be an aviator! I'm going to be an aviator!" Later, when he no longer flew actively, he declared, "Always, in some way, I want to be a part of aviation in Alaska."

10

Willing Hands and Feet

FRANK REYNOLDS is a carpenter at the hilltop University of Alaska, just outside Fairbanks. He is a dour, close-mouthed man and it was some time after I met him before I realized that he is an authority on Alaskan aviation. He took me once to the shed behind the college powerhouse where Eielson's old Jenny is stored.

"There it is," he told me, turning a flashlight into the gloom. "There's Ben's first ship. We wish we had room to show it better."

It hung from the rafters, the narrow, tapering fuselage, with the flimsy wings tied ignominiously along its sides. The engine was gone. The paint was scratched and peeling. Reynolds looked as proud as if he were displaying a Superfortress.

"I've helped him take her up many times," he said. "Two or three fellows would hold hands, you know, and the one on the end would reach out and spin the prop. Sometimes took a whole hour to get him going. 'Contact,' Ben'd say, 'switch off. Contact, switch off.' We'd have to pour ether in the gas. She was stubborn, that engine."

Alaskans gave more than dollars to build The Aviation. When Anchorage built its first airport, on May 25, 1923, the whole town turned out to help. A holiday was declared. "Marching to the tract," the Anchorage *Daily Times* reported, "swarming over the sixteen acres of stumps and undergrowth, volunteers cleared the field in a day." Men worked with horses and tractors, women and children with rakes. When the job was finished, they lit a bonfire and a committee passed out 250 pounds of wieners with coffee and lemonade.

Most old-time Alaskans have at one time or another helped to build an airport. Most know how to help a plane

104

into the sky. Even today, in the hinterland, you see people jockeying the tails around, holding the wings, swinging the props, to aid take-off. Frontiersmen are showered with snow, splattered with muck as planes plow skyward. A pilot may forget to wigwag the wings in thanks. It doesn't matter. Alaskans take it all as a matter of course.

They help their planes up and they help them down. Once Pilot Sampson came over the town of Brooks in rough air and didn't know which way to land. According to the *News-Miner*: "A farmer was espied near by and the pilot, stopping his engine at altitude, shouted to him to build a smudge. The farmer, accompanied by his dogs, ran to the field and quickly built a fire, so that the wind direction was learned and landing easily made." It was not so unusual.

Eielson and Wilkins lost their way on one of the historic Barrow trips. Their gas was running short when they sighted a small village below. They made a low pass over the roofs and dropped out a note asking the people to name their town.

"Remarkably comprehensive," Wilkins has written, "they soon set about stamping letters in the snow but the letters spelled the name of a town not mentioned on my maps."

The plane circled and Wilkins dropped another note asking the direction to Fairbanks.

"The people, without hesitation or troubling to stamp in the snow, formed themselves in the shape of an arrow."

Alaskans have become sophisticates of flight—the risky way. Every man, woman and child who boarded a plane in the early days had to have as much nerve as the pilot. "Took a lot of guts sometimes. We risked our necks with them birds—ridin' them old clunks. Why not?"

Once Dr. J. A. Sutherland, veteran Fairbanks physician, flew to Fort Yukon with Pilot Young to treat a fractured skull case. The trip was made in the dead of winter; it was so cold Sutherland stuffed newspaper inside his coat, so dark Young couldn't land till the people below lit a flare. The ship was in bad shape—altimeter out of whack, compass not working, gas gauges on the bum, engine missing on one mag. "Doc," Young warned, "you'll never ride in a plane that has more wrong with it than this!"

Another time Sutherland and E. B. Collins, Department of Justice agent, were called to Tanana on a rape case. Pilot Sampson rushed them there in his Standard. Collins had never been up in a plane. Sutherland had flown only once. Sampson had never been to Tanana, and Tanana had no airfield; but old-timers at Fairbanks told him he could land on the rifle range.

Sampson circled and circled when he reached Tanana. He scowled and scowled. Finally he handed his passengers a note:

> RIFLE RANGE COVERED WITH WATER
> RIVER BARS FLOODED
> NOT ENOUGH GAS TO GO BACK
> WHAT SHALL I DO?

They advised him to take a chance on the rifle range.

The Standard splashed onto the soggy runway and made it right side up.

Alaskans watch the load that goes into a ship, know when she's too heavy. They can tell a good take-off from a fair one. They hear any little off-beat in the engine. Sometimes in stormy weather they help the pilots navigate, watch the trees on one side, look for familiar hills. One passenger lit matches all the way through Rainy Pass at dusk so his pilot could see the instrument board. A miner called Big Hans had a tougher assignment than this.

It was a gloomy trip to begin with. Big Hans had a rupture. Another passenger, "Gus" Wilson, had a leg "big around as a ham" crushed by a collapsing wing dam. Also aboard were a prospector named Walter Culver, and a Scotty dog that had been attacked by Malamutes. Pilot Johnny Littley was flying the sick ones to the doctor.

In take-off from the mine field at Nyak the right wheel hit a grass-hidden mound. The lower strut broke. The wheel dangled high. Everybody knew what this meant. The ship would crack up when it came down to land.

Pilot Littley passed a note back to Big Hans:

WOULD YOU BE WILLING TO GO OUT THE
WINDOW AND ROPE THE STRUT AND PULL

IT UP PUTTING THE WHEEL IN POSITION SO
WE CAN LAND? CULVER CAN HOLD YOUR
LEGS.

Big Hans, hulking 200-pound Dane, said he was game if
Culver was. Culver grabbed his feet as he opened the window
and slid out headfirst.

Dangling from his ankles, Big Hans reached down into the
wind. His glasses, purse and fountain pen went spinning to
earth as he grabbed the strut, pulled it up and roped it.
Culver, with all the strength he could muster, hauled him
back inside.

Pilot Littley thanked them but he said one rope was not
enough.

Once more Big Hans slid out. He fastened the strut double. Once more Culver hauled him back.

When they reached the town of Flat, Littley buzzed the
field several times to show the people below that he was in
trouble. One of the men on the ground drove out a truck
with a stake body. As Littley landed, the ropes broke, the
holding strut gave way, the plane tipped sideways—but only
a few inches. The truck saved it. Racing along beside the
ship, it drove up under the wing and stopped—bracing it just
in time.

Nobody was hurt. Miners helped Littley mend the strut,
and he continued his trip.

A plane in Alaska "has nine lives, like a cat" and there is
hardly a town whose airfield has not been the scene of a
wreck. Miners, traders and trappers—women and children
too—have helped in time of need, "bandagin' props, shoein'
skis, mendin' struts." Bed sheets and tablecloths have been
used for fabric. Sourdough pancake batter has served as dope,
in freezing weather, to paste them on. Gas cans have often
been used to patch pontoons.

"Doc" LaRue, flying dentist, once used the side rail of an
old-fashioned bedstead for a lift strut.

Lon Cope broke a tail ski; somebody lent him a coal
shovel and he used that.

Russel Merrill wrecked a plane at Polly Creek; birch trees
were used to hold fast the interplane struts.

Chet Browne nosed over at Teller, breaking the back of his ship; volunteers helped him brace it with two-by-fours.

A. A. Bennett ran his Swallow into a bunch of stumps at the town of Chicken. Longerons were broken, fabric was torn, prop bent like a fishhook, lower wings badly smashed. "There's $10,000 shot to hell," he groaned.

The miners stood dolefully around. "That's tough, Bennett," they said. "Damn shame. Sorry it happened at Chicken."

Then a tall, gangling man named Springbett spoke up. He said he could repair the Swallow if Bennett would bring him the stuff to do it with. No, he hadn't been around planes much. Only flown two times. But he was a cabinetmaker and he'd been studying The Aviation, ever since the Wright brothers started it, in books and magazines.

Bennett took some of the others aside. "You bet," they told him. "Springbett's word's good. If he says he can fix it, he can fix it."

Bennett left Chicken by dog team and returned in another plane. The people of Chicken laughed when they saw it; "There it come, clatterin' over the woods, lookin' just like a porcupine; spikes all over it—spars, ribs and all kinds o' repair stuff sticking up out o' the cockpit, slung under the belly, tied along the sides."

Sprinbett got busy and had the Swallow ready to fly in six weeks. Bennett said she handled as good as new. He asked Springbett to come to work at the Fairbanks field. The cabinetmaker packed his bags, climbed in beside the pilot and soared away, delighted, in his own handicraft. He later became chief mechanic at Pan American's Fairbanks hangar.

There have been many others like Springbett, versatile frontiersmen who "just fell into it" and went to work servicing airplanes. Woodworkers, mechanics, garagemen, truck drivers, cat operators—they all used to hang around the fields in the early days. "There are a hundred volunteers of the Mechanician Class in our town," Wrong Font Thompson boasted in 1925, "who can assemble an airship in less than no time."

Many of those volunteers eventually became full-time aircraft mechanics. They have often been forgotten, these dauntless, ingenious workers on the ground. They should be remembered. Some became as important as the foremost men in the air. No pilot has contributed more to Alaskan aviation than Mechanic Jim Hutcheson.

"Hutch," a genial, nimble-fingered man, has lived at Fairbanks since 1911. He was working in a local hardware store when Eielson and Wien arrived. He soon drifted into aircraft jobs and has served on the local field ever since. He also traveled all over the Territory repairing wrecks and his services are always in heavy demand.

Hutch is proud of what the "airplane doctors" have accomplished. He is very jealous of their reputation. He brags: "There's no plane an Alaska mechanic ever fixed up in the hills that wasn't able to fly back to its home base." But when he talks about himself he is, like the best of the pilots, modest. "It was just *row*tine"—this is how he says it. "It was just a job to do, just *row*tine."

Once Hutch camped a month and a half alone in the Kantishna—living in a trapper's cabin, sawing his own wood, melting snow for water—as he repaired a wrecked Stinson. He kept the wings in a tent hangar and built a whole new trusswork inside with sixty splices in the ribs and capstrips.

When Ben Eielson made his first mail flights, Hutch did all the iron work on the skis.

When Pilot Crosson made the first commercial flight to Barrow in his open-cockpit Swallow, Hutch built heaters— long pipes with flexible tubes hooked onto the engine exhaust—"so Joe could at least warm his feet."

When a Wilkins expedition ship cracked up at Fairbanks, Hutch made new ski stands out of boiler pipe. "I was the only one who could weld 'em."

When Pilot Gillam broke a landing gear on the Eielson Relief Expedition, Hutch was flown all the way to Siberia to repair it. He welded it at 30 below zero in high winds.

When Pilot Reid crashed near Unalakleet during the relief expedition, cracking four feet off the end of his Fairchild's wing, Hutch and another mechanic repaired the broken ribs with baling wire and wood from a Christmas box.

Hutch is the most distinguished of the mechanics but there are other respected names: Loren Frenald, Ernie Hubbard,

Tom Appleton, Cecil Higgins, Burrass Smith, Fritz Wien, Matt Parvin, Harry Bowman and many more.

Most of these ground workers ached to fly. Many soloed. A few became successful pilots. More failed.

None tried harder than little Freddie Moller.

11
Fred Moller

WHEN A PAN AMERICAN mail plane crashed near Nome on April 6, 1944, it broke the company's northern record of eleven and a half years without a passenger fatality. Six men were killed.

For New York officials of the globe-circling organization this was bad news. For Alaskans it was something more. In the airline shacks and on the runways, people were hardly able to talk about it. The report spread fast. "Little Freddie was aboard. Little Freddie got it this time." Mechanics and pilots all over the Territory stopped hammering, welding, loading, checking, didn't know what to do, couldn't find words to say.

Slow old-timers, prospectors and dog-mushers, stopped one another all up and down the Fairbanks streets. "Did you hear? Freddie was killed this afternoon. Over to Nome." Some just stood. Others walked awkwardly away.

Nobody wanted to believe it. Nobody quite did till newsboys began shouting toward evening and people read his name. There it was for sure—in heavy black print, listed among the dead: FLIGHT MECHANIC FRED MOLLER.

Only a few weeks before, as he watched the same white land slide under the wings of the same silver ship, Fred Moller had told a friend: "The plane hasn't been built yet that can kill me."

He believed this. Alaskans believed it. Fred Moller, by his own account, had survived nine bad wrecks. Nine times the ships in which he traveled had plunged suddenly to earth. Wings had been demolished, cabins shattered, engines hurled off, props twisted. Always Moller had crawled out, still breathing, still cussing, still game for flying.

The year before his death he had been aboard another Pan

American plane when it crashed in an icing blizzard on the Koyukuk Divide. Pilots searched relentlessly through winter storm. All the old-timers had wanted to hunt for the ship that was down with Moller. When it was sighted, smashed against the mountainside, there was no sign of life. But Moller had survived as usual. He had tramped a big OK in the snow, helped his pilot out of the wreckage and started off on foot, leading him slowly and surely home.

On their return to Fairbanks, that time, the pilot made a radio speech, told Alaskans all about their grim adventure. Reporters wanted Fred Moller to talk too. But when he saw them coming he crossed the street, dodged through an alley and hustled out to the airfield. All he wanted was to fuel another ship, load the mail and ride aloft again.

Fred Moller was a proud little rascal. He stood only five feet high. He was wiry, skinny, spry as a rooster. On the load manifest Pan American listed him at 135 pounds. Everybody knew he was not that heavy but nobody knew his true weight. He refused to stand on the scales and he kept himself bundled up in a lot of clothes. "Two or three suits o' pants and two or three sweaters 'n' coveralls made a pretty big man of him."

Nobody knew Fred Moller's age either. For ten years before his death he had been telling people he was fifty-two. Some said he was in his sixties. Some said he must be in his seventies. Some said he was already getting bald when he hit Nome in 1901. Freddie was a wrinkled, weatherbeaten kid. In summer he wore a British cap on his head, in winter a fur hood.

Nobody could quite figure out Fred Moller's accent. He talked rough, like a foreigner. He said he had been born near London, England, but he had spent most of his life in the towns and gold camps of Alaska. He may have spoken a mixture of cockney and siwash.

Fred Moller lived many years with Barney Lashley, the Fairbanks gunsmith, in a pointed wooden shack at the edge of the airfield. Lashley ran a shooting gallery down cellar, and there was a sign painted on the side of the building: WIN A RIFLE WHILE YOU PRACTISE. One night Moller returned from a flight and found his partner dead. He put another sign on the front door: CLOSED. From that time on he lived alone. He had a gold pan for an ash tray, an old iron stove to warm him and two big alarm clocks to wake him early in the morning.

Fred Moller's heart was big and warm. He loved children; "liked to take a hungry waif home and feed him good. He'd cut their shaggy hair, give 'em presents. He'd buy candy for all the kids in town." Friends who sorted his effects after the final wreck found a satchel full of child snapshots. Moller had a weakness for women—especially Indian and Eskimo women, "the bigger the better." They had a weakness for him; when he hiked in to a village after one of his wrecks a swarm of dusky girls hugged and kissed him, laughing with relief. But he was leery of family life. "A woman," he said, "is liable to get too bossy." He never married. All of his savings—$16,000—were willed to an Alaskan boy, the son of neighbors.

So far as anyone knew, Moller left no blood relatives. But the double funeral with which he and a fellow victim were honored was one of the most crowded in Fairbanks history. Some of the roughest men in town wept as pilots and mechanics bore his coffin slowly down the aisle. Fred Moller was more than a flight mechanic, more than a man. To the people of Alaska he was an institution. There was never anyone else like him.

"Little Freddie," they called him, and often smiled as they said it. "Saw Little Freddie over in the Co-op, just come in from Nome.—There's Little Freddie, hoppin' down the street.—Say, what's your hurry, Freddie?"

He was so shy, so earnest, so busy and so fiercely proud that everybody liked to kid him. Yet everybody, even the senior pilots, stood in awe of him. He was a hard worker, a tough number, quite a kick. Everybody, in one way or another, loved him.

Most called him Little Freddie. Some called him Shorty. A few nicknamed him The Midget. Others dubbed him The Little Giant.

The Little Giant—that was the best name for Fred Moller, for he was a small man who tried to do big things. He was a great little pioneer, one of the truest pioneers Alaska has ever

had. He did not know success. But he kept on trying. His
spirit was sharp. His vision of the Territory's future was
large.

"You know," he said shortly before his death, "this is my
country. I want to see it develop."

Freddie and his father migrated to Alaska from England
during the Gold Rush. They lived a while at Nome, where
Freddie peddled papers and kindling and his father panned
the beach. Once, working for the Golden Goose Mining
Company, the elder Moller hit it rich. He took Freddie back
to London on a pleasure trip, returned to Alaska broke. Soon
after this, he went to the States and disappeared. Freddie
sent many letters trying to locate him. There was never a
reply.

For a while Freddie prospected, wandering alone far into
the Arctic, pitching his own camps, following the creeks to
many new places. But he had no luck, so he got a construction job on the Alaska Railroad. He helped build the famous
bridge at Nenana, one of the longest single spans in the
world. He was a "jolly good little worker," railroad old-
timers recall, dependable even in winter when the wind blew
up to forty miles an hour and the temperature fell to sixty
below. He knew every rivet on the Nenana bridge, and liked
to refer to himself as a "steel man." He was so tireless, so
meticulous, that one of the construction bosses offered him a
high-paying job in South America. He turned it down.

More than anything else Freddie wanted to go back into
the Arctic hills and look for gold. He liked the long suspense
of hunting colors and the rare excitement of finding pay dirt.
He was convinced he would hit it rich sometime. And he
loved to live and work in the wilderness—all alone.

"Why, it's the only country," he told me. "The sheep are so
tame the little fellows walk right up to you and the young
birds fly to your camp for crumbs. I had a pet fish one place,
a bullhead; that fellow was always around at mealtime for
me to throw him scraps. You know, out in the hills there's no
such thing as being lonely."

His feeling for the Arctic was more than sentimental. He
was a friend and disciple of Dr. Alfred Brooks, the United
States Geological Survey chief in Alaska, who knew the

Territory's resources better than anyone and maintained they could support ten million people. Freddie knew long ago what government geologists today, more than ever, confirm: the Arctic, virtually empty of humans, holds untold riches—coal, oil, gold, asbestos, nickel, lead, silver, tin, tungsten—even amber and jade. He knew that the most inaccessible parts of the Far North are full of promise. That is why he learned to fly.

To a man of Freddie's experience, the aviation idea came easy. He had tramped, mushed and floated hundreds of tedious miles. He had made his own automatic dams for sluicing, his own cabins, his own small boats. "You know, out in the hills we build everything and find a way to do anything. As I grew older I thought, by gosh, some means of transport must be invented to get over this country in the quickest way possible." In 1923, when Ben Eielson arrived at Nenana on his first Alaskan flight, Freddie was waiting in the front of the crowd. He helped tie down the Jenny. Then he cornered Eielson. "I told him I wanted something like that for prospecting. I asked him if he thought I could be a pilot too. He really encouraged me."

Freddie took his ambition very seriously. He made a trip to the States for instruction, and took a few lessons from the famous Spokane pilot Nick Mamer. But the trip ended badly. On one of Freddie's first solo flights his plane crashed into a line of electric light wires. He was in bandages after the accident for a year and a half. Returning to Alaska, he decided to learn more about motors. "I'd go to the dumps and dig them out, them old motors, to cut wood with woodsaws. I'd fix them up and get them running. After a while people found out I knew all about it and when they needed a man they'd send for me."

He worked a while as an airplane mechanic, servicing "machines" for the earliest pioneer flyers. "Those men are all dead now," he casually told me a week before his own fatal crash. "Cracked up, you know." He helped outfit planes for the Wilkins expeditions. "I shoed their skis with the proper metal. They had put wooden skis on. I told them they were liable to stick and recommended they use some tin." But Freddie was not content with ground work. He begged the pilots to let him borrow their planes. They usually refused, so he decided to get one of his own. "I rustled around till I heard there was a Waco cracked up that would be for sale. I bought her and we fixed her up."

He took more flying lessons—a great many more. The average pilot needs eight hours of instruction before soloing; Freddie required fifty-four. Noel Wien smiles indulgently when he remembers how hard the Little Giant worked at the controls. All the old-timers smile the same way when they remember how hard he worked over his plane and the two damaged Curtiss OX-5 motors he bought to go with it. Evening after evening he could be seen at the Fairbanks field intently welding the struts, covering the wings, puttering over the engine.

He painted the ship bright green and polished it, "rubbing and rubbing to make her shine bright." On the Fourth of July he strung small American flags over the wings and fuselage. He even built a model of the plane, perfect in every respect. And he gave his craft a name: *Anna*. Some insist it was named for an Indian girl. Others maintain he named it for his mother. Freddie would not say.

"The Anna," as he solemnly referred to his Waco, made history. He was never prouder than on the June evening of 1928 when the *News-Miner* announced his full-fledged entry into the aviation business:

What will probably be the first instance of a flyer-prospector using an airplane to carry him to the different mining regions in the Interior for the sole purpose of prospecting will start tonight with the departure of Fred Moller on an extended journey which will cover practically all the mining camps in this section of Alaska.

"The Anna" could hold one passenger, and Freddie decided to launch a flying company. He ran a large newspaper ad:

BEFORE YOU TRAVEL IN THE AIR,
SEE FAIRBANKS AIR EXPRESS.

THE ONLY FAIRBANKS COMPANY GIVING RATES
TO PROSPECTORS AND MINERS

HOT SANDWICHES AND COFFEE SERVED
DURING FLIGHTS
WARM FLYING CLOTHES FURNISHED

He made the sandwiches himself, slicing bread and meat in his shack. He "always had a few extra parkys around" to keep his customers warm. This was a real airline with all the trimmings. In fact, as he pointed out in the *News-Miner*, it was a more important venture than that. The Territory was planning to set aside a fund to aid prospectors. This project and its public meaning were featured with flourish in the little airman's big ad:

When I was a boy Alaska's greatest friend, Dr. Alfred Brooks, picked up a rock and told me a wonderful story about it—"Boy, this northern belt will produce in time four hundred million dollars."

THIS SPRING, BOYS, WE WILL HAVE $20,000 to prospect this northern belt. Be with me and realize what that means and more of it to come if we need it.

Boys, we will have to make this a success. We will just have to show Uncle Sam that he is an old duffer and that really Alaska is the most wonderful land he has in his possession and really it is God's country and we old-timers are right here to prove it.

Every dollar you can shove our way will mean one more prospector in the hills.

THINK OF IT AS YOU TRAVEL IN THE AIR.

For nearly two years Freddie flew "The Anna" through the inland mining country. He always carried a pick and shovel and gold pan in the cabin, ready to go to work wherever he came down. He took slight interest in hauling ordinary passengers, but he rode dozens of miners to their claims, free of charge, on the chance that they would find enough gold to pay him back. Often he chipped in with cash. He would make a fifty-fifty deal with a prospector any time.

Fairbanks Air Express was not a profitable venture. There were several reasons for this. Many of Freddie's passengers returned from the hills broke. Others met disaster, and he spent much of his time flying gratis to their rescue. "Their dogs would come back to a village, so we'd know the boys were in trouble—lost, drownded or killed by a bear, and I'd go out and hunt." He located one of his customers on a mountainside, "stiff as a board." Another had been eaten by a grizzly; "not much left of him, but I found a leg and one shoepac." There was always misfortune on the airline. If Freddie's customers were not in trouble, he was.

The aviation idea came easy to Freddie, but flying itself came continually hard. He was so small he had to perch on a pile of cushions to see out of the plane. He was high-strung and excitable in the cockpit—"just like a jumping jack." Beyond this, those who knew him best believe that his eyesight was poorer than he would admit even to himself. Although he spent a total of 500 hours at the controls of airships he was never able to master the knack of being a pilot.

Again and again Freddie cracked up, and he spent countless days on the ground, repairing his plane. "Always busy mending a busted stabilizer or rudder or a hole in a wing or ski." His sad landings were a common joke. People began calling him the "Slap-her-down-Kid."

One day Fairbanks mechanics heard the noise of an engine. "Hold your hats," said one, "here comes Freddie." The Waco dropped down in a sideways tilt, hit with a lurch and flipped over on its back.

"What happened? What happened?" the Little Giant shouted as he hung head down in the cockpit, silver dollars dropping out of his pockets.

"You just turned over," said a bystander, wounding Freddie's feelings so deeply that he would not speak to him for a week.

Once, landing at the town of Curry, Freddie knocked several branches off a tree. He patiently mended his ship, climbed in, and slithered into another tree on take-off. Another time, clad in a black-bear flying suit, he prepared for take-off from a snow-covered river bar near Shungnak. He pushed the boulders to one side and laid a row of flags to line himself up. Then he climbed onto his pile of cushions.

"All fixed?" bystanders asked.

"Yup," he replied, raising himself and peering ahead with the air of a submarine captain sighting through a periscope.

"Can you see all right?"

"Fine."

He started the engine. "Then," in the words of a witness, "by golly, he headed right for a pile of stones, smashed into it and broke twelve inches off the end of the prop."

He picked up the splinters and fitted them together like a jigsaw puzzle. He slipped a piece of stovepipe on the blade to hold them in place and wrapped the whole with wire. Propelled by this classic piece of patchwork, he managed to get his ship safely into the air and flew 300 miles home.

Freddie usually carried an extra propeller in the plane with him. He also carried tools and a "big butcher-knife and a saw to cut trees." They all came in handy. He couldn't learn to watch the winds. Nor, well as he knew the country, could he recognize it from the controls of his plane. Again and again he was blown off course. Again and again he got lost. Fairbanksans report that he could not even follow another pilot to Livengood, seventy-five miles away.

Since "The Anna" carried only thirty-five gallons of gas, these confusions led to repeated long walks. He was cheerful about this. Overland distance did not dismay him. Once he ran out of gas in the Koyukuk region and landed on a river bar. It was 200 miles to the nearest town. He built a raft of logs, floated downstream to the settlement and bought some motorboat gas. Loading it into a canoe, he paddled laboriously upstream, fueled his plane with the heavy stuff and took off.

Nothing and no one could persuade the little prospector that he could not fly. Ben Eielson, whom Freddie called his "staunchest friend," was one of the few pilots who ever gave him any encouragement. Freddie was enormously proud of this. "Ben came right up to my hangar every time I came back from a trip, and told me—'Attaboy! Keep going!'" Freddie did—until he lost the ship.

It happened in the spring of 1931. He left Fairbanks with a load of mail, heading for the town of Eagle in the Fortymile. By the time his gas ran out he was circling in the Nabesna, farther from his destination than when he took off. "The motor pooped as I was crossing a rocky ridge. I saw a little pond ahead and just made the edge of it. CRASH! 'The Anna' was gone."

So completely was the ship demolished that Freddie, mortified, made a bonfire of it before he left. Then, dutifully dragging the mail sack behind him on a ski, he trudged several weeks overland to Big Delta, where he was picked up by Pilot Ed Young. Young had tried to rescue him earlier. Learning Freddie's approximate position from settlements through which he passed, Young flew low over the dog trail many times, but Freddie hid in the woods each time he heard the plane. "His feelings were hurt, that's all," Alaskans explain. "He just wanted to come in under his own power."

Freddie did not have enough money for another plane so he made himself a twenty-six-foot poling boat. "He built it," Joe Crosson recalls, "with the loving care of a master." He announced that he was going off prospecting with it in the Arctic. A crowd of friends went down to the river bank on the day of his departure. Freddie shook hands all around, climbed aboard, pushed off and started cranking. The new engine would not run. He tried and tried, and was still cranking as the boat disappeared around the bend. That was the last Fairbansans saw of him for two years.

They were years of bad luck. He panned and panned, but found little gold. Then one day, floating down swift rapids on the Colville River, his boat tangled with low-hanging "sweepers" and capsized. His whole outfit sank to the bottom of the river. He swam to shore and hiked for weeks across the tundra, living as best he could off fish, rabbits and berries. He hurt his foot, but made a cane of forked willow and hobbled on. He arrived at Fairbanks "thin as a sliver, pale as a ghost," and was laid up six months with rheumatism.

The Little Giant worked a while as a mechanic, helped build Pan American's Fairbanks hangar and saved up enough money to buy part interest in another ship. Pilots were appalled when they learned his choice: a Stearman biplane—at the time one of the fastest-landing aircraft on the field. "You'll get killed, Freddie," they warned him. "That's too hot for you." So many told him this that he agreed to sell his interest in it.

Dolefully, he went to work as a Pan American flight mechanic. He held this job for the next ten years and became a legend in it. So exacting was he that it took him an hour to accomplish something another man could do in twenty minutes. Rising each morning at five or earlier, he walked to work along the edge of the field when most mechanics were still in bed. He serviced Pan American's ships as meticulously as if they were his own. "If he was assigned to a plane it was always the best." He developed a special method of folding wing covers and insisted that new mechanics learn it. He rubbed the cowling and waxed the wings as a housewife would polish silver. "A clean ship is a safe ship," he always said. Everything had to be just so.

Freddie worked nearly 10,000 hours aloft as a flight mechanic. Now and then, in Pan American's dual-equipped Electras, pilots let him have a feel of the controls. However, in the Pilgrims—workhorses of the company's Fairbanks-Nome winter mail run—he rode behind in the cabin with the passengers. He could hear the radio reports over his headphones, but his only means of communication with the pilot was by yelling or passing notes through a small aperture into the cockpit.

Crosson, who took Freddie along on many of the company's original survey trips, declares warmly that he was "the best flight mechanic in the world." It was not only that he was "nice and light to haul," allowing room for more pay load. He was an excellent radio operator; "that little so-and-so knew the code." He kept the ship's logbook in a neat, labored hand. In years of work he learned Pan American's routes by heart; their mountains, their rivers, their snow conditions and, equally important, their people.

Freddie knew all the natives at little stops like Ruby and Nulato and Golovin. He was generous: at Christmas time he never forgot a man, woman or child. But also he was stern. He bossed them sharply as they flocked about his ship to help refuel or unload. "He'd do anything for them—and they'd do anything for him."

Freddie bossed the Pan American pilots too. With himself and everyone else he was a hard taskmaster. The company assigned him the job of breaking in new men and familiarizing them with the country. He herded them like sheep. "You're just a kid at this game," he told one who had had many years of experience in the States. "You'd better listen to me." When another insisted on heading off course, he poked a fishing rod through the aperture and switched him on the neck. He threatened to spray a third with the fire extinguisher. There were several with whom he categorically refused to ride. No flyer, however high he stood in the company, escaped his vigilance.

Les McLennan, a large, burly captain who crashed with Freddie the year before the final wreck, reports that his small mechanic bossed him all the way back to civilization. When McLennan tried to chop a stump for firewood and missed, Freddie snatched the ax and refused to return it. "You damn fool," he said, "next thing you'll cut off your foot and then how will I get you home?" When they left the plane and started hiking cross-country through the deep snow, Freddie discovered that McLennan had brought along the ship's Very-pistol for a souvenir. "Didn't I tell you," he shouted, "not to pack anything you don't need?" He grabbed it and hurled it over a cliff.

Title meant less than nothing to Freddie. He bore an ill-concealed scorn toward desk workers and office executives. "So you're the new traffic manager?" he asked one pompous arrival from the States, and spat on the floor. When a group of visiting officials diverted a plane from the mail run to go polar bear hunting, he told them off as severely as he would the Eskimos. "Rich bawstards!" he snapped, fierce with indignation.

For years he wore on his cap the gold band that is reserved, by company regulation, for captains and first officers. No one wanted to tell him to take it off. Despite his age and his thistly independence the company kept him on the payroll and gave him the title of chief Fairbanks flight mechanic. In honor of his tenth year of service, Pan American staged a surprise party in the hangar. Crosson flew north from Seattle to attend. Freddie, who virtually worshiped Crosson, was pleased and "proud as a peacock." He prized the new two-starred company emblem on his lapel. Still he was restless.

All down the years he had been fretting. He missed the Far Arctic. He wanted to get back at the controls of his own plane and search for gold again. "I'm really a miner at heart," he said, "a prospector. I want to fly out and look for new places."

Pan American had done all it could to allay his discontent. Once the company tried to send him on a vacation trip to the States, but he did not like cities. He traveled only as far south as Juneau, and took the next plane back north. For years he had been granted extra time in addition to his vacation so that he could go prospecting. But this was not enough of the life he loved best.

In 1943 he decided to buy an airplane and strike out once more on his own. He paid $750 for a wrecked Curtiss Robin with a J-6-5 Wright engine. Moving to a tar-paper shack by the airfield, which also served as a nose-hangar, he worked in his spare time for months re-covering the fuselage and re-building the stabilizer of his new ship, NC-511-N. He painted the plane bright orange with a black stripe. In November he announced it was ready to fly.

The boys in the hangar tactfully suggested that he let someone else give it its initial test. He was too impatient. An anxious crowd watched as he climbed into the cockpit and revved up the engine. He waved happily, taxied out, began practicing S-turns—and ran straight into the Pan American tractor. The Wright engine was badly smashed.

He started all over again and worked many months in his spare time repairing it. When spring came and the warm sun melted the ice from the ponds he announced he had it fixed. "I'll be hanging the motor in another week," he told me. "Then I'll go out and just roam around. It's not the money; you know I could be living anyway. But I got my old maps, I know where the tin and tungsten are, and right now I want to look for vital minerals for the government."

Freddie's friends were all worried. He had not piloted a plane for many years. He wasn't young. He had used up enough luck for ten men. He would crash, people said, in no time. The Little Giant never had a chance to prove them wrong. He was not at the controls when death struck. He was riding on his last trip as flight mechanic, sitting in the cabin of a Pan American mail plane with the passengers.

He had notified Pan American that he would quit the flight mechanic job the first of April. The company had asked him to stay on a few days longer, as they were shorthanded that week. He had agreed.

It was a fair morning on April 5 when a Pan American Pilgrim piloted by young Robert Bullis, a newcomer in Alaska, prepared to leave Fairbanks on a routine mail flight to Nome. Aboard, along with Freddie, was his friend Ted Seltenreich, also an Alaska veteran, who was to replace him on the job. The hangar crowd kidded as they watched them load the plane. "Two mechanics," somebody said. "A sure sign of bad luck."

Freddie hustled over to the airport office to make out the flight plan. He was in a chipper mood.

"Well, Pop," he jubilantly told the manager, "this is my last trip with the PAA. From now on I'll be flying on my own."

The next day, seven minutes after take-off from Nome on the return trip, the plane plowed through white haze into a snowy hill. All members of the crew and three Eskimo passengers were instantly killed.

Fred Moller's body lies today on the steep slope of Birch Hill cemetery, just outside the "Golden Heart" town.

Beyond Fairbanks, for hundreds and hundreds of miles, spreads Arctic wilderness. Through jagged peaks the creeks rush unseen. Winds blow and blow, the sun beats down, and seldom a human feels them. Under the earth they lie as they have lain for centuries—rich minerals, wealth for the people, waiting to be dug.

"You know, it's my country. I want to see it develop."

He could not fly. He never hit it rich. But few men in the North have had the sharp pioneer spirit of Little Freddie Moller. "He had the kind of spirit that don't die easy." Few men have had as much right to call Alaska their own.

12
She Can Be Cruel

"SHE'S A BEAUTIFUL country," Pilot Jack Jefford has said of Alaska, "but she can be cruel."

Alaska's is a stern magnificence which seems both to threaten and invite. The pilots do not talk about it much, but they will fly out of their way to show it—the dreary ice-chunked glacier crumbling ponderously into earth and rock— the huge white cone of a "smoker" belching endless puffs into the sky—the water of a secret "hanging lake" cradled among the crags of lofty peaks. Sometimes a flyer will mutely point to splendor in the sky—glimmering "sundogs" above the Arctic snow, or the wild-weaving spokes of nothern lights, or the orb of a blood-red moon. From north to south, from east to west, in many weird and formidable ways, Alaska is beautiful.

But she can be cruel. In the decade preceding World War II more than a third of the planes in the Territory were demolished in major wrecks. Disaster has come to many of the bush pilots; near-disaster has been all in the day's work for all of them. Nevertheless, the man who has dropped to rough landing "somewhere in the wilderness" and seen people crowd to his plane for mail and meat will not again be content to slide monotonously along the concrete city airports of the main line. The man who has flown for hours alone above the northland, and mastered the techniques of doing so, will not again be content to be chained in traffic above a maze of roads, telephone poles, cities and towns.

Despite the frequency of wrecks and crack-ups, the safety record of Alaskan aviation is remarkable. When worse came to worst the bush pilots learned cagey ways of "cracking up easy"—knocking off the landing gear as they came down and sliding in on the belly, or "slipping in," where required, to let

125

one wing absorb the impact. The amazing fact is that in the decade prior to World War II, when more than thirty million miles were flown under the most primitive conditions, only sixty-three pilots' and passengers' lives were lost.

It was a special trade, flying in a land without airports. "You can always tell an Alaska pilot in the States. He staggers short onto a runway and has to taxi a mile to be refueled." The pilots prospected fields as miners prospected colors. They flattened propeller blades for utmost power in take-off, used flaps at the last split second for utmost lift and climb. They learned to feel for the ground in the Arctic winter whiteness, "dragging" runways that were almost invisible. Touching skis, they checked rivers for spider-webbing ice, logs or overflows. Flying on floats in summertime, they took off from small lakes by circling round and round on the water and making steep turns into the wind.

It was a special trade, navigating above wilderness. Pilots from the States, men with many thousands of hours of logged experience, have failed at it. Before the war-built airways were completed many Army flyers lost their way above Alaska. A military Search and Rescue Squadron was organized: pilots new to the North spent much of their time searching for and rescuing each other. Colonel Harold H. Carr, executive officer of the Army base at Fairbanks, once took off in a Norseman for Whitehouse, Canada. He wandered in the air for nine hours. "I'm following a medium-wide river-bed north and south," he finally reported over his radio. "I do not know where I am." Soon after this he ran out of gas and landed near the Salmon River in Alaska—farther from his destination than when he took off. A trapper led him to the nearest village and Noel Wien, in a Fairchild 71, flew him back to his base.

"Wrong-way Carr-again," the late Lieutenant General Simon Bolivar Buckner, Jr., commander of the Army in Alaska, wired him. But it is no disgrace to lose one's way above the northland. Noel Wien did so as late as 1932. Flying through misty dusk in the Seward Peninsula area he became completely confused. "Where are we?" a passenger asked. "I don't know," Wien told him. "We'll find a stream and follow it to its mouth and come out either on the Yukon or on the

Koyukuk." "Smiling Jack" Herman, after six years of capable work in the North, took a false turn in a well known mountain pass, ran out of gas and landed on a sand bar on the wrong side of the range. "I have never been lost in Alaska," wryly boasts Jack Jefford, one of the most accomplished younger flyers. "At least I always knew I was within the borders of the Territory."

Alaska has some of the crookedest rivers in the world. It took time, but the best of the pilots eventually learned to use them. "Two streams, when you get to know 'em, don't look no more alike than two people." They learned to follow these baffling courses even in winter, when they were blanketed with white, by following the line of timber along shore. It was difficult, in winter, to tell a river's direction; twists and turns were so frequent that a compass was useless. The flyers learned to judge by fallen trees—"The tops always lay downstream"—or if the river were too sluggish for this they judged by the lay of driftwood on the bars. "So many bends after the Fish Camp, and that village ought to show. . . . Three creeks from that hook, and you'll hit over Jimmy's cabin." This was their technique of navigation.

The best of the bush pilots, as the years passed, developed contact flying to a fine art. One, who lost his way in a foggy coastal area, landed on floats and tasted the water to see if it were fresh or salt. Pilots took their bearings on many subtle landmarks—the odd form of a hill, the curious shape of a nameless body of water. "I know hundreds of lakes," said one, "and none of them are on the map." They learned to "read" mountain passes and to follow these twisting gorges in bad weather, warily flying their ships at low speed with the stabilizer back—as one describes it—"almost hanging onto the prop."

"To get through Rainy Pass," a pioneer blithely told a new man, "you start where the Rhon River meets the south fork of the Kuskokwim. There's a cache on the mouth of the creek. Turn left and take the first canyon to your right. You'll see a canyon on your left that looks good—but don't take it, it's blind. Take the next left after that and fly up it—it makes a lazy turn to the left, then hard to the right. If you can crawl under the fog this far you'll make it through.

You'll go by a little green lake and come out on Ptarmigan Valley and start down the Happy River past Stillman Lake and then go into Happy River canyon . . ."

Merrill Pass is named for Russel Merrill, who discovered it. Mt. Eielson is named for Ben Eielson, who first landed at its base. S.E. Robbins found a crooked river which cut his initials, perfectly formed, in the tundra; delighted, he claimed it for his own. Noel Wien has a favorite lake, "pretty, with white sand beaches," where he once landed and shot a moose. Wien Lake, his friends call it. To other landmarks the pilots have given names both picturesque and bawdy: Windy Pass, Maggie's Crotch, Cloudy Mountain, Hour-Glass Lake, Bullshitna Lake, Fish-hook Lake, Breast Mountain. "You're damn right," says one of these flyers, "we got familiar with the country." Another more soberly sums up northern air navigation in the pioneer period: "We discovered the country because we had to learn to read it or else."

They learned, too, to read Alaskan sky. Their sharp judgment of weather time and again startled military pilots during the war. They confidently made zero-zero take-offs through the dense smoke-fog that forms above Interior towns in winter, knowing that it was merely local. They flew across wooded inland country under sluggish murk that hung as low as a hundred feet above the ground. But they shunned a hazy white day on the treeless Arctic coast when the ceiling was many times higher, and they were ever suspicious of the sudden, rolling fogs of the coastal southeast.*

Sixty-mile winds on the Arctic coast, the pilots learned, are not so bad;—"they tend to steady down and flatten out"— but the "Takus" and "Stikines" of the coastal southeast are violent and capricious. "There are times when you can take off okay from the small boat harbor at Juneau but a mile away the wind will blow you upside down." Flying in this region the pilots kept constant watch for the danger signal of

---

* Author's note: I regret that it has been impossible to include the stories of such distinguished southeastern pilots as Shell Simmons and Alex Holden. Their "float" work has been remarkable and thier company, Alaska Coastal Airlines, has been one of the busiest and most indispensable air services in the Territory.

boiling water. Flying through mountains, they skirted smoking ridges and stayed on the windward side of peaks. They learned not only to fear the winds, but also, when necessary, to use them. Trapped above fog, they found the holes that blowing gusts will make near rough terrain, and spiraled their small ships down through them.

The pioneers of Alaskan flight became past masters at outwitting the elements. They earned a reputation for being "among the best pilots in the world—because they had to be."

None has met stormy weather with the uncanny skill of Harold Gillam.

None has met rough terrain with the uncanny skill of Bob Reeve.

13
Harold Gillam

SNOWFLAKES WHITENED the windows of the roadhouse at McGrath. The panes rattled with wind. The dim afternoon was turning to dusk. Beside the Yukon stove a group of dispirited flyers settled down to the twentieth round of poker. They were fretful, tired of themselves and one another, tired of swapping stories and flipping through the pages of ancient magazines. For three days they had been grounded by a blizzard which still showed no sign of abating. "Really a storm," recalls Oscar Winchell. "I wouldn't 'a' whipped a cat out there that night."

They heard it faintly at first over the moan of the wind. Then the noise came loud overhead. The players left their game and went to the windows. They could not see it but there was a plane up there in the blizzard, coming in to land. No one wondered who the pilot was. Any man in the room would have staked his chips it was Harold Gillam.

The sound of the engine traveled back and forth, louder and louder, till it seemed as if the hidden plane would crash into the roof. Finally the blurred shape of Gillam's Pilgrim appeared just over the runway and plowed to a stop in deep drifts.

Gillam, bundled heavily in furs, climbed out, unloaded his sacks and came plodding through the snow with the air of a postman stepping up to ring a doorbell.

"Where's the mail, Charlie?" he asked the gangling veteran McGrath mechanic. "Will you gas me up? I'm going on to Fairbanks."

He asked for a cup of coffee and stood alone as he drank it, warming his back against the stove. He opened the door to see if the mechanic had finished, slammed it shut. He stood for a moment, hands in pockets, watching the poker game. Then he walked out without saying a word.

As they heard him taxi down the field the pilots once more crowded to the window. Gillam had turned on the landing lights for take-off: a ring of brightness broke the stormy dusk. All eyes followed the Pilgrim as it came growling back in a trail of white. The plane slowed to a sputtering stop. "By golly," said Charlie. "Don't believe Harold can make it. Snow must be over two foot deep."

Gillam tried again and failed. He walked back and asked Charlie to get a tractor. "Make a path just wide enough for the skis," he said. "That'll be okay." He sat alone in his ship as the chugging cat broke a runway. Then he gunned the engine and was gone.

One of the pilots turned up the radio receiver as they went back to their game. All evening they heard no report from Gillam. When they awoke the next day the snow was still flying, the wind still blowing. All morning the receiver gave forth nothing but empty crackles and zero-zero weather reports.

By afternoon the men began to worry. Perhaps Gillam was down in the storm. Perhaps they should go out and search. They sent a query to Fairbanks. The return news both relieved and annoyed them. Gillam had landed at his home base on schedule, as he always landed on schedule. Without beam he had flown through the night blizzard as he would fly through sunshine, so little concerned that he had not bothered to use his radio.

In the days before Alaska's airways were built, old-timers say, there were three kinds of weather in the north. There was "Pan American weather"—clear and unlimited. There was the whole gamut of good, bad and indifferent weather which ordinary men would fly. And there was "Gillam weather." Gillam's contempt for fog, snow, rain and wind is a legend from Barrow to Ketchikan. "He thought he could beat the elements." Other pilots made a grim jest of it. Hearing that he was aloft in a storm they claimed double reason for canceling their trips. "Don't believe I'll try it," one remarked. "God's plenty busy taking care of Harold."

In January, 1943, Gillam lost. But for more than ten years

he successfully flew Alaska with apparent indifference to nature's mood. "Thrill 'em, spill 'em, no kill 'em Gillam" the saying went. There were trips on which women screamed and men prayed as he battled wind and fog among the mountains. Some seasoned air travelers have been known to climb out of his plane at way stops and refuse to go on. There are others who declared his skill was superhuman, and who liked to travel with no one else.

Gillam had a brooding look. Short, burly, broad-shouldered, he had an aura of suppressed power. Before coming north he had been an amateur boxer. He looked the part. His coal-black eyes peered out from beneath heavy, overhanging brows. He was swarthy, of Irish descent. Some said he had Indian blood in him.

Gillam seldom laughed. Obsessed by aviation, he would sometimes join a technical argument with keen comment and incisive wit, but usually he was silent. He shunned other pilots. "How's the weather?" they would ask as he landed. "Not bad," he would reply. Invariably, with a dead-pan expression—"Not bad." That was all.

For several years Gillam kept two polar bears in a cage beside his hangar. No one understood why—least of all his mechanic, who frequently had to chase them when they broke loose and lumbered about the airfield. Gillam brought them in one day from a trip, had the cage built and kept them there. He was averse to discussing his actions—trivial or important—with anyone. Always he seemed deep in his own thoughts. Mechanics who have worked closely with Gillam for many years say they never had an inkling of what was on his mind. Women liked him.

In the air and on the ground Gillam was stern. Nothing seemed to have any effect on him. Oscar Winchell, who worked for Gillam a while, recalls a flight through rolling fog in a Zenith: "The average guy would 'a' been nervous, settin' to one side then the other—'Let's see, so much gas; my gosh, it'll take me an hour to get back. Well, I'm goin' in just a little ways more and beat it back to the field if she gets tough'—but Gillam, he was just as cool about it, like a doctor goin' to make an operation. Nothin' seemed to register. He set back there smokin' a cigarette, lookin' at the instruments, once he tipped the wings and showed me a moose on the mountainside. I kept lookin' at my watch and thinkin' he should go back, but he just seemed to know he was gonna make it—and he did."

Once, Winchell says, he and Gillam were circling at 16,000 feet above a sea of cloud. Mountains were hidden below. There was only fifteen minutes' gas left in the tank. "He was settin' there, lookin' around, found a few breaks in the fog but none big enough—there wasn't a worry on his face. Finally he pulled back the throttle and took her down. We could see a little, then she was too thick, we was blind a while again, right in the mountains—then we broke out in the clear just over the field. He landed and climbed out:

"I said: 'Aren't you gonna taxi over to the hangar?'

"He said: 'No, we'll tie her down right here.'

"I said: 'Wouldn't it be better to taxi her over to the hangar out of the wind?'

"But he told me: 'I *said*—we'll leave her here.'

"I looked at the gas gauge, and it showed empty. Not a drop left. He didn't say nothin' more—just took his grip and started walkin' to town."

Charles Harold Gillam, son of an auto salesman, was born in Kankakee, Illinois, in 1903 and grew up in Chadron, Nebraska. He ran away from home at the age of sixteen and joined the Navy. He spent several years in the Pacific in a destroyer. Mustered out in 1923, he drifted to Seattle and worked as a painter till he saw a sign in an American Legion hall advertising for construction men in Alaska. He went north and worked several years for the Road Commission, operating power shovels and driving tractors. Then he started his own freighting outfit.

Sourdoughs shook their heads when the newcomer signed a contract to move forty tons of supplies from Fairbanks to the Nome Creek dredge. It was a rough job and a rush job. Spring break-up was near, and the trip must be made before it came. Part of the trail must be cut through virgin wilderness. Gillam succeeded. When a formidable crag blocked his route he did not take time to detour but put a big block shive on top, linked tractors and sleds with cable and hauled the load up as the cats plunged down the other side. "Gillam liked tough work," pioneer freighting men say, "and he always found a way to do it."

Joe Crosson's first recollection of Gillam is of a husky kid bumping along in a tractor, smoothing the surface of the old Fairbanks field. After this job Gillam used to hang around the airport, dourly watching the planes. He asked Crosson a few questions. One day he told him he believed he would learn to fly.

As a student Gillam escaped death in the North's first fatal crash. He was riding in a two-place Swallow biplane with his instructor, M. L. Danforth, when the ship slid out of control and spun to earth. Danforth died two days later. Gillam, badly gashed in the head and hands, refused to stay in the hospital. Before the doctor had the stitches out of his wounds he was in the air again. Soon after this he was practicing spins alone. He was one of the first students to solo in Alaska.

Gillam did not have a pilot's license when he and Crosson made their perilous winter flights on the Eielson search. He had a total of only forty solo hours in the air. But of all the pilots gathered at Teller for rescue work, Gillam, the road-house manager says, was the least worried. "That little fellow didn't know what fear was." Crosson was amazed on their stormy trip to Asia when the cocky fledgling, barreling blind through fog, beat him to the *Nanuk*. The rest of the pilots were discomfited to think that he was the only one to reach Siberia and assist Crosson in the search. The following year, when Gillam applied for his license, he failed to pass the routine government examination, but the federal inspector laughed and certified him as an airman.

The first phase of Gillam's flying business was gloomy and violent. Pioneering service to the copper-mining region back of the seaport of Cordova with a Swallow, a Zenith and an Ireland amphibian "he scattered his airplanes all over the hills." In six months of 1931 he had six wrecks. He charged his passengers high rates but spent all of his income and more patching the aircraft. "He broke up so much stuff that half the time he hadn't a buck to his name." The merchants and miners who financed him lost more than $30,000.

He could hardly have found more difficult flying than in

the foggy, turbulent, mountainous coast region. At Cordova he landed on skis or floats on a small crag-cradled lake, or on wheels on a short glacier bar. The airport at McCarthy, near the Kennecott copper mine, was a narrow clearing on top of a bluff. "If you undershot," another pilot says, "you ran into the bluff—and when you took off, you hadn't a foot of spare." The short strip at the town of Copper was bordered on three sides by high brush. By day these wind-buffeted runways were "always Nearer My God to Thee." Gillam, often as not, slept till noon and flew late into the night.

"For some reason," says Winchell, "Harold seemed to like to fly in the dark. He would 'a' got killed but I think he had abnormally sharp eyes. I always grabbed a flashlight to walk from a field to the roadhouse but Gillam would never bother. He'd step along on a pitch-black night, sure-footed as a wild animal."

One night people at Copper heard the roar of Gillam's engine and looked out of their cabin windows. His Swallow, its navigation lights flashing against the bluffs, was circling to land. Men hurried down the trail to mark off the field with lanterns. But Gillam did not wait for their aid; his ship, heavily loaded with ore concentrates, descended and crashed. It rolled violently over a bank and a large stump broke through the windshield, missing him by inches.

He unbuckled his seat belt, climbed out and dourly surveyed the wreck. The tail was broken. Three wings were smashed. In one moment he had written off at least $8,000. "I'll be damned," he said, "if I think there's any money in this business." The next day he began figuring what parts could be salvaged to build another plane.

Gillam was not a neat workman, mechanics report, but he was ingenious. Once he landed on a river in winter and found he had forgotten to bring his fire pot. He built a brush fire to warm his engine for take-off. Often, when he had no mechanic along, he would mend a wrecked ship himself. "He'd just tie 'em together some way," says Winchell. "He knew they'd be busted up in a little while anyhow."

One bitter-cold day at Chitina an Indian firepotting Gillam's plane burned all the ignition wiring out of the engine. Gillam telephoned Copper and asked a mine-mechanic there how to rewire it with the magneto properly timed. Yelling over the crude frontier phone the mechanic suggested two different combinations which Gillam, working with bare hands at 30 below zero, tried. They failed. The engine remained dead.

"Well," he said, as a crowd gathered, "I'm going to figure this out myself."

It is no simple job to work out the wiring of the spark plugs on a nine-cylinder dual-ignition engine, and Gillam had not tried it before. He took a stick, scratched a diagram in the snow and spent a while pondering it. He worked the problem over twice and rechecked. Then he tried his scheme. Someone cranked the engine, and "by God, she turned over." He wired up the other side the same way.

By this time it was almost dark. He had planned to stay overnight; told onlookers he was merely going to taxi to the end of the lake to break trail for morning take-off. They watched the ship bump to the far shore and turn. Then, to their astonishment, it came thundering back. Men and women scattered like chickens and the plane sped straight across the place where they had stood. The plane rose, wings rocked in salute, and it faded into the night sky. "Never handled things like nobody else. There wasn't no telling about Gillam."

A trader at Copper, "Honest John" McCreary, fell down cellar and ran a nail through his stomach. He said he was feeling fine but nobody believed him. "Any time McCreary lies down in the daytime he must be pretty sick." There was no doctor at Copper. Late that afternoon an Indian rapped on the door of Gillam's cabin. "McCreary die," he said. Gillam loaded the groaning man into his plane, took off at dusk and flew 125 miles through driving snow to Kennecott. The doctor there said the patient might not last the night. Gillam left Kennecott after midnight and flew another 200 miles to fetch McCreary's son from Cordova.

As the plane came down on the lake at Cordova one wheel broke through ice and it sagged over. A spar of the lower wing was cracked. It took three hours to pull the ship out and drag it to shore. Meanwhile a telephone report came from Kennecott: McCreary was sinking fast.

A worried group watched as Gillam poured gas into the tanks.

"You taking off, Harold," asked one, "with that busted spar?"

"Ice is awful thin," said another.

"Oh, that's okay," Gillam told them as he screwed on the cap. "I think it'll be all right."

He motioned his passenger in, took off across the "rubber ice" and returned to Kennecott. McCreary lived. Whether he lived or died, it was all in a night's work to Gillam.

After several years of flight in the copper region Gillam was virtually penniless. He borrowed money for a second-hand Hornet-powered Pilgrim and moved to Fairbanks for a new try. Soon he got two more Pilgrims and began running back and forth from Fairbanks to meet the boats at Cordova. He did not care for charter freighting. He had his heart set on an airline. "The kind of cargo I like to haul," he told his mechanic, "is the kind that will walk itself into my plane."

He refused to have any numbering or lettering painted on these Pilgrims. His mechanic believes it was because he was superstitious. But from this time until his death in 1943 Gillam never washed out another plane. His flying entered a new phase. "Seems like he'd had an awful streak of bad luck and then BANG! he broke right out of it."

He did have three accidents. Once in foggy winter weather south of Barrow he ran out of gas and landed on the tundra. Calling over his radio, he described the terrain—"flat, white, cut up with rivers and creeks." A roomful of Eskimos, listening at the Barrow station, argued as to his location. For hundreds of miles the country looked like this. The only real clue they had was Gillam's hunch that he was "somewhere on the Meade River."

Ten dog teams started in this direction through the fog. Each Eskimo driver carried a timepiece and at appointed intervals Gillam lit oil flares to guide them to his wreck. He also walked out from his plane, each day in a different direction, hoping to meet them. Several times he came upon the scuffle of pawprints in the snow. The teams, he later said, seemed to be running round and round him in big circles.

The Eskimos wandered four days in the wild flats till one sighted a "pinpoint of light" in the distance and reached the plane. Gillam was on the Colville River, some seventy miles from where he had thought. The temperature was forty below zero but the drivers found him clad in coveralls and a pair of bedroom slippers, hunched in the cockpit as casually as if he were waiting in a hotel room for a telephone call. He refueled his ship with gas they had brought and flew on.

Another time the gas gave out as he burrowed stubbornly through fog in an attempt to land at Anchorage. His landplane plunged into the water of Cook Inlet, just off shore from town. As a powerful tide sucked the ship downward he helped his passengers out onto an ice floe. None even got his feet wet. Meanwhile the Anchorage fire chief blew his siren, and boats soon arrived to the rescue. The ship, by this time, had sunk so deep that only its rudder was showing. The Fire Department worked all night to save it, buoyed it up with oil drums. Next morning, when the tide swept in, a taxi pulled it back to shore with a length of cable.

A third time Gillam's plane was damaged when he landed on rough ice near the Arctic coast town of Cape Halkett. Villagers helped him repair it, and he proceeded.

These were the most serious mishaps he had in eight years of as bold flying as any man has ever done in the North. It was also very valuable flying. In the winter of 1936 he contracted with the United States Weather Bureau for a series of experimental high-altitude hops. Taking off from the Fairbanks field at dawn, and again at dusk, he spiraled to 17,000 feet and descended in precise circles to earth. Recording equipment carried in the ship registered temperature and humidity of the air masses at various altitudes, so that forecasts of weather in Alaska, Canada and the United States could be made more accurately. These were not the first flights of their kind in the North. Frank Pollack, the year before, had done some of this work, making two or three hops a week. But Gillam, aided by Pilot Bert Lien, had less leeway as to weather; his contract called for daily hops. Seldom did any kind of bad weather stop them.

Many of the flights were made virtually blind. At first the pilots had no ground aid to guide them back down through the fog. Gillam subsequently had a radio installed so that his mechanic could stand outside their shack hangar and bring him down by the sound of his engine. "You're over the lower Chena, Harold," the mechanic would shout. "Steer east ninety degrees." This arrangement helped some but was hardly windproof.

"You're west of town," the mechanic yelled one stormy day. "Head east."

"I'm headed east all the time," Gillam barked.

"You're still west, Harold," cried the mechanic. "You're drifting out of earshot."

The Pilgrim was blown twelve miles beyond town and Gillam, descending, broke into the clear only a few feet from the ridge of a small mountain called Ester Dome.

Once Gillam's banking ship, emerging from the fog over town, just missed the power company's smokestack. The plane was so close that witnesses could see the red reflection of the smokestack's obstruction lights on its silver wings. After several such episodes, Gillam installed a direction finder in his Pilgrim to complete the weather hops. Johnny Stump, local radio man, built the transmitter and a battery charger was used at the hangar as a homing device. It was the first such installation in the Territory.

In 1938 Gillam embarked on a still more spectacular aerial service. The record is registered in his logbook in proud, neat printing: a cross before each date, and at the top of the page the notation, "Cross-sign indicates all stops Kuskokwim mail route." But only the people of the Kuskokwim River settlements can tell the story of what this meant.

Ben Eielson, in 1924, had been the first pilot to carry official United States mail in Alaska; Gillam, beginning in 1938, was the first to do so with clocklike regularity. His Star Route contract called for stops at twenty river towns on the 525-mile route between Fairbanks and Bethel. When Pan American Airways previously handled this route the people had no idea what day of the week their mail would arrive. Gillam, although his contract did not require it, decided to haul the mail sacks on a precise schedule. Month in and month out, in all kinds of weather, he did so, reaching each village at the appointed time and never missing a trip.

Government officials report that Gillam's Kuskokwim delivery was one of the most perfect in the history of the United States mails—even compared to service by land or water transport. Alaskans at the river towns could almost set their watches by the coming and going of his silver Pilgrim. Trappers and traders would remind each other: "Today's Gillam day. Better finish that letter. Time to go out and meet the ship."

Gillam sometimes made the whole round trip while other planes on the route were stormbound. Landing repeatedly on drifting snow and thin ice, he never damaged his Pilgrims. Sometimes he flew the mail run high and barreled down through the overcast to make his stops. More often he flew it low, "sneaking under the fog" just level with treetops as he followed the twisting river bends. If the ski plane were forced too low for flight, he would land and taxi along on the ice. Once he taxied up the river for ten miles. He was bound to keep his self-imposed schedule.

Alaskans, accustomed as they were to aviation feats, were mystified by this infallible performance. They were also mystified by the flights which Gillam made from Fairbanks to Barrow at the time of the historic Levanevsky search. In the summer of 1937 Sigismund Levanevsky, one of the Soviet Union's foremost Arctic flyers, disappeared on an attempted flight across the North Pole from Moscow to California. His last report was made some two hours south of the Pole on the Alaska side. A Soviet party, equipped with a Fokker plane and the ice-breaker *Krasin*, promptly arrived at Barrow for search work. Americans now had a chance to repay their debt for Soviet aid on the search for Eielson.

Pilot Jimmy Mattern, who had been rescued by Levanevsky after a crack-up in Siberia on his 1933 round-the-world flight, made a much-publicized "mercy" trip from the States to Barrow, but did little serious work. However, the United States government set up a special weather-reporting system in Alaska to aid the Russian hunt, and other American flyers, in contrast to Mattern, gave generous assistance. Sir Hubert Wilkins, with Herbert Hollick-Kenyon and S.A. Cheesman in a PBY Consolidated flying boat, flew 1,000 miles a day over the ice pack during the next month and, navigating by moonlight, continued his search into the winter. Alaska pilots, including Joe Crosson, helped too—none more usefully than Gillam, who freighted crucial fuel and supplies to the Soviet party from Fairbanks. "Flying for the Russians," Charles Brower has written, "Harold Gillam wore this air route smooth."

Gillam was almost incredibly defiant of weather on the notorious route. The trip from Fairbanks to Barrow took him six and a half hours under favorable conditions. His Pilgrim, even with an extra tank, carried fuel for little more than seven hours. Despite this, he would leave Fairbanks under conditions of poor visibility, fly much of the long journey "on top" without sight of earth, and come down at Barrow through fog that "not even a seagull could land in."

The reckless performance is verified both by passengers and by spectators on the ground. Most impressive confirmation came from Danneld Cathcart, a United Airlines pilot who accompanied Gillam on one of the trips. Cathcart, describing the journey to other flyers, was hardly able to believe what he had seen with his own eyes. By his version Gillam climbed high to clear the Endicott Mountains and flew his single-engine Pilgrim for hours above unbroken murk. Then, without hesitation, he nosed the plane down into the fog. Cathcart saw nothing, vertically or horizontally, till a house and some antennae poles flashed past as the Pilgrim landed on the Barrow lagoon.

Gillam had radio contact with Barrow—but the weather reports would have driven most pilots away. "We were always worried," says Barrow's former Weather Officer, Stanley Morgan. "The antennae poles stood within 500 feet of the runway." Morgan watched all of Gillam's Barrow landings. "Harold," he relates, "would be circling in the soup above us. The Eskimos would stand in line and light flares, but often the fog was so thick he couldn't see them. Sometimes we'd try to direct him in by radio—other times he just came down on his own. Once he couldn't have seen the ice till he landed. And he hadn't enough gas, that time, to taxi his ship to shore. I frankly don't know how he did it."

"Gillam," Alaskans like to say, "was part bird." Even Tom Appleton, Gillam's ruddy-cheeked, matter-of-fact mechanic, was baffled by his navigation in stormy weather. "The mysterious part," Appleton declares, "was that when he said he was going somewhere he nearly always did. And he nearly always got home the same way. I'd get a telegram saying he'd be in. The fog would be on the ground and every other ship on the field would be setting by its hangar. By golly, just at the time he'd wired I'd hear a roar and the old ghost would come whistling in."

There were some partial answers, Appleton points out, to this riddle. The structure of Gillam's ships was important. The Pilgrims could "pack a load of ice"—as much as an inch and a half—on the leading edge of the wing. The Pilgrim cockpit, set high above motor and wings, allowed a pilot exceptionally good forward visibility. Other mechanics point out that much credit is due to Appleton himself; in the six years that he worked for Gillam the planes had no engine failures.

Beyond this, Gillam, contrary to popular legend, did not proceed "by guess and by gosh" alone. He bought many books on meteorology and studied the weather thoroughly. "Harold had a scientific mind. He was always figuring and plotting." In 1934, on his copper-country route, he installed some of the first air-ground radio stations in Alaska, hiring old-timers at the roadhouses to tend them. He later established such a station on his Kuskokwim mail route. As early as 1936, to gain experience for his high-altitude hops, he was draping a hood about the cockpit of his Pilgrim and flying "by the panel." He not only installed a direction-finder that year but also a directional gyro, sensitive altimeter and an artificial horizon—at a time when most of the bush pilots were content with compasses.

"Gillam," Appleton says, "had a theory that the weather is never as bad as it looks." Instruments enabled him to test this theory and to do many things which others could not. But there were no airways along his early routes, and instrument flight in the complete sense was not possible. His single-engine Pilgrim, which carried no de-icing equipment, was hardly a ship for instrument flight in any case. And always there was the unknown factor of winds. When all is said and done it is truly uncanny that Gillam was able to play the edge as close, as often, as long as he did. "He must have had an iron nerve," says one pilot, "to do it again and again." Another, who knew him better, puts it differently. "Harold," he asserts, "hadn't a nerve in his body."

Gillam developed such confidence in his own technique that he did not bother to keep pace with the scientific progress of the day. Although the Civil Aeronautics Administration began its Alaska construction in 1939, it was not until 1942 that Gillam sought training and secured an official instrument rating. More than once in the last few years of his life the C.A.A. filed charges against him for bizarre approaches on the new radio beams. "He got to the point where he almost acted like he was superhuman," says a colleague. "He was just plain asking for it."

Shortly after war struck in the Pacific the Morrison-Knudson Company, Idaho construction firm with large airport contracts in Alaska, looked for a flyer to speed its emergency job and chose Gillam. Gillam flew a twin-engine Lockheed Electra all over the Territory freighting for M.-K. "He gave that poor ship a workout," Appleton says. "He'd take her off with a thousand to fifteen hundred pound overload through the same kind of weather he used to buck in his Pilgrims." He hauled such heavy cargo that the two motors gave him no more safety than he had had with single-engine equipment.

His flying entered another phase, and Alaskans for the first time began to worry about him. In the past Gillam's work had been spasmodic. He had flown doggedly and daringly on special jobs, but there had been summers when he hardly left the ground. Now there was a war on; month in and month out, he logged 125 hours or more. (Airline pilots in the States are permitted a maximum of 100.) Allowing himself no let-up, he took as many chances as he ever had. "I'll bet," Oscar Winchell predicted, "the way he's goin', Harold don't live to work for M.-K. a year."

Winchell was wrong by a few weeks.

On the morning of January 5, 1943, Gillam left Seattle on a routine trip to Alaska. Aboard the Electra were five passengers: Robert Gebo, M.-K.'s Alaska general superintendent; Percy Cutting, M.K. mechanic; Joseph Tippets, C.A.A.

engineer; Dewey Metzdorf, Anchorage railroad and hotel man; and twenty-five-year-old Susan Baxter, who was going north for the first time to work as a C.A.A. stenographer.

Gillam was informed that a storm was moving toward the Alaskan coast. Other northbound flights were canceled that day but he, after considerable argument with Boeing Field clearance officers, loaded his ship and took off. So sure was he of his time-tested ability that he carried no medical supplies and almost no emergency equipment and made not one radio report all the way north.

Four hours out of Seattle the plane entered dense fog. Gillam went on instruments, but even then he maintained radio silence. He proceeded blind until he was over the southeast tip of Alaska. Planning to land at a new Army field at Annette Island, he approached on what he believed to be the southeast leg of its radio range. Actually he was following the northeast leg; the courses had been altered and the airways map which he carried was obsolete. Confused, he made a series of turns in an effort to orient himself. The Electra was flying at 6,000 feet, rocked by turbulence, with heavy ice forming on the wings, when one of the engines stopped.

By the account of Joseph Tippets: "We hit a violent downdraft and dropped 4,000 feet almost before we knew it. It was pitch dark and the fog was almost down to the ground, but now and then through a hole we could see peaks or trees flashing by. We were still flying at full speed.

"I yelled to Metzdorf to fasten his seat-belt. The plane swerved just in time to miss one mountain. Then we saw another one looming up straight ahead. There was an open spot toward the top and Harold gunned the engine trying to make it. But our right wing hit a tree. I could feel everything leaving my body, everything blacked out, then it all came back. I was lying in the dark in the drizzling rain. I called out to the others. There was no answer. All I could hear was the hissing of the hot engine in the snow."

When Gillam's plane was reported missing the C.A.A. sent an inquiry to every telegraph station along his entire route. Forty planes, Army and civilian, searched the coastal mountains. Coast Guard boats scouted deep into the bays and

inlets. The searchers had few clues. Gillam had belatedly
tried, as his ship plummeted earthward, to make a radio report. "I am in trouble," operators had heard him say. "One
engine is out." After this he had been too busy to give his
position—if he knew it. The Electra could have crashed
anywhere on the long route from the States to Alaska.

The wrecked plane, in fact, lay only seven miles from sea,
only sixteen minutes from the town of Ketchikan. But repeated sleet and snow storms, worst in half a century, beat
along this part of the coast and search pilots, flying only by
daylight, saw no sign of life in the jagged, heavily timbered
country. It was believed that Gillam's ship had dropped into
the ocean. One wonders what became of the dauntless tradition of northern rescue, which Gillam had honored so mag-
nificently in behalf of others. The reason is hard to find and
the fact disturbing to many today; the hunt, after only two
weeks, was called off.

Two more weeks passed before Coast Guardsmen aboard
a patrol boat sighted a bonfire on the shore of Boca de
Quadra Inlet. As the boat drew nearer, the crew saw two
bearded men running up and down the beach, shouting and
sobbing. The skipper thought they were isolation-crazed trappers.

"Who are you?" he yelled across the water as his skiff
drifted to shore.

The reply was electrifying. "We're survivors from the M.-
K. plane that crashed here over a month ago."

Tippets' ankles were sprained and Cutting had a fractured
back, but they, least injured of the survivors, had fought their
way down the forested mountain in a last desperate try for
help. Slipping and stumbling down steep, icy slopes, cutting
their way with knives through dense brush, they had spent
nine days covering a distance of less than ten miles. Their
shoes were so sheared that they threw them away and
wrapped their feet in rags. They found an old dory and tried
to row out of the bay but it capsized, and they were forced
to swim back through icy water to shore. For nine days they
had had nothing to eat but two crows, a few raw mussels,
and a half-cup of weeviled rice which they found in an
abandoned cabin. Their hands were cut and bleeding. Their

feet were bitten with frost. Each had lost more than fifty
pounds.

The patrol boat took them to the Ketchikan Coast Guard
sickbay, where they told their story. They said they felt as if
years, not weeks, had passed since the crash of the Electra.

In the collision the nose of the plane had been buried in
deep snow, and one wing had been snapped off. The fuselage,
which had dropped into a gully, was shattered by a falling
tree and the right engine smashed to pieces. The girl had
been most gravely hurt. She had suffered head injuries and
her right arm, trapped in the wreckage, was broken and
bleeding. The men applied tourniquets and did all they could
for her comfort but she lived only forty-eight hours. Gebo
and Metzdorf had survived but were lying in a critical condition on the side of the mountain. As for Gillam, his fate was
not known.

It was remarkable that Gillam had not been killed in the
crash: the cockpit had been crushed on top of him. There
was a gash on his head, and he had seemed dazed, but he
worked doggedly after the accident tearing up aluminum for
shovels, building snow shelters, tending signal fires and cooking meals, till the food was nearly gone. On the sixth day he
had taken a few provisions, and a parachute for warmth.
"I'm going up on a ridge," he had said. "Maybe I can sight a
definite landmark. If I do I'll go to it." They had tried to
dissuade him from setting out alone in his condition, but
without further comment he had disappeared into the wintry
forest. That was the last time they had seen him.

Search for Gillam was renewed and Tippets and Cutting,
after only a few hours' rest at Ketchikan, insisted on starting
out at the head of a rescue party toward the other survivors.
Despite their injuries and weakened condition they urged the
Coast Guardsmen up the mountain at a relentless pace,
threatening them with violence when they sought rest. "We
weren't supermen," Tippets explains. "I guess we were just
used to it." Gebo and Metzdorf were close to death when the
group reached them. One had a broken arm and leg, the
other a fractured collarbone. Unable to move, they had lain
inside a crude lean-to for nine days in a pool of alternately
freezing and thawing water. Their condition was so pitiful

and their relief so great that almost everyone, including the Coast Guardsmen, wept.

Other air disasters have caused more fatalities, but none in the history of Alaskan civil aviation has caused so much prolonged suffering to so many people. There was the cruelty of the terrain—so steep and sharp that several young Coast Guardsmen had to be carried down the mountain. There was the mercilessness of the weather, so wet the survivors could not build fires for warmth, but cold enough so that frost formed everywhere inside the make-shift shelters. These things were endured for weeks by men sick with pain and weak with hunger. And not the least torment was psychological.

Time and again the survivors heard search planes roar past above the storm and fog. On occasion they even saw the planes soar overhead or circle in valleys below. The men signaled and signaled. When all sound stopped after two weeks they mentally prepared themselves to die. Even today some of them have a haunted look in their eyes which tells how little hope they had of return to the world of the living.

And Gillam? Alaskans were as mystified by the circumstances of his tragic end as they had been mystified by his performance in life. After several days of renewed search a Coast Guard party found his frozen body, wrapped in the parachute, on a shore of Boca de Quadra Inlet. It lay only one mile from the place where Tippets and Cutting had been rescued. Gillam had removed his red underwear and tied it to surrounding spruce trees. He had hung his flying boots, bottom up, on two tall poles nearby. It was evident that he had been dead for several weeks.

Some said he knew the end was coming and hung his boots to mark his own grave. But those who knew him best do not accept this theory. A few bouillon cubes and packages of dry matches were found in his pocket. "He wouldn't have starved," they say. "He wouldn't have let himself freeze to death. Harold was a tough hombre. He knew how to take care of himself in the winter. Guys like him don't just lie down and die with their boots hanging up. As long as he had matches and bouillon cubes Gillam was good."

Cutting, exploring the surrounding area, found signs that

Gillam had broken through a stream. He believes the flyer hung up his clothes to dry and lay down for a rest. His body, when found, rested on a slope with the injured head slightly lower than the feet. Cutting believes that blood rushing to his head caused a cerebral hemorrhage. Doctors consider this theory plausible. However, no autopsy was made and the cause of his untimely death is not known.

The Civil Aeronautics Board, citing, among other things, Gillam's procedure into a storm and his failure to use his radio, officially designated the basic cause of the wreck as pilot error. Most of his fellow flyers prefer to judge it another way. "His engine quit him," they say. "That could happen to any of us. . . . If his engine hadn't quit him he would have made it again." None, talking about his final accident, care to discuss the matter of recklessness. It was mechanical failure, they stress, that sent the Electra plunging earthward and rendered Gillam helpless, at last, against the violent elements which he had foiled so amazingly, so usefully, so long.

14
Bob Reeve

BOB REEVE, aged forty-four, has a thatch of snow-white hair. This is not surprising: he has made a practice of landing on glaciers. He is probably the world's only specialist at this frosty and risky line of work.

Reeve has other distinctions. During World War II he was a legend with the armed forces in Alaska. He hauled military freight out the stormy Aleutian chain in a fourteen-year-old single-engine Fairchild, bucking some of the world's worst weather in one of the world's most ancient operating airships. Army pilots laughed at his dilapidated craft. They called it "The Ironing Board." But they regarded Reeve with respect, even awe. They knew he is one of the most accomplished bush flyers in the world, with 11,000 hours of logged time over South America, the United States and Alaska.

During his career Reeve has had twenty-one forced landings, but until 1943, when he crashed in Aleutian fog, he never damaged a ship beyond repair. Till then, the most serious injury he suffered was when he dropped into a hayfield, climbed out and was kicked in the face by a horse. Sixteen of his sudden descents were caused by failure of old models of the Wright Whirlwind engine. "I was a guinea pig for those engines," he says. "I helped take out the bugs." Today, as he watches formations of Wright-powered bombers go thundering overhead, he proudly shakes his fist. "There's part of old Reeve in every one of those damn things," he boasts.

Reeve has not only logged 11,000 hours bush-style; he expects to log many more the same way. He is one of the last active old-timers. You can often see him at Merrill Field, in oil-stained duck pants and a worn leather jacket, loading a small red ship.* REEVE AIRWAYS—he has lettered on the fuselage. His hangar is a tar-paper shack. He employs one mechanic but he does most of the repair work on the plane himself.

"What kind of rig is that, old man?" a pink-cheeked Major once asked him.

"It's a Fairchild," replied Reeve, who was lying flat on his back mending the tail wheel.

"What model?" persisted the officer.

"It's a Fairchild DGA," said Reeve, sticking his head out from under the ship. "That means Damn Good Airplane. And if you call me an old man again I'll take you over my knee."

Reeve talks fast and suavely, his conversation interspersed with wisecracks. His white hair contrasts startlingly with coal-black eyebrows. After work hours, his genial face ruddy above a well tailored suit, he has the air of a successful bond salesman. He likes fine clothes; owns a dozen custom-made hats and adds to this collection whenever he has a chance. He likes parties, has an addiction for imported champagne and always carries a case in the back of his LaSalle car. "Too busy," he explains, "to take it in the house. Besides, if I want to celebrate I have it right handy."

Reeve is racy, restless and high-strung. "Let's vamoose," he will snap at a tardy passenger. "Okay, let's vamoose!" Slowness in anything visibly annoys him. Until his doctor ordered him to quit, he was a heavy chain-smoker. More than once he has seared his chest as a cigarette dropped inside his shirt during landing. "I have spent more time flying sideways to see if my ship was on fire," he claims, "than any pilot in history."

Reeve and a twin brother, sons of a railroad depot agent, were born at Waunakee, Wisconsin. Like Gillam, Bob Reeve ran away from home. At fifteen he faked his age and joined the Army. He earned an infantry sergeancy in World War I. Later he studied law at the University of Wisconsin. "I wasn't any legal fireball," he says, "but I learned two things—

---

* Early in 1946 Reeve bought several larger planes, including two DC-3s, for expansion of his service.

how to make gin and not to bet into a one-card draw." He sold ads, worked in the business office of a newspaper. Then he soloed, barnstormed with the usual number of forced landings and missed meals, and test-hopped some of the first tri-motor Fords.

In 1929 he struck out to South America "for adventure" and was one of the first pilots on Pan American-Grace Airways' original mail run. He set a speed record between Santiago, Chile and Lima, Peru, and made the second night flight in history up the west coast of the continent. In 1930 he flew the mail 1,476 hours—a world record at the time. For two years scorched pampas, dense jungles and tropical peaks slid beneath him as he pioneered these southern routes. "I returned to the States a well-to-do man," he relates. "I'd earned money like a horse—but I spent it like a jackass." Then he decided to head for Alaska. "I'd seen every country to the south and wanted to have a look at the north."

Stowing away in the chain-locker of a steamboat, Reeve arrived in Alaska with two dollars in his pocket in the spring of 1932. He stopped at Valdez, a small seaside town at the foot of lofty snowcaps. Locating a wrecked Eaglerock bi-plane, he repaired it and rented it from its owner at $10 an hour. Neighbors helped clear a cow pasture for a field, and he was ready for business.

His first customers were two grizzled prospectors. They offered him two hundred dollars to fly them to Middleton, a small island 150 miles offshore in the Gulf of Alaska, where they wanted to stake claims. No boatman, they admitted, was willing to take them out through the heavy seas to this lone, storm-lashed dot of land. But they had been there before and had seen a "big long beach" that would be ideal for a landing field.

Reeve trusted them. He flew above the tossing waves for two hours in his single-engine craft. "Where's your beach?" he shouted when the bleak isle was sighted. He followed the shores around, looking down on steep, boulder-strewn, surf-beaten banks. His passengers couldn't find the beach, and he decided to land on the likeliest-looking sandspit.

It was not as likely as he judged. The ship nosed up in "fluffy pea soup sand" a thousand feet from shore with the propeller bent. The tide was rising fast. Reeve straightened the prop blades with a wrench and started the engine, but the plane would not budge. The three men pushed and pulled. They could not move it. Only luck saved them. Wading to the island, Reeve found an old block and tackle washed in from a shipwreck banging against the rocks. He and his passengers buried one end deep in the sand, tied the other to the Eaglerock's wheel axles, pushed planks under the wheels and inch by inch pulled the plane through the surf to land.

The return trip was no better. They dragged the Eaglerock a mile overland to the longest, firmest stretch of sand they could find. The ship slithered skyward and soon flew into a lashing hailstorm. With the engine at full power Reeve could barely keep his plane in the air. It was a long, harrowing journey over the crashing breakers, and when Valdez was reached landing was impossible. The town was completely hidden—only the cloud-wreathed mountains showed where it must be. He made a try for Seward, an hour away, which had the only other landing field within two hundred miles. Five minutes' gas remained in the tank when he set the Eaglerock down.

"Then and there," he says, "I started sharpening my wits, a process which has continued ever since." In fourteen years he has met every treachery of the elements, and his reactions have become lightning-swift, his judgments sharp as edged steel. As a contact—"seat of the pants"—pilot he has few equals anywhere.

Reeve earned his reputation on snow and ice. He is known throughout Alaska as "the glacier pilot." He began this work early in 1933. Only once before had landing been made on one of the North's lofty rivers of ice. Pilots Crosson and S. E. Robbins, servicing a scientific expedition, had come down on a frozen slope of Mt. McKinley the previous year. They had done their utmost—but with such risk and such damage to one of the aircraft that the company for which they worked refused to allow any more trips. Glacier-flying was hardly a trade the hardiest airman would enter by choice. Even Gillam shunned it. Reeve did not try it as a stunt. There was a practical reason.

Valdez, when he arrived, was as broke as he was. It was

much the same story as that of Fairbanks: the nearby mines had been worked out. There were promising claims in this steep coastal region, but they lay high on the slopes of the Chugach Range. On the tipsy boardwalks of the ghost town, in dingy pool halls and shabby cabins, men talked of the wealth that was so near and yet so inaccessible. Everybody said there was rich ore up there. Everybody wanted to take a chance on it.

Reeve, who by this time had acquired a Fairchild 51, was willing to take the chance that would make the whole thing possible. "I had to eat to fly" he comments, "also—I had to fly to eat." He agreed to make an experimental trip, taking a prospector named Jack Cook to a site called Big Four, six thousand feet high on the slopes of Brevier Glacier. If he succeeded in landing, Cook would give him a contract to haul supplies to convert the prospect into a working mine. It took only twenty minutes to lift Jack Cook to the Big Four, a journey which had hitherto taken days of climbing. The trial trip, however, was hardly auspicious. As Reeve sums it up: "The first time I landed on a glacier I flew into the side of a mountain."

"That's the place!" Cook yelled as they hovered along the vast slope of a snowcap. It took a knowing eye to find it; only the tiny dot of an ore pile marked the miner's claim. Reeve flew to the bottom of Brevier Glacier, banked, and started climbing. Whiteness "plumb fooled" him. The grade, which appeared to be no more than three percent, was more than fifteen percent. His plane began to stall. He could not turn; he was locked in by towering walls on either side. "I was flying," he says, "straight into a booby trap." He cut the engine, and his ship plowed smack into the snow at the top of the incline.

The depth of the drifts saved aircraft and men from injury. Reeve and Cook worked all day digging the ship out and shoveling the start of a runway—"kind of a shelf"—for take-off. As they climbed aboard for the return trip they looked down a sheer 6,000-foot drop with the ocean glimmering far below. Like riders on a mammoth shoot-the-chutes, they were plunged into space as the plane shot down the steep slope and dropped into the sky.

The next day Reeve returned to the Big Four. "I couldn't back out. I told them I could do it." This time he flew in at a steep climb and landed at the bottom of the glacial slope. Hitting the snow at eighty miles an hour the plane moved less than 400 feet before it stopped.

Reeve flew eighteen tons of equipment to the Big Four, including a mill, a crusher, tables, a compressor, oil, coal, pipe and building materials for houses. The mill shell weighed a thousand pounds and there was hardly an inch to spare as he hoisted it with jacks through the door of his Fairchild. To haul all this equipment by horses, said Clarence Poy, manager of the new mine, would have taken many weeks and cost the company thirty-five cents a pound. Reeve, at four cents a pound, delivered the whole works in seven days. Later, he delivered a shipment of Diesel engines, wrapping the heavy parts in mattresses and dropping them by parachute. "Airplanes," Poy declared in a speech to the American Institute of Mining and Metallurgical Engineers in New York, "will be instrumental in re-pioneering Alaska in double-quick time."

Reeve gave year-round service to the glaciers. In summer, when the snow melted at Valdez, he used the mud flats at low tide for take-off on skis. Steamboat tourists from the States stared incredulously at his airport. ALWAYS USE REEVE AIRWAYS, advised a sign painted on the side of his shed hangar. SLOW UNRELIABLE UNFAIR AND CROOKED. SCARED AND UNLICENSED AND NUTS. REEVE AIRWAYS—THE BEST. He hadn't written it, but he liked it. Grass and daisies clustered in the muck of his 600-foot runway. A red flag planted at the end warned of a deep ditch and a swift mountain stream.

Reeve drove to work in a Model T Ford labeled "Airways Officials." At night he bolstered his plane against the tide by hoisting the tail on empty oil drums. He used stainless steel from an abandoned cocktail bar to sheath his homemade skis. His ship was held together by baling wire. The floor was patched with old grocery boxes, labels still on. It was a bizarre operation but in the next ten years Reeve expanded it and lifted more than 1,500 tons of equipment from the seaport town to the gold-producing areas of the glacier country.

He charged $100 per flying hour for these charter trips. There were days when he took in as much as a thousand dollars. He put part of his earnings into the mines and grubstaked prospecting passengers. One man owed him $400 for six years. Finally pursuing him to a remote camp, Reeve found that his debtor had "beat it back to the creek" when he saw the plane coming. He followed through deep snow up a mountain and demanded his pay. The old prospector declared that since the price of gold had doubled, he owed only half the original amount. They settled the matter by flipping a coin in a teacup. Reeve won, and the prospector paid $400 in gold dust.

But like other Alaska pilots Reeve has taken fifty cents on the dollar for bills as high as $2,000. He didn't make a fortune for himself in the Valdez country, but he earned enough to buy several secondhand planes, and his pioneer achievement was large. He made operation possible at the Big Four, the Mayfield, the Rough and Tough, the Little Giant, the Little Rose, the Gibraltar and a dozen other mines, enabling them to get in on the gold boom of early Roosevelt days. The population of Valdez doubled. The town came back to life.

Only by trial and error did the white-thatched flyer master his unique trade. It required nerve and a highly experimental frame of mind. There were no precedents. Trips to the land of perpetual snow have an unearthly quality.

As Reeve describes the glacier country, there is no horizon, no perspective, and glare of sun on the crystallized snow can be blinding. Even on a cloudy day this glare is so bewildering that no altitude below a thousand feet is safe. Dropping down to land is "like sticking your head in an appear flat. Once, landing on an icy grade, he had just impossible for a man in the air to judge the angle of the glacial surface below. Steep slopes, if they are visible at all, enamel pail." Every descent has the elements of a forced one. "Judging where the snow is, that's the first thing, judging where the snow is. You might level off 500 feet too high and come tumbling down in a stall—or you might approach too low and smack into the drifts."

As he learned on his first trip to the Big Four, it is nearly stopped the engine when his ship began tobogganing backward toward a precipice. He started the engine just in time to pull the plane back into control. After this lesson he always landed with his foot poised to kick the rudder and skid the ship at right angles to an incline.

The depth of the snow is also impossible to judge in the weird light, and the unpredictable runways trick not only a man's vision but also his sense of feel. Once Prospector Charlie Elwood, riding on top of a load of freight, was terrified to see Reeve open the cockpit door and thrust his foot out.

"Don't leave me!" he cried, grabbing his pilot's shoulder. "Don't leave me!"

"What's the matter?" said Reeve. "We're there. Those are the Black Mountains, and there is your claim."

Elwood looked out. Snow pressed against the panes. The plane had silently sunk to window level in soft drifts.

"By God," he replied, "I didn't know we landed. I thought we were still in the air and you were trying to jump out."

Reeve himself could not always tell when his plane had met the earth. He would set up rows of black or orange flags ten at a time. "When I saw all ten," he relates, "I knew I was approaching. When I saw only one I knew I was on the ground." Once, landing in deep snow, he was marooned eight days. The shovel he habitually carried in the ship was not adequate to break a runway. Unable to raise his plane from the frosty featherbed, he could only sit in the cockpit till wind came to blow the drifts away.

But the greatest hazard of Reeve's work was not deep snow. The huge, grinding glaciers of the Chugach Range are among the most treacherous areas on the face of the earth. Much of their surface, rough as shattered glass, is broken with icy pinnacles and with jagged unitaks (crags of rock) which sometimes tower a thousand feet high. Ridges of bouldered moraine crisscross the frozen mass and it is cut throughout by yawning crevasses, some big enough to hold cathedrals. Subterranean rivers roar below. The snow often forms a deceptive thin roof above such death traps.

Reeve once flew into one of the snow-covered moraines. The impact deflected his plane upward 200 feet, nearly snapping his head off and cracking the landing-gear tubing. Another time, when drifts melted under summer sun, he discovered to his horror that he had been landing on the snow roof of a crevasse twenty feet wide and hundreds of feet deep. Dozens of corpses lie in the dark chasms of the Chugach glaciers. One winter night Reeve nearly joined them.

He was eating at the Merchants' Café when two men stumbled in. They asked if he could take them to Valdez Glacier. At first he believed them drunk, so disjointed were their movements, so halting and jumbled their words. "Martin's up there!" they stammered. They had been on their way across the glacier, heading toward a mine, when a blizzard struck. It was 20 below zero that night and their companion, George Martin, had frozen his feet. He could go no further and they had left him alone on the high slope. Unless he were rescued immediately he would die.

Valdez is the most dangerous of all the Chugach glaciers, so jagged a maze of ice pinnacles that Reeve had never attempted landing on it even in daylight. Dusk was falling. The three men hurried to the airfield and Reeve took off. He could not see well enough in the gloom to consider landing on the frozen surface of the glacier but he managed to bring his plane down safely on one of the bouldered moraines. He and his passengers snowshoed four miles over the glacier to the gulch where Martin lay. They found him dead. By this time it was pitch-dark. As they felt their way back to the ship Reeve stepped over the edge of a deep crevasse. He caught himself on a ledge and hung there till his companions managed to pull him out. The fall so shocked him that he has not since been able to walk confidently at night on a level sidewalk.

In thousands of glacier flights this accident, suffered on foot, was the most serious Reeve ever had. "Part bird," Alaskans say, as they said of Gillam. Reeve, one of the North's few talkative pilots, is strangely inarticulate if you ask him about his glacier-flying technique. Much of the work he calls "just plain drudgery." Taxying across unpredictable surfaces, he stopped every 1,000 feet or so, leaned out of the cockpit and studied the terrain ahead. He circled repeatedly before a dubious landing. "Just a kind of dim outline of a depression, maybe the way the sun shone on the snow, a little glazed look to the surface, a little deeper shade than the rest"—these were the subtle warnings that saved him from disaster.

He memorized the tortured face of a glacier in summertime, when the snow was gone from the lower slopes, and observed, for example, that the safest place to taxi is along the edge of a moraine, where the crevasses tend to be narrower and shallower than elsewhere. He improvised many devices to mark his runways, sometimes setting up flags, sometimes arranging for men on the ground to sprinkle the snow with lampblack when his plane approached. Venturing to new places where no human had been, he judged his altitude as best he could from the dark streaks of moraine or rock or, if natural markers were missing, hurled out black gunny-sacks for perspective. He learned these tricks and many more. But it was a good share of luck, as well as skill, that made his record possible. "Fantastic luck," he says.

Winds were unpredictable. No man can foretell the torrents of air which spill through the Chugach Range like sudden waterfalls. Once Reeve's plane was smacked down five times as he attempted take-off. Another time, as he landed on a mountaintop, a williwaw lifted his Fairchild and tossed it over a sheer 5,000 foot drop. He opened the engine full-throttle and fought for control, but the plane went from a fall into a semi-flat spin, skis, wing tips and tail surfaces striking snow benches on the way down. By his account the next thing he knew he was leveled out again, flying through a canyon at an altitude of only 200 feet.

This story is almost too much for other pilots to believe. However, witnesses at the mountaintop mine saw the plane blasted over the precipice and watched it tumble out of sight. They were astonished when Reeve returned on his next trip, so certain had they been that he crashed to death below. "In those twenty seconds," Reeve says, "I figure I should have run out of luck 100 years in advance."

Like Gillam, Reeve became insolent in his duels with the elements. Once he was forced down by fog at the mouth of a canyon. He noticed that the mists, blowing like a curtain, cleared at surprisingly regular intervals. He had never flown low through this gorge, and it was so narrow that his Fairchild, once in, could not turn back but he decided to risk it. Timing his take-off to meet the next clearing, he flew in between the rock walls.

Fog blinded him. All he could see was a dim streak of moraine leading steeply up the mountain to one side. A strong updraft gave him enough lift and climb to follow it; ordinarily, he estimates, the plane could have ascended no more than a thousand feet a minute at the precipitous angle, but the wind forced it up at twice this rate. Thick scud blew all around but he managed to follow the rutted dark line all the way and he emerged into clear sunshine, at 6,000 feet, "on top."

Only a few rocky peaks broke the fog. Only twenty minutes of fuel remained in the tank. But to Reeve a group of sawtooth pinnacles looming off to the west were familiar as an old friend. This mountain, he knew, sloped into the valley of Dutch Flats. He flew to the crags, nosed his plane under the edge of the fog till he found another streak of moraine and followed it back down to the lowlands. Still another pass—twisting, wind-swept Keystone Canyon—threatened his way home. He started into it, dodging mists and fighting violent updrafts that repeatedly "sucked him into the soup." But the fog ahead was too thick. He could not proceed. Spiraling down, he landed on a small snow-covered bar in the middle of a river.

Then it happened. With deafening thunder "the whole side of a big white peak broke loose." A mammoth avalanche, "thousands and thousands of tons of snow and ice," crashed down the canyon wall, damming the stream and blocking a road which highway workers had worked two weeks to clear for spring traffic. Men who witnessed this monstrous fall believe it was caused by the vibration of Reeve's engine. He likes to think so. "Not every pilot," he brags, "has set off a major snow-slide!"

Reeve's most spectacular glacier flight was made in 1937 to service a New England Museum of Natural History mountain-climbing expedition in the Canadian Yukon. The party, headed by Brad Washburn, wanted to climb 17,000-foot Mt.

Lucania—at the time the highest unscaled peak in North America. Many men had talked of climbing Lucania but none had tried. The mountain stood in the midst of the vast, desolate St. Elias "ice cap," largest glacier system in the world. It would be a staggering task to reach the base of Lucania overland. Only an airplane would make the project feasible. Washburn wrote Reeve from Boston, asking whether he could land on Walsh Glacier, at the foot of the mountain, with the expedition and its supplies.

It would be a long trip over mean and little-known country: more than 240 miles of mountains and ice-choked valleys lie between the town of Valdez and Walsh Glacier. The glacier itself, lying a hundred miles from solid land to the west, was hardly a place in which to risk an accident. Landing would be something of an experiment, for Walsh is 8,500 feet above sea level. Specially equipped light planes had operated from slopes this high in the Swiss Alps, but nowhere in the world had a ski plane with a load of freight landed and taken off at such an altitude. Reeve promptly agreed to service the Washburn expedition at his usual charter rate in a single-engine Fairchild.

Early in May he flew the bulk of the expedition's supplies to the base camp site, hauling them first to snow-landing at the Kennecott Mine (halfway point) and ferrying them on from there. The snow at Walsh Glacier was hard and fairly smooth. The Wright engine, operating with a leaned fuel mixture, performed as well during take-off and landing at 8,500 feet as at sea level. As it turned out, it was not altitude that endangered Reeve's Lucania flights, nor, as some would believe, was it the "frigid bitterness" of a northern clime.

He had planned to make all the flights under winter conditions but Washburn was delayed and did not arrive at Valdez until late June. By this time the snow was melting on all but the loftiest slopes. Walsh Glacier, high and well sheltered, would still be deep in white but a re-fueling stop at the Kennecott Mine was no longer possible. There was now no place along the entire route from Valdez to Walsh where the plane could land with safety.

Washburn was anxious. "Can you make it?" he asked.

"I can try it," Reeve told him. "Anywhere you'll ride, I'll fly."

On the morning of June 21, Washburn and another mountaineer, Robert Bates, wading in mud at the Valdez flats, helped load 350 pounds of extra gas and equipment into the Fairchild. Reeve removed the plane door so the freight could be thrown overboard in case of trouble. Without these supplies the expedition could not proceed; with them the ship could carry just enough gas in the cabin for the return trip. Fuel in the tank was just enough to reach Lucania. The heavily weighted Fairchild sloshed up from the muck and flew northeast.

The plane was slowed by a thirty-mile headwind, which brought the gas margin very low. After two hours the halfway point was reached. Now a stern decision must be made. Was the weather favorable enough to justify continuing? If Walsh Glacier should be fogged in, forced landing would have to be made elsewhere. The panorama ahead left much room for doubt. Low fog wreathed the ice fields. Scattered squalls swirled among the peaks. Sheets of moisture, traveling sideways, warned of turbulence. Reeve hesitated only a moment. "You know," he says with a smile, "if you turn back that first time you're liable to find yourself doing it over and over."

Dark rain clouds bore down and down as the Fairchild flew on. The wind grew gustier. In another hour and a half the plane approached the foot of Walsh Glacier. As Washburn tells it,[*] "Flying into that valley was like entering a tunnel with a dead end. A mile on either side of us almost vertical cliffs of ice and rock rose into the clouds. Below us tossed the rough surface of our glacier. Seven or eight miles ahead the valley floor and walls melted into the murky ceiling, the lower surfaces of which we were just skimming. Behind us the storm was dropping down.

"He used the 'black slits' of open crevasses to come in safely. He throttled back the motor and dropped steeply to a point in the middle of the cracks. With the stabilizer slightly tailheavy and the motor idle, we dropped at a fast rate.

[*] *Sportsman Pilot*, January, 1938.

About fifty feet above the crevasses Bob gave the motor full throttle and pulled sharply back on the stick. He cleared all the cracks but the last little ones; the tails of the skis touched these and we settled to a perfect three-point landing in the snow a dozen yards beyond."

In this "perfect" landing, however, the skis dropped deeply and the ship sank up to its belly in hidden cracks. Snow conditions had changed since Reeve's April trip—a fact which he could not recognize from the air. There was less moisture at this inland site, and accordingly less settling and packing than in the coastal country he had known. "Fluffy white stuff like hoarfrost" had piled up into a more deceptive cover than any he had experienced in his flights around Valdez.

It took two hours to dig the Fairchild out, shovel a channel, and move the plane to a firmer spot. Reeve shook hands with the mountaineers, wished them luck and climbed aboard for take-off. The Fairchild wallowed twenty feet and dropped clumsily into another crevasse. Soon after this the air filled with melting flakes. The men pitched tents and crawled inside. A few hours later they heard a maddening patter. It was no longer snow that beat down on the face of the glacier. It was heavy, gray, drenching rain.

The storm lasted four days. The snowy surface of the glacier softened to slush. Three times during this period the group dug the Fairchild out and dragged it to ice ridges from which Reeve attempted take-off. Each time he failed. The temperature steadily rose to 58 degrees above and the glacial ice became so rotten that even the men, stepping carefully, broke through as they walked.

On the fifth night the storm broke and the temperature dropped to freezing. By morning a slick two-inch crust had formed. Washburn declares he will never forget the sight of Reeve, silhouetted against the rising sun, soberly calculating his chances. Reeve knew this might be his last opportunity for take-off until the following winter.

A ten-mile downwind was against him. The ice was thin and the slope short. Chasms yawned below. He could abandon the Fairchild and walk out. There were two ways of hiking to civilization. Skirting canyons and fording swollen rivers, he might struggle to Kennecott Mine, 150 miles away. Or, inching up and down the precipices of a 16,000-foot snowcap, he might toil sixty miles to the tiny Canadian settlement of Burwash Landing. He had little time to deliberate. Minute by minute the rising sun was thawing his fragile runway. "I'm no mountain-climber," he told Washburn. "I'm a pilot. You can skin your skunk and I'll skin mine."

He hastily emptied his plane of food, tools and emergency supplies and loosened the blades of the prop, flattening each one a degree for utmost power. He brushed frost from the wings and fuselage. He turned the engine toward the sun to save fuel in warming it. He climbed in, waved to his companions; the Wright growled and the Fairchild started ahead.

In Reeve's words: "I got up pretty good speed till I hit the crevassed part, then I went right through again but I pulled her out—I wasn't stopping—that was an awful strong plane and I figured sooner or later I'd get it in the air. It ran about ten thousand feet—bang, bang, bang, like a surfboard—there wasn't enough lift and I was getting no place fast. Ahead I could see big open crevasses two to twenty feet wide. Just to the left was a smooth icefall and a five-hundred-foot drop-off.

"I made a sharp turn and dove right over it toward the valley wall. The drop-off gave the ship just enough forward speed; it missed a huge crack and sailed into the air. That was the greatest feeling in my life bar none."

Washburn and Bates reached the summit of Lucania several days later and were heralded by journalists and scientists throughout the world. Few heard of the gambling Alaskan who had made the ascent possible. Washburn, who has worked with many aviators in Switzerland, Canada and Alaska, declares, "Bob Reeve is without question the finest ski pilot and rough-country flyer I have seen anywhere."

In such exploits as this Reeve has gained the reputation of being a man without fear. This is not completely justified by the facts. Once, riding aboard an airliner in New York State, he got off before he reached his destination because he did not like the pilots' decisions in a snowstorm. The rest of the passengers flew safely on. Reeve often feels uneasy on the airlines of the States. But year after year he has enthusiastically continued the most hair-raising kind of bush flying in the North.

He left Valdez in 1941 but continued his "one-horse" freighting operation—first out of Fairbanks, then out of Anchorage. He scoffed when other bush pilots went to work for Pan American and Alaska Airlines, discarding their rough garb for tailored uniforms. "Hi, Captains," he shouts when he meets them. Unlike Gillam, he has never had any interest in mastering instrument techniques. Nor was he pleased when the C.A.A. and the Army began their airways construction, rendering flight safer and easier. "All you need to be a pilot in Alaska today," he complains, "is a duckbill cap, a brief-case, a watch with seven hands on it, a slide rule and 300 hours in the air—100 dual, 100 solo and 100 padded."

The Army and the C.A.A. found Reeve a hard case when they arrived in the North. "What do I want with a radio?" he asked them. "I have enough troubles of my own without fooling with a gadget like that." Required by law to install one in his plane, he refused for months to learn how to use it. The C.A.A., in a period of three months, grounded and reprimanded him at least a dozen times for various offenses. He refused to recognize military approach procedures on the new Army airports during the war. Landing at Juneau at dusk, he caused an air-raid alarm. "What's the matter with you?" an irate brass hat asked. "We nearly shot you down!" Another time, almost out of fuel, he landed at Fairbanks during a practice air-raid black-out. "Who gave you permission to come down?" a sentinel demanded. "Come down?" Reeve snapped. "What am I supposed to do, hang up there like a balloon?"

But he could be forgiven many things. Reeve did a superb job in World War II. In 1941, to speed construction of a strategic airport at Northway he hauled 1,100 tons in four months in a Fairchild 71 and a Boeing 80-A. He hauled a total of more than 1,000 soldiers, more than 1,600 tons of military freight in the war period, in supposedly obsolete ships. He was the only bush operator under exclusive contract to the Army, and he is the only bush pilot who has ever flown regularly out the Aleutians.

To the layman Reeve's glacier flights may seem more

uncanny than his military flights—but not to the sophisticated airman. It is well-known that Aleutian weather is among the worst in the world. Fog and storm roll ceaselessly across the bleak rock chain; ceaselessly and violently. Hundred-mile squalls windmill the props of bombers, scatter piles of lumber, send heavy oil drums whirring through the air, tear off tin roofs. Few of the Army's high aircraft losses in this theater were directly caused by the Japanese. Most of the planes crashed in foul weather.

Reeve signed a contract with the Alaska Communications System (Signal Corps) to haul key men and rush radio equipment into this gale-swept area. He made more than 200 trips "to the westward,"* most of them in his Fairchild 71. The Fairchild has no de-icing equipment. Powered with a Wasp engine which Reeve used in South America in 1929, the ancient red ship cruises at only 110 miles an hour, lands at only fifty-five. Army pilots, many of whom had never seen a plane of this vintage, were appalled. Reeve laughed. "When the boys go into Tokyo," he wisecracked, "I'll be with them. I fly so low and so slow the Japs wouldn't have the heart to shoot me down."

I traveled with Reeve from Merrill Field on one of his trips "to the westward." He showed me to a seat in the rear of the Fairchild's cabin. I was lucky to have it. The rest had been removed; a towering pile of freight, lashed with rope, nearly filled the narrow fuselage. "I guess that's where you sit, Sarge," Reeve told a soldier, pointing to a duffel bag. The soldier took his place, straddling a box of radio tubes. "Have you got your lunches?" Reeve asked us. "Where we're going we'll run out of hamburger stands awful fast."

As we headed out the Alaska Peninsula toward the "Chain" I saw what he meant. The scraggly spruce tapered down to brush. Soon the trees were gone. This was volcanic country, gaunt, eerie country where geography was not something to read about but something to see and feel in an overpowering way. To our right tossed the waters of the Bering Sea—reaching north for 700 miles to the strait where

---

* Reeve never flew to the tip of the "Chain," but he made many trips as far west as Dutch Harbor and Umnak.

America and Soviet Asia nearly meet. To our left loomed a line of big, fog-wreathed snowcaps which seemed to march in ponderous procession—as the Army's Aleutian air forces were daily striking—toward Japan. The first few hours of the trip passed in bright sunshine. But as we neared the Army base at Cold Bay it came.

It came in a matter of minutes. We could almost tell it from the look of Reeve's shoulders—and the way he kept peering to the right. Wisps of scud were drifting in across the sea. There it was, "ugly, ugly stuff," blowing in over the water, piling up and pouring across the narrow neck of land that we must fly. Before long, patches of mist were playing all around us. Drops slid across the windowpanes. Reeve throttled down the engine, flying slow and low. We moved only a few feet above the earth at a speed of eighty miles an hour.

Marshes below were blurred, ponds dim slivers. The fog was dense and ever changing. Now the dark outline of a hill rose ahead; then it was blotted out and another mound appeared. Reeve sat erect, working fast. The plane dodged one way, then another in a narrow, shifting channel of dim light. Suddenly there was nothing outside the windows. Reeve jerked the stick back; the Wasp roared again at full power and the Fairchild climbed steeply. It was ten minutes by the watch before a faint haze appeared above, the fog broke into blowing wisps and we emerged into sunlight. The altimeter registered 7,000 feet.

They looked unreal, those snowy volcanic cones to the left—one of them sending puffs of black smoke into the sky. There was no other sign of earth; billowing clouds were massed below us, spreading into the distance as far as we could see. Reeve banked the plane right and left, studying the surface of the fog, hunting a break and a way down. There was none.

A cluster of specks appeared in the air behind: a flight of bombers. They soon overtook us—gray-green, camouflaged ships of war with the Air Forces emblem on their sides. They dipped their wings. The freight groaned and shifted as our plane rocked to right and left in answering salute. Speeding past, the Army planes scattered, circled and disappeared at precise intervals into the fog for routine instrument let-downs on the Cold Bay radio range.

But Reeve was not equipped to follow this beam of science. We were held aloft—at the mercy of the steady sinking of the sun, the relentless draining of fuel in the Fairchild's tank, the capricious drift of cloud. He circled repeatedly. He flew west a while, throttled back and descended again into the murk, dropping as low as he dared. It was no use. He approached the edge of a mountain and hovered close among the frosty crags, looking for a wind-blown hole. Finally he pointed the Fairchild south. In a few minutes we had left the Bering side, crossed the peaks and were heading out over the Pacific Ocean.

For nearly half an hour we proceeded out over the shrouded sea. Then we descended once more into the gloom, the roar of the Wasp sounding ominously muffled. Five hundred feet, the altimeter read. Four hundred feet. Three hundred feet. It read less than two hundred when I caught a glimpse of flashing combers which widened into a vast expanse of ocean. Turning north again, the plane sped back under the low mists, almost skimming the waves, till we came to the dark outline of land.

Reeve followed the side of a bay, and once more we were hovering over swampy flats in a yellowish murky light. The fog rolled all around; we could see no more than a quarter of a mile ahead, and it appeared, second by second, that we would be blinded altogether. Sea gulls scattered before the Fairchild over the dismal wastes and it seemed as aimless as they. Then, like a mirage, a jumble of Quonsets, revetments, and wooden hangars loomed ahead and among them, looking both beautiful and unreal, lay long, wide runways sparkling with colored lights. Reeve did not circle for his approach. He banked steeply, cut the engine and glided onto the Cold Bay airdrome. Flight control men in a red-flagged jeep drove up as we landed. By the time we had signed their papers the fog was sheeting across the runway and the control tower was hidden from sight.

"Well, kid," Reeve remarked, "you were in the luck. I had a good trip for a change."

Personally and professionally, Reeve was a tradition at

lonely bases of the "Chain." Good friend of majors, colonels and generals, he joined them at poker and helped them many a stormy evening "kick the gong." Good friend of enlisted men, he did them many favors, arriving with camera film, magazines, fresh milk and other supplies that livened their spirits more. Everybody liked the witty, friendly, informal Alaskan. Officers and men alike talked of him as if he were something from Ripley. "He scares hell out of us," one dispatcher told me. "We've given him up for lost plenty of times. But someway he always makes it down."

Parked on one of the Army airdromes beside a row of Mitchells and Liberators, the Fairchild looked ridiculous, like a child who had toddled into a row of troops. The small red plane was not as big as the gas trucks that rumbled up to refuel it. Time and again winds tore it loose from heavy oil-drum moorings. Ground crews chuckled as they telephoned Reeve late at night: "Sorry, your ship got away." Pilots smiled as he slammed down the receiver. "Damn it—there goes Leaping Lena again."

One stormy day flight-control men picked up an emergency call.

"This is Seven Zero Three Four. Will you give me a report on the day's tide? I say again, I want the *tide*, the *tide*—how high is today's *tide*?"

"What's he flying?" asked a new soldier, "a plane or a boat?"

Bad weather had forced Reeve down on a seaside mud flat. The ocean was rising. That day's tide was the highest of the year. Informed of this, he splashed off, climbed up through the fog, circled till he found a hole, spiraled down and fought his way to the nearest field.

The most serious accident of Reeve's career occurred when he lost a Boeing in 1943 near Cold Bay. Fog forced him "on top"; all fields within range were shrouded. Darkness fell. The gas ran out. Only a glimpse of phosphorescent breakers, sighted through a hole in the overcast, enabled him to make a controlled landing on a strip of beach. His back was hurt and some of his passengers were also injured. The plane was demolished by wind and sea.

Friends say that Reeve was sobered by this accident. He

was also sobered when his twin brother Richard, an Air Corps captain, crashed to death in Illinois. But he continued his work with bravado. "I enjoy every minute of flying down the Islands," he told me. "You get to Unimak, the jumping-off point and the ceiling's only a hundred feet and you can see maybe a mile beyond Scotch Cap. You start out heading west and you tell yourself, 'Well, after all, you can't live forever so you may as well enjoy this flight.' . . ."

"It's sharpening my wits," he briskly added. "I want to keep sharpening my wits."

15
Jesus and the Whale

WHEN Eielson and Wilkins made their 1928 hop across the top of the world Charles Brower was proud. It was on the homemade tables of his Barrow whaling station that Wilkins prepared his navigational charts. The aviators ate at Brower's table and were his guests for twenty-three days.

"Wilkins and Eielson," Brower wrote in his diary, "flew to Spitsbergen right from my front door."

The Eskimos at Barrow were still prouder.

It was they who shoveled snow from the ice to make a slick runway. It was a tough job. The first three strips they cleared were too short. They had to drag the plane up the coast by dog team to an open place and shovel a path a mile and a quarter long so the heavily loaded Vega could take off.

When Charles and Anne Lindbergh flew North to the Orient in 1931 Jimmy Sirlock, an Eskimo at Nome, carved an ivory model of their plane and made them a present of it. He labored over it, and it was perfect in every respect.

The Eskimos of Alaska have not always felt so friendly toward airplanes.

When the Black Wolf Squadron flew over in 1920 natives scampered, dove into their huts.

Years later, when an Anchorage pilot kindly tossed out a load of oranges to a group of hunters, the men scattered as if the fruit were a load of bombs.

Another pilot dropped flares for night landing and a whole frightened village decamped.

In 1926, after the dirigible *Norge* had crossed the polar sea to Alaska, it wallowed uncertainly above the Arctic Coast. The exhausted crew was lost. Spying a man on the tundra far below, they nosed the huge silver ship down toward him, briefly cut the engines, and Explorer Roald Amundsen shouted "WHERE ARE WE?"

The Eskimo's mouth dropped open. He stood there speechless till the *Norge* floated away.

All the natives heard about this wonder in the sky. Later that year, when a government geologist traveled into the Arctic, he asked them what had happened since his last trip north.

"Plenty happen," they told him. "Jesus and the whale, they fly right over!"

When the Lomen family at Nome hired a plane for survey of its reindeer herds an Eskimo named Thomas Sequinas said the scheme would not be practical. "Cannot see reindeer from air," he argued. "When birds fly over they cannot see man on ground, or why we shoot?"

One of the Lomens took Sequinas on a flight. The Eskimo grinned and grinned. "Oh, my," he said. "All same dream. Can see *plenty* reindeer from air!"

When the first plane circled over the Eskimo village of Unalakleet an old woman, bedridden many years, hobbled to her feet to see it. She was no longer an invalid.

Today these cheerful, keen, farthest-north Alaskans are as much for aviation as the white population of the Territory.

When the noise of an engine is heard, as it may be for fully ten minutes clattering above the Arctic shore, Eskimos at one of the lone towns begin calling. "Tingun! (Machine that flies!)" they cry, in the soft, dignified enunciation of their people. It echoes all over the village—"Tingun! Tingun!" The teacher dismisses school and everyone hurries to meet the plane. There is no excitement. Many of the natives have never seen an automobile, but they take aviation for granted. Dusky children will swarm happily on a taxying ship and hop rides, swinging on the struts, standing on the skis.

For a while the Eskimos used aircraft for letter paper. They'd pick out a nice, light-colored ship and scratch on the fabric with knife or pencil:

HELLO FROM THE DIOMEDE PEOPLE WE GOT
TWO WHALES THIS YEAR
PLENTY WALRUS

OUR PEOPLE ARE ALL WELL
MAYBE I FLY OVER SEE YOU SOON

Messages and replies would travel this way for hundreds of
miles. But the scribbling was tough on the fabric. Pilots were
annoyed. They asked the Eskimos not to do it. You seldom
see it any more.

In winter the Eskimos border runways with flaming oil
pots, or stand in two rows in the snow so a plane can land
between. These natives will do anything for aviation and
often, with their intimate knowledge of wind and weather,
they can help better than white men can.

Once a pilot landed at Unalakleet, left his plane on the
river ice and went to bed. Eskimos came and waked him.
"Wind comes from west," they said. "Maybe ice go out
tonight. More better you move plane."

They helped him wheel it to shore. By morning the ice was
swept away.

Few Eskimos have had the money to learn to fly but many
have served as mechanics. One helped Crosson complete his
celebrated Arctic flight in 1927. Crosson was in despair when
he broke a strut of his Swallow at Noorvik. The damage was
bad, and the nearest repair shop was 500 miles away. It was
a native boy who had never before seen an airplane who
did the mending job. He sawed splints from a plank, fitted
them to the strut, and wrapped around some babish. Crosson
flew a long time with this strut and had no trouble.

One of the most painstakingly skillful mechanics in Alaska
is an Eskimo named Peter Lazarus. He has been employed
by Ferguson Airways at Kotzebue nine years. Lazarus does
fine wing work, knows engines too and can heat a motor in
high winds, his boss says, "when a white man would get it on
fire in five minutes."

Lazarus has repaired many wrecks. I stood with him in his
wooden hangar and gazed around at broken wings and struts
and skis. "Oh, my," he softly told me, "I no like to fly."

But other Eskimos would like to be pilots, and most love
to fly. Pilots say they are good passengers, casual on even
their first trips, never get frightened, seldom sick. They are

canny passengers, too. They usually recognize ground land-marks better than white men do.

One of the Wien brothers, flying 190 miles to Fairbanks, wondered why his ship was tail-heavy. On arrival he found three little Eskimo girls stowed away behind. They laughed and said they had come to town to go to the show.

He took them to the movies, bought them supper with ice cream for dessert and flew them, gratis, 190 miles home.

16
Sig Wien

IF PILOT SIG WIEN should take a notion to run for the Presidency of the United States, and if ballots should be distributed to the Eskimos, he would probably receive almost every vote on the Arctic coast of Alaska.

"Sigwien," they call him, softly slurring together the words. Often simply Sig. Several dusky babies have been named in his honor. The spotted seal parka which he wears in winter was the gift of an Eskimo friend. So were his mukluks and fur traveling bag.

"Sig! Sig come in," children shout when his plane appears. The people recognize his ship instantly. They have seen the black and orange Bellanca many times. As they watch it glide earthward dark eyes are shining under fur ruffs. As he climbs out of the cockpit broad smiles greet him, spreading like a newly lighted fire.

Sig, younger brother of Noel, is carrying on the family tradition. He has done his pioneering in the last few years. A graduate of the Boeing School of Aeronautics, he decided to develop an airline from Fairbanks and Nome to the very top of the continent. Until he established his route the far Arctic coast had not been regularly flown. It still has few airway facilities. Wien, mostly in his single-engine Bellanca, has made regular trips to Barrow since 1943, giving that farthest-north town the first year-round transportation it has ever known.

Sig is a big silent man. Tall and heavily built, he has a stubborn Scandinavian face and baldish head. He knows all the Eskimos and calls them by name, but seldom, except in the line of work, does he speak to anyone. "Must be the tightest-mouthed devil in the world. A hard guy to understand." No other pilot in Alaska is so leery of reporters. The first time I tried to interview him, at Barrow, he hustled upstairs in the schoolteacher's house and hid when he saw me coming.

Once, after Sig had been marooned a month in the Arctic with a broken landing gear, a friend saw him eating breakfast in a Nome restaurant. He hurried to his table. "Sig!" he cried. "You're back! What happened? How are you?"

Sig looked at him slowly. "Well," he replied, with a characteristic long pause. "Well"—in close-clipped words—"I'm back in business."

Another friend who sat beside him in the cockpit during a five-hour flight reports that Sig spoke only once during the long journey.

"See the wolves?" he asked.

"Yeah," said the man, overwhelmed by this burst of loquaciousness. "Three of 'em."

"No," returned Sig, peering carefully earthward. "Looks like five."

Sig is a big silent man—and it is a big silent land that he has chosen to fly. He may travel for hours without seeing a town. Point Lay, one of the stops on Sig's airline, consists of only a dozen or so sod-banked shacks. Wainwright is not much larger. At the Barrow terminal no more than sixty houses straggle around the red-steepled church and green wooden schoolhouse. But the Stars and Stripes fly there. People live there. Regularly Sig flies there.

By title Sig is a company executive. Since he bought out Noel's interest in the family firm he has been the president of Wien Alaska Airlines, the oldest company operating out of Fairbanks. Wien Alaska Airlines has fourteen pilots and does some $500,000 worth of business a year. In a month its seventeen planes may fly more than 50,000 miles, serving not only Nome and Barrow but also dozens of scattered settlements throughout the Interior. Many decisions confront the chief of this busy, far-ranging little outfit.

Sig seldom appears in Fairbanks to make them. If he does appear it is little help. He ignores government forms. He has forgotten to keep up his logbook. "Well," he may reply, as young assistants bombard him with questions, "well ... that sounds like it might be a good idea." Then, leaving matters dangling, he will climb into his plane and head toward the Arctic and Barrow. He may not return for weeks—or months.

He can hardly be called a high-pressure salesman. Once, spectators recall, a contractor from the States strode into his office.

"I have to go to Moses Point immediately," he announced. "I want to charter your plane."

Sig gave him a blank look and a long silence.

"Well," he finally replied, "maybe."

The man bristled. He was a big shot, a go-getter. "I've got to get to Moses Point," he shouted, banging his fist on the table. "When can you take me?"

Sig, leaning back against the wall, scratched his head. It was some time before he answered. "Well ... I don't know. I don't know just when I could take you."

His prospective passenger walked away in a huff.

Sig is a man of strong likes and dislikes and he can afford to be choosy. He has too much business as it is. By the same token he has no time to be an executive. He is a tireless flyer but he never catches up with the demand.

Wander into his painted airline shack on Nome's main street some day and you will see what his Barrow service means. Freight piles high beside the old-fashioned scales. The room is full of restless people. Where is Sig? The pretty blonde girl behind the counter is patient. "Two days ago he was at Wainwright heading this way. He hasn't reported since. We'll let you know." People straggle disconsolately out, drop into the North Pole Bakery for coffee or the Polar Bar for a drink. If it is summer they may find another pilot to take them. If it is winter and they are traveling all the way to Barrow it is likely that they will have to wait for Sig. There is usually no other way to go except by dog team.

Many pilots have flown to Barrow in summer; none before Sig has made regular trips in winter. Even at Nome and Fairbanks the days are dim and short, and the farther north Sig flies the more tightly the cloak of darkness is drawn. On a high December noon Barrow is shrouded in dusk and he will use his landing lights to come down. Sig holds an instrument rating, but because of the dearth of airway facilities along his routes he must fly contact much of the way. As a result he has become a specialist in Arctic winter daylight; he probably knows it more intimately than any other man in America.

In fair weather he may sometimes stretch his flying time, crossing the snow country in the reflected light of the moon. Otherwise he must use the scanty piece of day for all it is worth. Allowing for weather, latitude and season, he has tested it in flight until he has a sixth sense of its ever changing margins. Knowing how soon he may trust the glow after the gloom, how far he may dare the gloom after the glow, he does not waste a minute. He takes off as soon past the edge of night as he is able to distinguish shoreline bearings. He probes deep into the dusk and feels his way down onto runways bordered with burning oil pots.

A winter flight with Sig Wien is fantastic. In the diffused Arctic light nothing outside the windows seems real. All around, above and below, is whiteness; not the usual whiteness of fog or snow but a luminous whiteness without depth, beginning, or end.

If you fly long enough this way your eyes play you tricks. The icy path of a river below seems to unreel like an endless belt. The plane seems to hang suspended with a tide of nothingness rushing past. The roar of the engine begins to sound strange. That loud noise, is it really pounding out there, or is it in your own head?

"My God, where are we?" a passenger solemnly shouted on one of these trips. "How did we get here?"

The silent pilot in the wolfskin cap threw back his head and laughed.

No airline route in Alaska has been more difficult to pioneer. Dimness is Sig's routine. Sometimes the coastal villages are almost buried, with only a few chimneys sticking up from the snow. In this part of the North, where so many flyers have lost their way, Sig never misses. He makes his way from point to point like the engineer of a shuttle train, with never a sign of confusion. He knows the coast so well that he uses small mounds and twists in the shore for checkpoints as another Alaska pilot would use a large mountain or a wide river. He flies the Arctic as precisely as a woman threads a needle.

Tortoise-slow in his motions, deliberate in his judgments, Sig is one of the most calculating pilots in the Territory. He will sometimes wait on the ground in bad weather when brasher pilots are taking off. He is cagey with the elements. Sudden storm, however, may blind him anywhere along his lone routes. His ski planes have been forced to earth a number of times. He has had to siwash it, waiting for clear sky. But he has coolly prepared for emergencies like these by caching supplies along the way. Never in all his flying along the Arctic coast has fog or blizzard caused him to wreck a ship.

He is equally cagey with terrain. Although his runways are among the most primitive in Alaska, they have caused him only a few minor crack-ups. He approaches the fickle strips of sand and ice with never-ending suspicion. Once, a passenger recalls, he approached Point Lay in wintertime for what, by all indications, would be a routine landing on the frozen sea. Eskimos formed in two lines to show him the best place to come down. Sig dropped low, throttling back as he studied the snow condition. It looked fine to the passenger. "A nice smooth place. I couldn't see a single thing wrong with it."

To his surprise, Sig flew around again and descended again, gingerly touching the snow with one ski. He repeated this. Seven times in all he circled and "dragged" the runway. Then he flew away, soaring down the coast till he found a stretch of snow beside a sheltering cliff. The passenger tightened his safety belt. He says the spot looked "plenty rough." Sig made only one pass and glided gently down.

He spent the next hour and a half laboriously taxiing a twisting path back through the ice ridges to Point Lay. All this time the passenger was doubting his pilot's judgment. "There was nothing wrong with the Eskimos' runway. That was one time I figured Sig missed." But when they inspected the Point Lay strip he found that Sig was right. There was a large, sharp-edged chunk of ice hidden just under the surface.

Sig's astute piloting aided the Army and Navy during World War II. He and his pilots made many wilderness landings to service the "star-gazers"—Army parties who used astronomical calculations to map the northern part of the continent. Rugged charter flying was also done in connection with the Navy's Arctic oil-drilling program. In the opinion of Lieutenant Commander William T. Foran, geologist in charge, Sig speeded the Navy's oil work by many months.

This involved some highly sensational flying in a race against the summer thaw. In June of 1943 a Navy group flew north in three Douglas transports for a rush survey. The Barrow runway was too short for these planes. Sig scouted the sea ice till he found a 3,000-foot path between pressure ridges. The Navy group came down safely, unloaded and took off in the nick of time; three days later the ice went out to sea. During these three days Sig shuttled incessantly in his Bellanca, transferring cargo and geologists to shore. Then he faced the problem of moving them all to the Navy's survey ground in the Colville River area, 180 miles inland.

There was a river bar seven miles from the intended work site where landing, for Sig Wien, would be easy. But this would require the men to back-pack all their supplies across the tundra. Time was precious. Sig found the remnant of a snowdrift, landing on soggy slush until it nearly melted where they wanted to work. He made seven trips to this snowdrift, landing on soggy slush until it nearly melted away. "Every time, it was really like a forced landing," Lieutenant Commander Foran told me. "Smartest piece of navigation in an airplane I've ever seen."

The Eskimos have learned to expect things like this from "Sigwien." His flying has brought the people a new way of life. Barrow, until he began his air service, received only four mails a year. Now he delivers mail the year round, almost every week. Dora Adams had her baby. Oopiksoun is dead. Takpuk killed a whale. The belugas are running. Letters of news he brings, and love letters. "Sometimes," Charles Brower told me, "they would be a lot better off without those." But the Eskimos do not agree.

When the first boat arrives at Nome (several months earlier, each summer, than at Barrow), Sig loads his plane with celery, cabbage and oranges for towns that are still icelocked. The year round he brings needles, soap, cigarettes, calico—anything the trading posts may need. If a tractor breaks down he will bring repair parts and sometimes sit down and mend it himself. Sig once took a course at Dunwoody Industrial Institute. He is a good welder; he can repair his plane or anything else.

Sig notices things. Once he saw an old gas lamp that was not working. On his next trip he brought parts to fix it. Sig tells Eskimos where the walrus or caribou are moving, saving the hunters days of fruitless search. He does big favors and small ones. On each trip he picks up a chessboard at Point Lay and hauls it ninety miles to Wainwright. The next trip he hauls it back so that Tom Anayak, schoolteacher, and David Panik, store manager, can carry on a game.

Sig will come when trouble strikes. One autumn Father Tom Cunningham, Catholic priest, was stricken with pneumonia at Cape Prince of Wales. There was no doctor there. The people feared he had little chance to live. When Sig got the news he dumped a load of passengers at Kotzebue and although he was on wheels and the Sound was not yet frozen over, he took a short cut across the water, his ship dragging under a load of ice. He bundled Father Cunningham warmly inside the cabin and flew him to the hospital at Nome. Their return trip was made in a blizzard. Father Cunningham lived. When the priest tried to pay for this trip Sig shrugged his shoulders.

David Vincent, thirteen-year-old son of the Barrow schoolteacher, was lost. He had wandered off from a reindeer camp into the fog. For three days he had been missing. It was summertime, but grown men, plagued by mosquitoes, wandering alone across the tundra, have been known to lose their minds, and David had no food.

His parents asked the radio station to call Sig. He was in the air well on his way to Nome when he got the message. He turned, flew back to Barrow and located the little shape of the child in less than half an hour. Toiling through a mass of lakes and marshes, David was already fourteen miles from the coast camp and steadily moving farther into the wilderness.

Even Sig could not land in these sticky bogs. He circled and dropped candy bars with a note telling David to follow in the direction he would fly. He struck back to the reindeer camp and picked up several herders. He flew them over the lost boy and landed them as close to him as he could. Then, cruising back and forth, he guided David and his rescuers until they met. He would take no pay for this.

There are many times when Sig will take no pay. On occasion, when the spirit moves, he will fly out of his way with mail or fresh fruit for a settlement off his route. The people ask for a bill. "Well," he is likely to say, vaguely scratching his head, "this isn't on my regular run. I really don't know how much it would be. . . ."

It cannot be said that he is oblivious to money. A passenger pays $150 to fly from Nome or Fairbanks to Barrow. A round-trip charter costs $750 to $1,000. Freight brings Sig sixty cents a pound, and he has been known to heft a package for a full minute, judging its borderline weight. He once scolded a pilot for using office stationery for personal mail. He may drive a hard bargain with a customer from the States, but up in Eskimoland he dislikes to take cash from his friends. He frequently hauls people on credit and almost as frequently forgets. If it were not for the fact that the Eskimos are conscientious about paying their debts, this harassed office girl reports, Wien Alaska Airlines would lose a lot of money.

"Did you take Leo Shaffer from Barrow to Kotzebue?" she may ask. "He was in yesterday to pay you, but I have no record of it."

Sig, pulling a sheaf of scribbled slips from his pocket, will thumb slowly through them and stuff them back.

"Well . . . I can't find it but I believe I did."

Practical men wonder why Sig handles money so casually, why he neglects management to fly this solitary and hazardous Arctic route. "Well," he once replied when the question was put to him, "I don't know. Up here there's lots of room."

For the full answer you must see Sig with the Eskimos, watch their faces as they crowd about him in a friendly, almost worshipful group. You must hear the people talk about him, or read what the children write about him in their school papers.

One day Sig Wien came to Barrow
We ran down to the landing field.
The A.T.G. guardmen were all
  in a straight line.
The guardmen said "Halt!"
We all stopped.
One guardman said,
"We want to help the boys and girls.
We don't want anyone to get hurt,
We don't want anyone to get killed."

You must watch the children scampering eagerly around Sig's plane as he lands, so close that pilot and parents are worried. Four years ago at Christmastime Sig played Santa Claus in the Barrow schoolhouse, handing out village gifts. He wore a red-and-white suit instead of his flying clothes. But he was doing nothing very different from what he does every day.

In the happy faces of the Eskimos Sig earns a live and never-ending reward for his work. He likes these people and knows their life so well it has become a part of his own. In winter he dresses as they do from head to foot, in the fur of squirrel, reindeer, seal and wolf. He eats their "muktuk" —whale-skin and blubber. When he stops for the night at the Arctic towns he stays sometimes in the home of the missionary or schoolteacher, other times in native sod huts. Always he is welcome. Always he seems content.

When Sig's landing gear snapped on rough ice at Point Lay in 1944 he found he was marooned in a town without coal. He slept thirty-six nights in a sleeping bag in the schoolhouse attic. It was so cold that school was dismissed. Frost formed on the desks, and his sleeping bag was coated white. He did not seem to mind. He did not even mind spending Christmas at this lone settlement. The Eskimos gathered willow boughs along the timberless flats, fitted them onto a wooden post and hung their home-made tree with ornaments. A dusky girl, who had never before seen such a bird, cooked a turkey he had brought in his plane. "She did an A-1 job," he comments.

"We had a turkey New Year's Day, too," he proudly told me, "at Wainwright. We always have a turkey at Christmas and New Year's wherever I happen to be."

17
A Man Can Do Anything

SOME old-timers thought they could fly too—"land and take off, don't need no lessons, nothing to it—a man can do anything in Alaska."

Tom Roust, "one of the roughest, toughest old boys ever hit the country," was a carpenter by trade. He arrived in the North during the Gold Rush and made a lot of money building boats. When Roust was in his fifties he bought a wrecked Hisso-Standard at Nome and doctored it up. He said he was going to fly it.

"I can handle her," he told everybody, "I know wood."

One morning he got in his plane and started running it back and forth in the snow to see how fast it would taxi.

As a witness tells the story:

"By golly, next thing Old Tom knew the throttle froze—he was six hundred foot in the air. It was around zero that day and he had no coat, no goggles, not much gas in the ship. Christ, he took her up to fifteen hundred 'n' sashayed over town, skiddin' 'n' slippin' somethin' terrible. He didn't know how to bank, so he'd go into steep climbin' stalls tryin' to turn.

"Then he decided to come down and land.

"First time he tried he hit a ski on a drift; BINGO! she jumped back up in the air again. Then he come back in a wild maneuver—overshot—went around again. Third try he come down grittin' his teeth: 'You bastard, you stay down this time'—

"She stayed down all right—all in a heap."

Tom Roust climbed out of the wreck with two broken ribs. "Never mind," he angrily told the crowd. "If my eyes hadn't froze I'd 'a' made it."

They put him to bed in the room above the bar in the

Lincoln Hotel. Everybody said: "That'll take the flyin' out o' that tinhorn sport."

But a few days later he was up again, working on his plane. He took it off again, brought it down again, and crashed again—breaking four inches off the prop.

After that Roust flew many times. Eskimos would dive into their huts. Mothers would call their kids in from the streets.

"LOOK OUT! THERE GOES TOM!"

But he never had another wreck. It was a gang of Nome boys who tried to fly his plane one night and smashed it to pieces. He went to the States after that, took some lessons, bought another ship, hired a pilot and operated a regular service out of Nome: Roust Airways.

"Joe Skoric never had a license," Alaskans say, "but he sure had plenty of gall." Skoric, a high-strung little Russian, paddled over from Siberia all alone in a skinboat shortly after World War I. He got a job stringing telephone wires around Nome and has lived in Alaska ever since. He smiles, waves his hands, speaks in a pleased, shrill voice when he talks about aviation. He always wants to make plans. He loves the idea of an airplane.

"Long time ago," he says, "I'm out hunting on skis. I run down one hill, gotta climb da next, run down one hill, gotta climb da next—and always I see da fox running up other side. I say to myself gee I wish I have a wing so I can jump over da big hill. I make up my mind to go Outside and get some training. I go to Boeing Field—gee it's awful high, eleven dollar an hour is cheapest I can find. I spend six hundred dollar trying to learn to fly but then I quit."

Skoric returned to Alaska, but year after year he kept thinking of an airplane. In 1934 he made another trip to the States and brought one—"clean, nice little ship, forty horsepower Taylorcraft"—and tried again.

Skoric has a total of ninety-eight hours in the air. Few of them have been good ones.

He wrecked his first ship soon after he bought it, near the town of Crescent, Oregon.

"I'm flying 'em along, was 8,000 feet up, motor starts coughing, coughing—some kind of trouble—then I see great big gray wall. Da fog is moving right toward me, I don't know how I'm gonna keep 'em up there—you know you gotta see where to go to fly.

"I climb, fog it's all under me—wind pushes me east, I look below, it is all gray mass everywhere, funny little motor always missing, I open throttle more, it is a bad time till I see a hole, wind drifting—I dive. I was glad to come down but I don't know where I was, motor coughing, I see a big white lake, lotta big high trees, where can I find a place to put my plane? Then way toward the east I see da smoke; I says now somebody live there, where people live they usually got some kind of space—I go for it but I see smoke is moving—it was a railroad train.

"Well, I put 'em in gliding position, I keep on down, keep on down, see da shiny highway, keep eye on highway but from the air is different—I don't know how wide. I see little bit space between woods and creek, two smokestack, just then da motor cough bad and stops. I try one two three time with throttle, no good, so I just switch off. By this time I see a tree higher than I was, I just miss it and make for open spot, tourist camp parking ground shaped like a horseshoe—there is my chance.

"I coasted, just skim trees, start slipping on wing but pretty soon I see right in front of me telephone wire. I just jerk it on da stick and got 'em over but when you jerk it once, dat's da limit. Now I see horse and wagon so I try to jerk 'em once more and I just pull 'em over. I was practically half stiff. Now I'm just over da ground, I see little root stuck in ground right ahead of me, root bent some kind looks to me, I pass dat but root lifted and stick in belly of plane, seem like. I hit the ground, it is a soft ground, whole wheels sink in, I turn my head, expects to go over on nose but plane stops short. I am so happy cold sweat come out all over me!"

There was little damage to the plane. Skoric repaired it and decided to use the highway for take-off.

"Ditch this side, ditch other side, highway only fifty foot wide, trees, trees, all branches and ditches, it was a tough place, I tell you. A man he come with me to give advice. He look both ways, when no car coming he give me da signal. I grab throttle, start taxying to take off, I was in a hurry, didn't want to block road, maybe foolishness too, when I taxi I turn to left, open throttle, jerk da plane and lift it—there she go, I got 'em floating already but motor cluk-cluk too cold, I pull on stick maybe too fast, I see dat fellow waving his white cap telling me to come down. Twice she stall me down. Third time I make it, just miss tree—funny thing, you know why I make it?—because I don't know any better! Dat man he make a fun of me, just laugh."

This was only one of Skoric's adventures. As he told another pilot:

"I'm flying 'em along on top, listening to sweet music over them headphones. Engine she was purring good. Then sudden all I hear is sweet music. My ship she start dropping, I fall, fall, fall, hit 'em smash."

Skoric bought a second Taylorcraft, a newer model with a 65-h.p. engine. He took this plane to Alaska and flew it out of Nome—but not for long. One windy day he tried to land at Bluff on a narrow beach with a cliff at each end.

"Well I got too much air speed, gotta get 'em slower.

"I glide down. I keep looking. I got 'em sixty. I got 'em fifty. Now I got 'em forty.

"Then I got no air speed.

"Then I got no airplane.

"Wind tips tail, swings it in da ocean, I got to swim to shore."

Today Skoric is planning to buy another airplane.

"Pusher type, that's what I get now, little bit of motor on top in back, like little eggshell, so light, so simple, nothing to it. Dat's the only thing for our country. No wind in face, no oil on windshield, can open it, stand up, look around, figure things out. I want to hunt da big wolves. Plane you can just tie 'em up anywhere, leave 'em; dog team you got to feed 'em every day. I'm getting old. I want to just fly around, fly around, take life easy."

There has never been a pilot in Alaska like Henry Kroll, the "Mad Trapper." Kroll is heavy-set. He has a crop of shaggy blond hair and a fine tenor voice. When he was a boy of thirteen in the States he got a job as a one-man band in a circus. Later he went to work in a steel mill, figured out a trick way of unloading gondolas which he sold to his boss. Then he moved to Alaska to prospect and trap.

He arrived one night at Cordova and signed for a room in the Northern Hotel.

"I'm the Mad Trapper," he told the desk clerk. "That's all you need to know tonight."

The name stuck.

The Mad Trapper has been out in the hills alone so much Alaskans say he knows how the animals think. He is tough and powerful. He can handle anything—even a live wolverine, one of the fiercest animals for its size there is. When Dr. Will Chase of Cordova wanted some live wolverines to sell to a zoo Henry Kroll went out in the hills and caught three.

He forced splints in their mouths, muzzled them and brought them all back to town at once.

"There he come, walkin' down the street with all three of 'em, nobody could believe their eyes. He was pushin' one ahead of him on a long pole, pullin' the second on a dog chain—the third, it was ridin' on his back in a sack, strugglin' and growlin'. Henry got mad at the one in the sack. He turned his head. 'What's the matter, you bastard?' he snapped. 'You're ridin', ain't you?' "

The Mad Trapper is more than tough. Maybe he's mad, his friends say, but they wish they had a mind like his. "Never went to college—but Henry is an inventor, everything he tries he goes at hammer and tongs. In a way he is a genius."

Once he decided to build a machine to grind gold. He bought books on hydraulics and made himself an arrastra from a bicycle wheel, the rear axle of an auto and an old fire hose. It was the only one in the North; "two rocks hangin' in a cement pit, geared to waterpower, turnin' and turnin'—the damn thing worked." He built another machine to recover gold from mossy creek banks—"gadget with teeth in a box—run by rope and pulley, tearin' the moss apart like a big comb." It wasn't very efficient, his helper Leon Vincent says—but it worked, too.

In 1937 the Mad Trapper decided to get a plane so he could hunt wolves and coyotes and look for quartz outcroppings from the air.

He went Outside and bought a pusher type Curtiss Wright, Jr. He had one flying lesson; the instructor refused to take him up a second time, so he soloed without further help. Returning to Alaska, he decided to base at the cannery town of Seldovia.

The Mad Trapper was a mad flyer—"would come in low overtown, idle the engine, play a banjo and sing and yell to people in the streets." But he logged 500 hours and had only one bad wreck. He even went to Anchorage to take a test for a license. Five men took the exam that day but he was the only one who passed it. A government inspector said he was a natural-born pilot.

He handled his plane as he handled a wolverine—nothing fazed him. Once he landed his plane on a mountainside on wheels and left it a few days while he went prospecting. When he returned the snow had fallen too deep for wheel take-off. He hiked ten miles to timber line, chopped trees and whittled out a pair of skis. Still he couldn't make it. He pushed and dragged his plane a long way till he found a wind-swept slope—and soared into the sky. On the way home his engine quit. It was the first time he'd ever flown on skis but he made a perfect forced landing on a sand beach. After this trip he built himself a pair of skis which could be strapped onto the wheels in a matter of minutes.

He was proud of his flying. When a sailor laughed at his little ship and kicked it he ran after him in a rage and beat him up. But the Mad Trapper was a pilot for only two years. One day his plane was smashed in a windstorm and he decided he was through with aviation. He hiked back to town and built a floating cannery.

William Dunkle, a tall, gray-haired, dignified man, is one of the leading citizens of Anchorage. He has lived in Alaska thirty-six years. He worked a while as engineer and assayer for a copper company, then managed a small gold mine near Anchorage called the Lucky Shot. In 1932 Dunkle soloed, went to the States and bought a three-place Travel Air. He started for Alaska in it but cracked up at Warren, Pennsylvania—right in front of a football game.

He bought a sister ship and started again. This time he

reached Alaska and became the first commuting mine-owner in the North. He also bought more planes and traveled around Alaska looking at prospects. He flew the Travel Air 800 miles on floats—all the way from Anchorage to the Arctic town of Shungnak—in search of asbestos.

Once, taking off from Spenard Lake, Dunkle landed in the trees, broke a Travel Air to pieces. Once, at Slippery Creek, just beyond Muddy Glacier, he took off uphill in a Stinson— didn't make it—smashed a wing. Once as he was flying over mountains the motor quit right above the summit of a range. He landed on a glacier, tried to repair the engine and took off, but he had three more forced descents on the way home. "These deadstick landings," he says, "are not so good."

Altogether Dunkle has logged 2,000 hours, spent $100,000 on aviation, bought eight planes, suffered eight crackups.

Aged sixty, he plans to buy another plane soon. "I wouldn't own a ship Outside," he says, "but this country is easy to fly in."

Many old-timers have tried to become pilots. One has built a full-fledged aviation business which has been important for many years. His name is Archie Ferguson.

18

Archie Ferguson

"NOME RADIO, Nome Radio," the pilot yelled. "This is Cessna Two Zero Seven Six Six. Christ, it's startin' ta rain up here! Looks like some awful dirty stuff ahead. I'm comin' in! I'm comin' in! Gimme yer weather in the clear!"

The operator on the ground gruffly reminded him that Alaskan wartime weather information must, except in cases of extreme urgency, be broadcast in code. "Cessna Two Zero Seven Six Six," he asked, "do you declare this an emergency?"

"Yer damn right!" returned the pilot. "Yer damn right it's an emergency! Christ, any time I'm in the air it's an emergency!"

It happened. Archie Ferguson is one of the craziest pilots in the world. "But crazy like a fox," Alaskans say. "You have to know Archie."

All over the northland, wherever planes fly, stories about Archie Ferguson fly too. All over the northland people are talking and laughing about him. "Say, did you hear the latest on Archie? . . . Heard a good one on Archie last night. . . . Listen to what that little devil done now." When Archie radioed that he had sighted a Jap submarine moving north along the Arctic coast the Army took his observation seriously—but not too seriously—for he is always seeing and doing things which rock the imagination of the average man.

Gnarled and dumpy, with fat cheeks and friendly eyes, Archie looks very much like one of the Seven Dwarfs. Aged fifty-two, he has lived in Alaska since he was a boy. For many years he trapped muskrats, mined gold and mushed dogs. He married a full-blooded Eskimo. Later he decided to become a pilot and, basing at Kotzebue beside the Arctic

Sea, he pioneered the farthest-north flying service under the American flag.

FERGUSON AIRWAYS, he proudly advertises, ANY-WHERE, ANY TIME. The name is splashed in huge white letters on the side of his chalk-red wooden hangar. His single-engine Cessna, ordered from the States, once belonged to Paul du Pont. "Ya know du Pont, that powder magazine boy?" he explains, "he sure had her rigged up nice. Nawthin's too good for me and the millionaires."

Archie owns several ships—Cessnas, Stinsons and a Waco. He and his staff, serving a large area around Kotzebue, sell more than $50,000 worth of air transportation a year. Ferguson Airways seldom flies as far north as Barrow but Archie, like Sig Wien, reaches Arctic settlements hundreds of miles from the nearest standard road or railroad. Archie did an important war job, freighting for strategic mineral surveys, airport construction and mapping projects. The "Little Man," as he is affectionately nicknamed, is a big name at the top of the continent. But he goes about his business in the prankish manner of a clown:

The late Lieutenant General Buckner, when he was in Alaska, declared he considered Archie Ferguson the greatest comic character he had ever known. Airline captains from the States, meeting Archie, are amused, amazed, and somewhat annoyed. "Maybe he's a pilot," one remarked, "but he shouldn't be." Alaska has produced a flock of rugged and colorful airmen, but Archie is in a class by himself.

"Christ," he says, with a broad, toothless grin, "I sure love ta fly." He captains his Cessna with a kind of frantic enthusiasm, shouting so loud over his radio that operators at airways ground stations must tune down their receivers to save their eardrums. Time and again he has been asked to lower his voice, to make his reports formal and brief. He does not seem to understand.

He monopolizes the circuit for twenty minutes at a time, giving a mile-by-mile account of his lone journeys. If he fails to receive a response from one station he twirls the dial in a frenzy of annoyance, calling several others. "Jeezus," he snarls, "don't ya fellers never keep yer radios on?" Hearing another pilot aloft he will defy air regulations and babble a line of profanity and gossip to him. "When ya goin' Outside, Frank? Say, I hear Woodley's got a Boeing. Christ, I wish I could get a Boeing! Wonder if I could fly a Boeing? Where ya at now, Frank? Jeezus, she's blowin' up here! How's the weather over there?"

"Ya hear that noise?" he yelled one day to the station at Nome. "Christ, that ain't static; that's a bear. Yeah, I gotta bear in the plane with me, and he's broke loose. He's climbin' right up here beside me, growlin' 'n' showin' his teeth—big sharp teeth! . . . Oh, Jeezus, he's tryin' ta eat up the fuselage. There's two of us up here now, but it looks like purty soon there's only gonna be one 'n' it ain't gonna be me. Stand by, I'll call ya every other minute."

No one was surprised when he reached his destination safely. Narrow escapes like this are routine with Archie. Rumor spread, Alaska style, that the bear was at the controls as the Cessna slid onto the runway. "The best landing," someone wisecracked, "Archie Ferguson ever made."

He hauled this bear on a sudden impulse, planning to keep it as a pet. "Oh, Jeezus," he recalls, "when I picked him up at Point Hope he looked real tame like a dog. I led him on a rope—jest a cub, ya know. The Eskimo there said: 'Now Whitey yer goin' away, not see ya no more, be a good bear.' Gee he was sad, that boy.

"When I threw the damn bear in the plane he began ta git mad. I tied him down but soon as we hit some rough air he broke loose. Boy, I was travelin' along at three thousand feet 'n' he come up 'n' growled at me—*Grrrrrrr, Grrrrrrr*, oh *Jeee*zus! But when we got out o' rough air he quieted down 'n' we made it okay. I sure made a purty landing! He jumped right out 'n' Christ ya should 'a' seen the Eskimos scatter!"

A tame trip is irksome to Archie. An incurable practical joker, he likes to frighten passengers by switching off the gas, momentarily, in mid-air. He especially likes to frighten women schoolteachers newly arrived from the States. "We're comin' ta the Arctic Circle!" he will shout like a sight-seeing bus-driver.

"Can we see it?" they eagerly ask.

"Naw ya can't see it," he tells them, "but ya'll sure know

when we hit it. The engine'll quit—there's no air in that
damn circle for eight hundred feet."

More than one teacher has screamed as he slyly cut the
motor. He never tires of this trick. "Oh boy, I'd oughta teach
school myself," he says, shaking with laughter. "At least I got
more learnin' than that."

Archie has a high, rasping laugh, and shakes with mirth till
the tears roll down his cheeks. "He loves a lot of things,"
Alaskans say, "but nothing so much as laughter." Archie does
not talk, but cackles, like Donald Duck. He does not walk,
but half-runs, half-hobbles wherever he is going. On the
ground and in the air his nervous energy is inexhaustible.
"He will fly three hundred miles," a Nome businessman told
me, "ask three hundred questions, answer them all himself
and fly three hundred miles back."

I first met Archie on the main street of Fairbanks. "Ya
wanta fly with me ta Kotzebue?" he asked. "I ain't got
nawthin' but a load o' candy. Jeezus, I gotta go ta the depot,
I gotta go git some freight, I gotta see if I got any passengers. Ya wanta fly with me ta Kotzebue? Ya wanta buy a
parky? I got some nice parkys, all built nice, ya wanta buy
one? Christ, I love ta fly." Before I could answer he was off
down the street darting into a bakery.

When I traveled to Kotzebue for an interview with Archie
I made the trip with another pilot. It was past midnight when
we reached the shoreline of the top of America. A red June
sun blazed low above the Arctic ice as we dropped toward a
straggle of specks at the edge of the land. "Kotzebue," the
pilot told me. Slipping in past a row of antennae poles, we
bumped onto the narrow dog-leg strip of the Ferguson Airways field. Eskimos in gaily colored calico parkas came
crowding about the plane. Among them, wearing rumpled
pants and a sport blouse open at the neck, stood Archie.

"What's the matter, Harry?" he yelled, slapping the pilot
on the back. "Can't ya land a plane no better'n that? Jeezus
she was blowin' over by the Hogg River today, stronger'n
that plane would fly! Oh Christ, that was a blower, so rough,
she was blowin' me right backward toward Siberia!" Suddenly he noticed me. "So ya come ta see us?" he cried. "That's
fine, that's fine! Come 'n' have some coffee! Christ I like

coffee, but it sure don't help me ta sleep. Ya wanta see my boats?"

The Eskimos smiled broadly as he trotted along a sandy path and I tried to keep pace. All the people in town seemed to be up and about on this bright, warm summer night, wandering among the tumbledown turf-topped huts. "The ice is jest breakin'," Archie jubilantly shouted over his shoulder. "The whales'll be comin' in purty soon. Oh Christ the summer's come! Listen ta that ice!"

It was a loud noise, crunching of floes and hissing of slush. The white mass glittered and shone in the ruddy glow to the far horizon. "Boy, it's nice here," Archie mused, as we gazed out across the polar sea. "Not too hot, and in summer the sun never goes down. She's up all day 'n' she's up all night 'n' the kids play till they fall on the ground 'n' go ta sleep!"

He saw a large cat sitting in the grass. He lunged toward it. The animal leapt away. "Christ," he shouted, "I gotta git a cat for a guy. . . . I'll give ya a dollar," he told an Eskimo, "if ya'll git me that pussy. Oh *Jeeee*zus, where the hell is it at?" He hurried on past fish racks and driftwood. "I got seven lighters 'n' two tugs," he told me. "The Airways is only one o' my lines. I own the whole Kobuk River. Christ, the whole country is workin' fer me. Boatin' I git two cents a pound, flyin' I git two bits. Ya wanta see my store?"

A cowbell jangled as we entered his spick-and-span trading post. Furs, calico, tents and groceries were piled neatly on the shelves. A box of matches cost twenty-five cents. A candy bar fifteen. "We do business in trade money," Archie said. He showed me a large coin marked FERGUSON STORES. "I got three stores," he said. "This'n 'n' one at Kiana 'n' one at Selawik." He led me into an office where a grandfather clock and old-fashioned painted safe were reminiscent of doughty corporations in New England. "Lookit this quartz," he shouted, picking up a large paperweight. He ran his knotty hand over the smooth-polished surface. "If they'd make a few mountains like that we wouldn't hafta worry. Jeezus, wouldn't that make a swell place ta land?"

He ran out the door and I followed him to his green wooden house. "All built with six-by-six timbers," he told me, "from our own sawmill. This damn place is strong." The large living room was cluttered with radios, shovels, duffel bags, parkas and freight. Hanging by the stove was a Ferguson Airways calendar, illustrated with a painting of a voluptuous nude. "How d'ya like that?" he asked. "I sent that to the president o' United Airlines 'n' he told a guy no *wonder* Ferguson Airways has a lot o' business with passengers like that! . . . But I usually have monkeys on my calendars," he added with an air of grave confidence. "I love pictures o' monkeys. The travel man saves 'em for me every year."

We sat down at a linoleum-covered table as a pretty young Eskimo girl appeared. "We want lots o' coffee, Flo-Flo," he told her, "lots o' coffee." She had just served it, with bread and cheese, when there was a knock at the door. "Come in!" Archie yelled. A small dusky boy entered, hauling a load of ice. "Okay, Isaac," Archie sternly told him, handing him a quarter. "Go 'n' buy yourself some candy 'n' be sure ya go ta my store." "Yes, sir," said the boy, softly.

No sooner had he departed than there was another knock. "Come in!" Archie yelled again. Three rough-clad men, Bureau of Mines geologists, entered the room. "There y'are," Archie shouted. "I wondered where the hell ya zulus went. We'll run ya over ta Kobuk in the mornin'. Now what d'ya want from my store? I tell ya what yer gonna need. Some eggs 'n' bacon 'n' potatoes 'n' salt pork. Ya got any Stayaway? Oh Jeezus, the mosquitoes are gettin' good 'n' big! Come 'n' set down 'n' have some coffee."

Clippings and pictures of airplane wrecks lined the walls of the room. There was a broken propeller nailed over each of the doors. Archie saw me looking at them. "They say I got more crack-ups than any pilot in Alaska," he amiably explained, "but I ain't killed nobody yet. Oh gosh, I wouldn't do that." He began to laugh. "Ya wanta fly with me ta Shungnak?"

I made elaborate excuses. "Christ," he insisted, "we'll have a nice trip! Awful purty country over there." Shungnak, he told me, was located 175 miles up the Kobuk River. There was a C.A.A. radio station there and an Eskimo village nearby. "What's the matter with ya?" he challenged when I still demurred. He seemed sad. "Oh *Jeez*us, here yer writin' a book on aviation 'n' ya don't even have no faith in it!" I told him I would like to go.

We returned late. I was wakened very early by violent rapping on my door. "Christ," Archie yelled, "ain't ya never gonna get up?" I found him shaving in his living room with an electric razor. "Ain't that sumpin' ta have in the Arctic?" he chortled. "Gotta Disel motor 'n' pump works it. Jeezus, it wakes up everybody in town. I gotta shower too, boy she r-e-e-e-ly works! Everything I got is the latest ya can get. Christ, I like ta get up early in the mornin'!"

I looked out the window. The day had an evil look. Fog hung low above the roofs. Blowing sand raced along the path.

"Are you going to Shungnak?" I asked tentatively.

"Yer damn right," he replied. "We'll be takin' off right away." Flo-Flo gave me coffee and bread. Archie gulped some coffee and paced back and forth between the table and the door. "I never eat no breakfast," he told me. "Hurry up!" Although it was a warm, muggy day, he insisted on helping me into one of his fur parkas. "Ya sure look swell in that," he exclaimed, trotting outside.

I followed him to his black and yellow single-engine Cessna. "This is a Cessen," he told me. "I paint all my ships black 'n' yaller," he added as the Eskimos untied the ropes. "They show good, yer damn right." I climbed in beside him and he started the engine. We jounced to the end of the strip and turned. "See?" he yelled, "I can taxi!" A roll of mist swirled before us. The engine roared loud, we bumped down the runway and rose past a graveyard into the sky.

"There ya are," he shouted over the racket of the motor. "Don't I know my stuff?" Smiling delightedly, he grabbed the headphones and fitted them to his ears. His stubby hands jerked as he adjusted the power. "Kotzebue Radio, Kotzebue Radio," he yelled. "This is Cessen Two Zero Seven Six Six. I'm jest takin' off fer Shungnak. Jest headin' over Kobuk Lake. Everythin's all o-o-o-kay, all o-o-o-kay. Call ya again in a few minutes. Roger!"

He whistled as we flew low under fog. Soon the water below us changed to swampy green-speckled tundra and we began to follow a wide muddy river. Countless streams and little lakes glimmered beyond. "Sure a lot o' rivers, ain't they, huh?" he said, well pleased. "The Kobuk's got eighty mouths out on the flats. Gee, I can make this baby talk! Ain't this nice now?" Every few minutes he called in to Kotzebue. "I'm o-o-o-kay!" he repeatedly screeched, as if this were something remarkable. "I'm all o-o-o-kay! We're rollin' right along! Yer comin' in sweet, Gray. I'm makin' purty good time."

There was no sign of life beneath us but the Arctic wilds made a curiously civilized pattern: pointed trees were grouped along the river banks as precisely as if they had been landscaped by an architect. As we flew inland we left the fog behind; the sky was blue, the earth had a soft greenish cast. He twirled the dial to another frequency. "Selawik Radio, Selawik Radio," he yelled. "Ya there, Hadley? Okay, Hadley, I'm on my way ta Shungnak. Did ya get any more mushrats? I'll be over, say, I got a load ta put inta Noorvik fer the Bureau o' Mines, yeah, I want ya ta find out how's the condition there 'n' give it to me, yeah, that's right, Hadley, 'n' I'll call ya again. O-o-o-kay, Hadley, o-o-o-kay!"

"That's my wife," he explained. "She runs one o' my aer'nautic stations. Damn fine woman. There ain't a white can copy code any better'n she can. Hadley's smart too. Oh Christ, it's hot taday, gosh I'm thirsty, I wish I had a watermelon. Jeezus, I love watermelon!" He began to whistle again.

We were passing low mountains now, a jumble of shaggy peaks in shades of blue and brown. "This is sure nice country," he told me. "I got a sheep ranch up in the Noatak. God had nawthin' to do so he built me a runway. Land on a big flat bench five thousand foot long. All I gotta do is step out 'n' shoot the sheep. Nice cold stream runnin' out o' the hill, I fish for grayling on one side, hunt on the other, oh boy, nobody else knows where it's at!"

Laughing complacently to himself, he twirled the dial again. "Kotzebue Radio, Kotzebue Radio," he yelled. "I'm stickin' purty close to the Kobuk. Christ, there's so much static I can't hear a thing yer sayin'. I'm gonna work Shungnak. O-o-o-kay, Gray. Roger." He turned to me. "Christ, this is a big country up here 'n' it's all full o' minerals. Someday we're gonna have a big stampede 'n' I'll be flyin' all day 'n' all night. Jeezus, the gold is bound ta go higher, how else we gonna pay off the goddamn war debt? See that mountain over there, that big green mountain? The whole damn thing is jade. We sure got a rich country. Right over there, all green, Christ don't ya see it? Y'oughta have a color test made on yer eyes."

He turned indignantly to his radio. "I'm jest a little north o' the sandblow," he told the Shungnak station. "Guess we'll be there purty soon." To our south a weird expanse of gray appeared on the face of the land. "That's a sandblow," he told me. "It's all sand over there, trees is all blew away. Great big sandblow, eight mile long by three, all covered o' stumps, Jeezus ya can see holes all through that damn thing— ya can't land an airplane on nawthin' like that!"

The plane lurched. It lurched again. As we proceeded the air became rougher. "They say at Shungnak if I go up," he mused, "I'll get out o' this blower. Well, we'll find out if they're lyin'." The Cessna steadily rose. "We're *climb*in' up the Kobuk!" he shouted, "*climb*in' up the Kobuk! Lookit her go up, that's a little baby, lookit her climb, she's really goin' upstairs now! Don't ya worry, ya know they designed these airplanes for wind, that's why they put wings on 'em."

He whistled a few more notes and began to sing. *"Jest in case I love ya!"* he idly chanted, off key, in his cracked falsetto voice. *"Jest in case I do! I love ya little darlin', I love ya little dear! Ya'll always be my sweetheart, no matter WHAT they say!"* Then, abruptly, he stopped. Raindrops were spattering against the windshield. Soon we were flying through a gray drizzle with fog rolling all around. He began complaining over his radio. "Oh, Christ!" he told Shungnak, "we're runnin' inta some awful dirty weather. Jeezus, it's hot in this airplane!"

"What's the ceiling at Shungnak?" I asked.

"Oh I dunno," he said. "Must be okay, they said ta come on in. I'm so rumdum from all the coffee I've had I don't know what I'm doin'." He glanced at my face. "Don't ya worry, honey," he told me kindly, "I'll set ya down nice 'n' easy. Nice 'n' easy."

He did. He made a good landing at Shungnak and we

returned safely that afternoon to Kotzebue. He started out immediately on another trip that evening. *"Nawthin'* to it," he told me. *"Nawthin'* to it! Christ, I love ta fly!"

Archie, with his parents and a brother named Warren, arrived in Alaska in 1917. "Times was bum Outside 'n' Papa read some story so we hit north." He has been to the States only three times since, visiting Seattle to buy boats and store supplies. "God it's awful out there," he says, scowling at the recollection. "I started across the street 'n' nearly hit seven cars. Oh Christ, so much noise I couldn't sleep, I couldn't do *nawthin'*."

On one of these visits a friend drove him down Seattle's main street and they went through a traffic signal. "What's the matter with you?" snarled a policeman. "Didn't you see the color of that light?" "Yer damn right," Archie snarled back. "It was bright red." So many things confused him in Seattle that although he had planned to remain a month he returned to Kotzebue after five days. "I shouldn't 'a' even stayed that long," he says. "Up here at least a man's his own boss. Oh God, I'd die Outside."

The Ferguson family traveled from Nome far into the Arctic looking for gold. They operated a mine at California Creek. "I used ta run a nozzle on the Giant," Archie says. "Oh God I liked that." They traveled many hundreds of miles by dog team. "Jeezus, the snow got deep 'n' we had nice great big dogs." Archie also hauled freight along the Kobuk River in a homemade scow. "It's a long, long ways up the Kobuk in a boat, yer damn right. I'd never hardly sleep. Drunk coffee ta stay awake. Christ, every year the channel changes, gittin' wider 'n' shorter. Once I got stuck on a bar for three weeks, but when she raises she raises fast. I sure liked ta run the river!" He trapped, too, in the Colville River region. "I sure liked that. I'd skin the Eskimos, damn right, I was good, really went ta work 'n' caught a lot o' foxes. Hardly a year I wasn't the high man."

In 1919 Archie was married by a missionary to Hadley Wood, grand-daughter of the chief of the Kobuk Eskimos, in the Friends' Church at Shungnak. Warren also took an Eskimo wife. The Fergusons, a restless and hard-working clan, pioneered importantly in this part of Alaska. They built a sawmill and opened several trading posts and a mink farm. They started the first and still the only civilian movie house north of the Arctic Circle. They brought the first automobile, an International "pickup," to their part of the country and rode it up and down the sea ice between villages. They also imported the first motorcycle and the first cow.

Archie is pleased when he tells about most of these achievements, but thought of the cow fills him with wrath. "She was a good cow," he says. "Gee, we shipped in alfalfa 'n' the milk was rich. I wanted to get her a partner 'n' raise a herd." He sent to the States for a bull, but his dream of expansion was frustrated. When the steamer arrived a small calf came trotting down the gangplank. "Oh Christ, only ten months old. We didn't git a damn bit o' milk after he arrived!"

The family also pioneered in radio. In 1932 Archie and Warren hitched a Ford spark and battery to an aerial, their Eskimo wives learned code, and they all went on the air. Other "hams" joined them and an uproar of gossip crackled from Arctic towns. "It was swell," Archie says. "We was all in a mood for it." However the unlicensed sets were so powerful that they drowned out reception all over Alaska. It was not long before the United States Marshal had them silenced.

Warren, by all accounts, was the business head of the Ferguson empire. He had all of Archie's energy, harnessed by an orderly mind. Warren built shrewdly. But his Arctic career came to a tragic end. In 1939, as he was driving over the frozen sea, his automobile dropped through thin ice and he was drowned. His body and those of his parents, marked by elaborate tombstones, rest in a graveyard at Kotzebue. Archie, sole survivor, has fallen heir to the family enterprises.

The Little Man is as reticent about his finances as a Wall Street executive. "Christ," he airily replies when questioned about them, "I make plenty o' money. I don't do anythin' fer nawthin'." By informed estimates, he grosses some $200,000 a year from all his operations. Little more than a quarter of this comes directly from "The Airways," as he calls his flying service. But The Airways means everything to him.

No civilian pilot in Alaska, government records show, has put in longer hours aloft than this high-strung, erratic little sourdough. In summertime he has averaged well over the hundred-hours-a-month maximum allowed airline pilots in the States; one month he totaled 185. On a stormy day, when it is impossible for him to make a trip, he will climb into his plane and buzz dizzily round and round above the village. "Christ," he says, "I dunno, somehow in a plane I feel differ'nt. I'd go nuts if I couldn't fly."

He got the aviation idea from his ski-equipped motorcycle, which hurtled over the winter sea ice at a speed of forty-five miles an hour. "Christ, Hadley 'n' I'd put on our nice parkys 'n' ride between towns. It was a great big police model, a Harley. Jeezus, we had a lot o' fun with that thing!" One sub-zero day he stopped short just in time before an open crack four feet wide. Confidently, he built a snow ramp on the ice and froze it. He tied a log to the cycle in case it dropped through. Then he told his wife to stand beside the crack. He drove away and roared back toward her with the engine wide open. "I hopped right over 'n' lit ten foot on the other side. Jeezus, I was re-e-ely flyin' then!"

Archie had his first plane ride with Noel Wien in 1926 in a Standard. The Little Man was badly frightened. "Wien looped me 'n' I purty near fell out. Christ, I was so scared I couldn't get my hands loose from the sides of that plane." From this time on, however, he could talk of little but The Aviation. Visitors report that he kept them awake half the night "cackling and cackling about a bunch of planes." In 1931 the Fergusons spent four thousand dollars for a Great Lakes trainer and another thousand dollars to have it shipped from the States by boat. They hired Pilot Chet Browne of Colorado, whose name they had seen in a magazine ad, to teach Archie how to fly.

Browne gave Archie sixty hours of instruction. He would have given him still more—but Archie's impatience won out. "Christ," he complained, "ain't ya never gonna solo me?" On the great day Browne hid an alarm clock under the seat and set it to ring in ten minutes. "Go right up over town," he told Archie. "Climb to a thousand feet and circle around and be sure and take your time." Archie flew steadily, circled smoothly till the alarm went off. Then his plane banked crazily and went into a steep dive as he forgot the controls and tried to climb under the seat to locate the noise. "Oh *Jeezus*," he relates. "I was scairt, I thought it was some kind of a signal." He managed to regain control but was so unnerved that he came down on a sand bar instead of returning to the field.

Archie's shrewd, soft-spoken Eskimo wife was not enthusiastic about her husband's flying. "That's one thing," she says, "I didn't encourage him in." His first trip with a passenger hardly reassured her. Archie set out in great excitement with a miner named Jimmy Donovan for Shungnak. "Christ," he recalls, "that guy must 'a' had on four suits o' underwear 'n' three suits o' pants. I could hardly stuff him in the cockpit. I come down ta land at Shungnak on a smooth place in the river but Jeezus I missed it 'n' hit on the next bend. If he hadn't 'a' had so many clothes on I'd 'a' killed him fer sure."

Archie's parents, then living at Shungnak, were always terrified when they heard him approaching to land. He scolded them bitterly after his first crack-up. "I couldn't tell the wind. I told Mother when I came back to be sure 'n' put up a sock or make some smoke fer me. Christ, next time I went over 'n' buzzed the store she made that fire damn quick 'n' I landed fine. I went in 'n' Papa was askin' her 'Where's my new pants?' They couldn't find 'em nowhere. 'Oh dear,' she told Papa, 'ya know I betcha I burned 'em, I musta used 'em to make Archie's smoke with!' Jeezus she was so scairt, she burned up his nice new pants—oh Christ! Poor Papa!"

The Fergusons went into the aviation business in a big way. They purchased more planes and some expensive radio equipment. "I figger," Archie says, "that money's sumpin' to buy with. But I wish they'd hurry up with that damn television so I wouldn't have ta buy blind." More pilots were hired to instruct Archie and to fly the ships. "I've been trained by experts," he boasts. "I've had an awful lot o' instructors but I still need a lot more."

A surprising number of Alaska's younger pilots have, at one time or another, worked for Archie. "The Ferguson College of Technical Knowledge," they call his operation. He pays well, on a commission basis. "I want 'em ta steal passengers. Christ, we love ta steal passengers!" In summer weather a Ferguson Airways pilot has made fifteen hundred dollars a month—nearly twice as much as Alaska Airlines, the north's largest local operator, would have paid him in salary. But turnover has been high. This is not only because of the hazards of coastal Arctic flying. There are other drawbacks.

The Little Man is strict. He does not smoke, never drinks anything stronger than beer, and frowns on such habits in his men. "*Nawthin*' runs a guy down," he snaps, "like boozin'." Always an early riser, he expects the same of his pilots. He will rouse them from their beds in wintertime long before it is light enough to fly. "Oh, *Jeee*zus!" he will wail, if one does not appear when he is called. "Oh Christ!"—pacing the floor and looking out into pitch darkness with the sun still to rise. "That zulu's still snoozin' 'n' we have a trip ta make. Christ, we'll jest have ta cancel out, that's all, 'n' such a nice day too."

Archie's pilots work hard, but none can keep up with him. "God," he will say. "Think o' that, they actually made a trip." He is driven to distraction when one of his men is weather bound away from Kotzebue. "Christ," he will yell over the radio, with other airway stations listening, "I suppose yer boozin' or God knows what yer doin'. The weather's fine here. Come on back!" He is enraged if one of the pilots muffs a take-off from Kotzebue's frozen winter runway. He will stand by the field jumping, hitching up his pants, shouting, and swearing. "Christ, hurry up! I'm losin' five hundred bucks a day! Oh *Jeez*us, I guess I'll have ta do all the flyin' myself!"

Archie's pilots do not care to travel with him. Harry Swanton, newly arrived in the North, was caught in fog as he hauled the Little Man toward Nome. Treetops flashed past the windows. "Okay," Archie told him, "ya got an instrument rating, fly her on instruments." Swanton tried to comply but could not orient himself to the Nome radio range. "Christ, yer headin' right back ta Kotzebue," Archie screeched as he recognized a mountain through a hole in the mists. "What's the matter with ya? Can't ya fly?" Swanton pointed to the compass. "Oh," said Archie, "that damn thing, it don't work.

I took a screwdriver 'n' give it a coupla twists but it ain't good for *nawthin'*. Christ let's git out o' here!"

Archie dislikes scientific air navigation and all that goes with it. "I can foller a dog trail awful dirty," he says, "but the beam, it's sure hard ta figger out." He was first angered during World War II when an engineer surveying for a military installation failed to recognize his Kotzebue strip as a runway and started building a transmission line right down the middle of it. The Little Man jumped in his plane, flew to see a general. The general had the work stopped. But Archie does not forget easily, and he is still continuing a vigorous one-man fight against Alaska's new airways.

Once in a while, typing rapidly with two fingers, he sits still long enough to write a letter of protest to the C.A.A. In one of these classic documents he complained about a "very dangerous obstruction near Fairbanks. . . ." "It is a bunch of radio towers," he indignantly wrote. "It seems the C.A.A. are not happy unless they can stick up a bunch of towers on the sides to the fields and on the approach to the fields. . . . The one in Fairbanks I believe is most dangerous of them all . . . built rite side of a good road that shows up in bad weather and pilots are sure to follow this road in bad weather if they get caught. . .

"Fairbanks weather was not so bad but heavy rainy swalls and was following the Chena Slough and all at once this nice road showed up. I at once got on the road and was doing fine till I saw this tower go by and I won't try to tell you how far I missed it but it was so close they nearly had no tower. . . .

"Kotzebue had a pretty nice field till the C.A.A. moved in but it is now surroned by towers, wires, etc., and it is quite a trick to get into it without losing a wing. I think the only way we are going to be able to operate a plane in Alaska if the C.A.A. keeps improving is to have underground airways . . ."

The Little Man talks bitterly of Alaska's large Army airports. "I went inta Galena," he recalls of a base on the Soviet Lend-Lease ferry route. "Some soldier told me ta call him on the down wind leg o' the beam. I said where the hell is that at? Oh, Christ, I musta been right on it, I landed okay but it took me an hour ta git out o' that place. They told me I gotta git the weather. I told 'em 'I don't need no weather, I ain't had no weather all day, God it's gonna git dark let me out o' here.' They tell me every bend in the river, what clouds ta fly between, look out fer a certain plane, oh Jeeezus! Then they give me a little piece o' paper 'n' tell me ta give it ta the clearance officer.

"I must 'a' asked ten men—nobody knew where the hell he was at. I seen a guy diggin' a ditch by the runway and I says ta him 'Will ya take this piece o' paper so I can git out o' here?' He says sure 'n' puts it in his pocket. I take off but Jeezus when I get in ta Fairbanks they jump me 'n' ask me why I left Galena without a clearance. I tell 'em I give it ta some guy, he was the only guy who would take it. Oh Christ, if I ever have ta go back there I'm gonna land on a sand bar, you bet."

Archie prefers to "run a plane" by trial and error, as he used to drive a dog team. Nor has he much use for the kind of learning that comes in books. A C.A.A. inspector once advised him to study meteorology. "Metrinology?" he snarled. "What the hell is that?" He cares nothing for the precise paraphernalia of the flying fraternity. "I never keep no logbook," he told me, "just when I crack up, that's all."

Since 1936, Archie admits, he and his pilots have demolished at least ten planes and had so many accidents that he cannot begin to count them. Archie has had more crack-ups than any of his men. "But don't ya think," he boasts, "it's got me worried. I never git hurt in a wreck. Ya gotta know how to do it."

He was badly hurt three years ago when he flew a Cessna into the ice in a snowstorm. The ship crashed violently and a thirty-six-pound battery missed Archie by inches as it hurtled out the windshield. "I sure scattered that plane," he says ruefully. "All that was left was one ski 'n' the fuselage." His back was fractured, he bit a large chunk out of his tongue and he was so frightened that he refused to board a rescue plane—preferring, despite his injuries, a slow, rough journey home by dog team.

But few of his crack-ups have been major ones. "The main thing in flyin'," he preaches, "is airplanes are jest material 'n' ya can rebuild 'em. Pilots and passengers hafta be born." The Little Man seems to have a charmed life. The record is startling; the performance must be known at first hand to be believed. "The more I see Archie Ferguson fly," one airline veteran wryly remarked, "the less I fear an airplane."

One winter day Archie's ship, heavily loaded, approached Shungnak. The radio station warned him that the river ice was only three and a half inches thick. This did not deter him: he had landed the week before on only three inches. He came down, "sassy-like, singing a tune." The plane broke through. Several inches were broken off one blade of the wooden prop. Archie grabbed an ax and chopped off the other side to match. "Christ," he told his nervous passenger, "I'll fix this baby. We're r-e-e-e-ly gonna fly taday!"

The plane ran three miles down the river, rattling like a sawmill, before it rose aloft. "Jeeesus," he relates, "I rolled the stabilizer way ahead 'n' used the belly-flaps, 'n' the little devil went right up in the air with me. She flew me practically like a stall, till I got her up ta eighty 'n' then she stayed that way. I guess it just happened ta be right." As he gabbled over the radio, describing his predicament, operators could hardly believe their ears. "NC-18799 heard on 02042," flashed one airways dispatch, "says broke propeller, now en route to Kotzebue." He landed safely. C.A.A. inspectors, examining the stubby prop, were appalled. Incredulous that it could have supported flight, they declare it belongs in an aeronautical museum.

Archie seldom bothers to reel in his radio antenna, but lets it drag along behind him as his plane lands. "It works swell," he retorts, when criticized for this. "An airplane will do what ya make it." He proved this masterful philosophy to himself, and incidentally made aviation history, when he ran into trouble three years ago at the town of Kiana. He parked his Cessna at Kiana one summer evening on a short river bar. The water rose during the night, swirling to the belly of the plane. "Think o' that," he recalls. "My whole damn runway was gone." But he was far from stumped. "I'll take her away by boat," he told the Eskimos.

Seven dusky women helped him pull the Cessna over to the bank and haul it onto a barge. They blocked the wheels and tail. Some of the women climbed aboard for the ride. Archie mounted into the cockpit and opened the engine and the hybrid contraption roared along the river by aircraft power to the nearest field. "Talk about power!" he brags. "Ya'd oughta seen that thing walk up the river! Ten miles an hour, she made upstream. I'd cut her close 'n' let the wings clear the banks. The engine, she never got hot—I run her at 1200 'n' she stayed at 375 Farnite. I went around them bends so fast the natives thought the Japs was comin'! That rig looked like a big bulldog! I never seen an airplane done better'n that!"

Archie was one of the first pilots in Alaska to use a plane for wolf-hunting. Today the Territory pays a bounty for the skins of these predatory animals, and many flyers collect it every year. Archie, with Pilot Maurice King, first tried the challenging sport in 1935. As King flew the ship, Archie pointed a shotgun out the window toward a large wolf and fired. He hit the propeller and the ship crashed, but he remained enthusiastic. Altogether, he claims, he has killed sixteen wolves with the aid of an airplane " 'n' cracked up every time."

In the saga of the Little Man's life and flight there is no episode more characteristic than that of the profane parrot. This fateful tale is his favorite. "I jest sent Outside for that bird," he relates, "ta keep us company. Jeezus, a bunch o' sailors on the boat learned him ta swear 'n' by the time I picked him up at Fairbanks he knew every cussword in the English language. I put him in a cartoon box in the end of the plane 'n' took off with one o' my pilots, Maurice King, fer home. Christ we run inta the roughest air in my life. Maurice was flyin' 'n' fightin' the plane 'n' I was fightin' the parrot—oh *Jeeee*zus, that bird was screamin' callin' me names, sumpin' awful.

"We kep' that parrot three years before Sunday, my big lead-dog, killed him 'n' ate him up. He was purty that bird—green, ya know how they're green? But he didn't like me—I really figger he thought I tried ta kill him that day. He'd scream 'n' dive for me—no question, he didn't like me at all. But ya know that damn bird—in the end he saved my life."

It happened in 1941 when Archie, flying in foggy weather, was forced off his usual route. He cruised uncertainly among blurred hills, believing he was near the village of Hughes.

"I'll be in in ten minutes, Mrs. James," he shouted to the Hughes operator. "Put the coffee pot on."

"Okay, Archie," she answered. "Where are you?"

"Never mind where I'm at," he shouted defensively. "Put the coffee pot on."

Ten minutes later he crashed in the winter wilderness at least a hundred miles from Hughes. As the plane heaved under a load of ice, he opened the engine full throttle, heading for a clearing. One of the wings hit a tree. "Then she quit flyin'. She was in a half-turn 'n' hit flat. Christ, that's a nice way ta put an airplane in, it sure is hell on the airplane though."

The wing was sheared, the engine torn out, and Archie was knocked unconscious. His two passengers—a restaurant man and a doctor—mistook oil spattered against the windshield for blood. They believed their pilot was dead. Archie revived in time to hear them talking about this. "Christ," he relates excitedly, "I really thought I was killed, I was afraid ta open my eyes—death was so nice, so quiet! Then I come to, reached up ta shut off the switch 'n' saw it was disconnected. My darn arm was broke 'n' there we was—radio tore out, motor tore out, not much grub, twenty below zero 'n' a hundred miles from anywhere."

The party was down in one of the bleakest, remotest parts of Alaska—"mountains all over, all low timber, no lakes or nawthin' there. God that's lonely country 'n' there wasn't even no rabbits around, the snow was so deep." There was only one sleeping bag in the plane, only one pair of snowshoes, no gun and little food. Most serious: search parties had only a false clue to the wreck's location. But Archie was cheerful as usual. He began building snow houses and chopping trees. "Christ, fellers," he said as soon as the weather cleared, "we're in too deep here. We can't get over the divide. Best thing we can do is to git a bear 'n' kill it with an ax."

He found a ring of iced bushes which marked the "breather" of a bear hole. "Come on," he told his dubious passengers. He gave the snowshoes to one, the ax to another, and they wallowed through the deep drifts. They cleared away the brush "so them bears could come right out ta battle." Archie rammed a long stick deep into the hole and started stirring.

"Christ," he yelled, "I can feel 'em."

"More than one?"

"Oh God, yes, I can feel sometimes one, sometimes two. Now I can see 'em, the sons o' bitches, I can see their pink eyes shinin' in the dark! Oh *Jeeee*zus, here they come!"

The passengers turned and ran floundering toward the plane. Archie, stranded without a weapon, floundered hastily after them. He was indignant. They were more so. They refused to return to the animals' lair. "You've got us in enough trouble, Archie," they told him. "You're not going to get us in any more."

"The only way out," he then told them, "is the radio." Slowly but ingeniously he retraced the wires of the receiver. He found the battery in a snowdrift. He "couldn't git no call out of her" but he remembered from his boating days that a dead battery may be revived by heating it in a stove—"at least ya can git out a half-hour more." He heated theirs by a bonfire and began yelling. The frontier repair job worked: a voice came back from Fairbanks, more than three hundred miles away: "Archie, we hear you. Planes are out looking for you. What is your position?" He tried to answer but his battery went dead.

Four days and nights the men waited. The planes did not appear. "Jeezus those nights was long and we was hungry. I started dreamin' about turkeys, tables o' turkeys, Christ I'd start eatin' 'em—life was really sweet! I et so much at night I wasn't hungry in the day." Archie's passengers, however, were very hungry and as time passed, the Little Man began to have misgivings. He had heard the gruesome story of the Donner party.* "Jeezus, them two was off whisperin', that restaurant guy was a big man, had great big whiskers—Christ

---

* The Donnor party of frontiersman, crossing the Rockies toward California in 1846–47, experienced such rigors of starvation that some of the group resorted to cannibalism.

I thought maybe they was gonna eat me up. I kep' the snowshoes and laid awake all night so if they started fer me I could git away."

The fifth day Archie made another try with the battery—"If you let her lay a while she may work again." He heated it and made another call. "Tell Maurice King," he screeched, "I'm right where we had all that trouble with the parrot." The call was heard. Operators relayed the bizarre message to Pilot King. "Sure," he said, "I know where that is." Two years had passed since King's violent ride with the profane bird and the profane Little Man, but he remembered it well. He located the wreck without delay and other pilots, including C.A.A. Inspection Chief Burleigh Putnam, soon arrived for the rescue.

Archie was determined to salvage his ship, although it lay more than 200 miles from Kotzebue. On return to his base he hired a group of Eskimos with sixty dogs to drag it back. The gang had to cut slowly through many miles of virgin timber. When they reached the site they found the wreck covered with new snow. It took two days to dig it out. Altogether the expedition cost Archie $1,000.

"Sixty dogpower on it," he exultantly wrote the C.A.A., "boys sure done a fine job getting it out. . . . I am tearing her completely down and she will be as good as ever again. I hit awful hard as the big round stand on the smith greb skies, I put a one-turn twist in them. . . . I wish you people could see this ship. Motor is not hurt at all. . . . I got one spar four foot from end and I got all new parts from factory—spar, ribs etc. . . . Both skie boards were snaped off rite at bottom of smith greb stand, the boards could not keep up with the ship HA-HA. I sure know how to handle them in a crack-up HA-HA. My arm is getting along fine, only thing is a bend in it, I may have to have part of bone removed later. . . . Now I see a man has to have a real wreck to have any sence and when I see ice on my wings now I don't have to be told what to do and when I see a tree I go around it, HA-HA."

Soon after this disaster, as Archie flew with Pilot Sam Shafsky above the same forbidding region, he reached down and shut off the gas. "Oh Christ," he wailed as Shafsky frantically checked the controls, "Oh Jeezus"—peering out the window in mock terror—"lookit them trees out there, lookit that steep canyon, we're gonna crack up 'n' this time they'll never find us! We're goners!"

Long after Shafsky had started the engine Archie was chortling and punching him on the shoulder. "God," The Little Man shouted, "that was sure a close one!"

One of Archie's friends, some time after this, approached him with a solemn face.

"I think you ought to know," he told him, "that Shafsky's telling the inspectors a lot of things about your flying."

Archie's face clouded. "What's he telling 'em?"

"He says you're flying a plane without a Ph.D."

"That lousy bastard," Archie snapped. "You tell Shafsky ta keep his mouth shut. I got a lotta things just as bad I could tell on him."

It is like a comic short run off at double speed. The show never stops. But the flying of Archie Ferguson calls for more than laughter. For all his antics, The Little Man has worked both hard and usefully, risking some of the Territory's worst weather and crossing some of its loneliest wilds. American Airlines is no more important than Ferguson Airways to the people it serves. And the fact remains that none of Archie's crack-ups has taken the life of a passenger.

"Only yesterday," he proudly wrote the C.A.A. inspectors, "on a take-off in Kiana, I snapped the nut-cracker off on landing gear, and when that comes off as you know the skie is free to rotat like an auto-giro and it stopped rotating straight across which is bad for the insurance people and the blood pressure. . . .

"The ship wanted to turn to the right and as I was sure something was wrong I asked the passenger to stick his head out the window. He nearly passed out. He said the skie is sticking out the same direction as the wing which is not the way skiees should be installed. . . .

"When I approached the place for giving the insurance people a headache I had the passenger sitting beside me move back in the back end of said ship and get on my side with one more passenger. I decide to give the people of Kiana a real show. I brot the ship in on power slow as she would fly and when she was about six feet from the ground I cut off the master switch and motor prop stopped straight across. The ship stayed on the good skie as my stick was way over in the left hand side where it should not be in normal times and ship stopped without ground-looping which again shows I am a pilot regardless of what anyone else thinks of me. . . .

"I am getting along o.k. again as the sun gets higher and I can see the ground once again.

"It is sure nice to fly!"*

* A year after this was written Archie Ferguson decided to sell his airline to Sig Wien. According to those in the know, he had become discouraged by the business end of the operation. He kept his own Cessna, however. "She sure looks nice," he wrote me, "all polished up so you can see yourself in it. Nobody flies this ship but me and when you come back to Alaska I will sure take you for another ride, HA-HA."

19
New Skyways

ALASKAN AVIATION is changing fast.

During World War II the Army, Navy and Civil Aeronautics Administration spent more than $400,000,000 to build Alaska into a giant air base, and today the Territory is probably more completely equipped for flight than any land at the rim of the polar sea.

Thirty large airports and two dozen auxiliary and intermediate fields have been hacked from the wilderness. Fifty-six radio ranges and sixty-six weather-reporting and communications stations have been erected on the frosty peaks, boggy tundra and gaunt isles. For 8,000 miles the safe, guiding courses of the radio beams crisscross the northern sky, and instrument flight has become routine. During the war United Air Lines, Northwest Airlines and Western Air Lines, operating Alaskan routes for the Air Transport Command, experienced fewer weather delays than on their commercial routes in the States.

Most of the Territory's bush pilots are learning to use the new airways where possible. One has done more. A former Nome flyer, he has worked full time since 1939 to help install these devices of science. Today, as chief patrol pilot for the C.A.A., he is flying king of the entire 8,000-mile system. His name is Jack Jefford.

20
Jack Jefford

THE C.A.A. has built radio ranges all over America—in swamp and desert and on the tops of mountains—but never in a more forbidding spot than Wales, Alaska. Wales is no place to build anything. But the bleak, wind- and fog-swept Arctic town, only fifty-eight miles from the mainland of Soviet Asia, was strategic in the war. It lay on the Lend-Lease ferry route which thousands of Soviet bombers and fighters were flying from the States to Europe. So, in the winter of 1944, the range was installed.

To boss this Arctic job the C.A.A. picked a big, bearded Alaskan named Otto Nelson, one of the toughest construction men in the North and one of the most profane. Otto spoke hardly a civil word all winter. Living at Wales was rugged. The bunkhouse and cookhouse were buried in snow up to the chimneys. Otto and his gang had to dig tunnels to get in and out. Month after month the fur-clad men struggled in foul sub-zero weather. This was bad enough. Then one day the Diesel engine on which they depended for heat, light and power broke a crankshaft and "tore itself to pieces."

Otto radioed for help to C.A.A. headquarters in Anchorage, 740 miles away. The men went out over the sea ice with a tractor and tried to smooth a runway between the pressure ridges but before they were done the tractor broke down. They sent another dispatch asking for a new connecting rod. Hopefully, they marked off the edges of the unfinished runway with oil drums. For two days they swore and shivered as they waited. Then they heard the roar of a plane.

"There he is!" yelled Otto. "There's Jack!" They climbed out through the tunnel. Staring up into swirling fog, they could see nothing; but directly above there traveled the steady thunder of a ship with two engines.

"I bet," Otto growled, "he don't make it down."

The sound moved out over the frozen sea, fading until they could hardly hear it. Growing louder, it returned. The workers waited anxiously, their parkas flapping in the frigid wind. They were not disappointed. A big silver transport with orange tail and wing tips came plunging down out of the gloom.

"He must 'a' dropped through one o' them windholes," said Otto, "over by the mountain."

The plane, bucking heavy gusts, approached low over the ice.

"Hell," shouted one of the men, "he ain't even lined up with the runway!"

"He can't make it anyhow," another said. "Must be a thirty-mile crosswind."

The engines were idling as the transport floated past. Then they burst into a loud roar and the plane climbed out of sight. The sound moved away again, returned again. The plane reappeared, dropping low and gliding directly toward the narrow strip. But it did not land. Speeding past, it flew up into the fog once more and was gone.

"Sonofabitch," said Otto, whose beard was white with frost. "The bastard's going home."

But the plane returned a third time. Now the flaps were dropped. Evenly the ship descended, its right wing tipped to the wind. Just before touching, it leveled off. The wheels met the snow neatly and the plane began its run in the hundred-foot-wide path between towering ice ridges. The windward engine growled as the pilot steadied his craft against blasts which threatened to weathercock it to one side. Trailed by blowing whiteness, the transport rolled to a smooth, even stop. Both engines roared loud and ran down with a couple of chugs into silence.

One of the men whistled low. "There's a Jefford landing for you," he remarked.

Safe on the ground it sat—America's standard airliner, the DC-3. Painted on its silver side was the international-orange, winged emblem of the C.A.A., the nation's foremost civil aviation agency. This was NC-14. Resting on the sea ice, its gleaming wings almost spanning the narrow track, the Doug looked much larger than it does on LaGuardia Field. There was no loudspeaker "Announcing the arrival of American Flight Number Five at Gate Three." Only the howl of Arctic wind. There was no gate, no railed ramp, no crowd of uniformed attendants, porters and passengers hurrying for five-minute departure. Only the gang of grizzled workmen tramping through the snowdrifts, pushing close to the plane, their eyes all fastened on the door.

It snapped open from the inside and the captain of the ship stepped out. A big, rawboned man with a keen, friendly face, he was wearing an open fur parka over a pair of rumpled pants and a bright green woolen shirt. One of his mukluks was untied, his tie was askew and a few locks of his unruly black hair were fallen across his forehead. This was Jack Jefford, the hard-working, fun-loving ex-Nebraskan who is the C.A.A.'s top pilot in Alaska.

His co-pilot, grinning, curly-headed "Fuzz" Rogers, followed as the workers crowded around to shake hands.

"Shall we tie her down, Jack?" they asked. "You staying overnight?"

"No," Jefford replied in his deliberate western drawl, "I'll be going right out."

He fumbled in his pocket with the air of a schoolboy looking for a penny. "Say, Otto," he added, "I believe I've got something for you." He pulled out a mass of crumpled papers and thumbed through them till he found a letter. "Sorry," he told the others, "that's all the mail there is."

"You got the generator?" asked one of the crew.

"She's aboard," Jefford replied, flourishing his hand toward the plane. "All set to go."

A group of Eskimos came through the snow and stood about, smiling broadly. "I got a helluva big engine in here," Otto told them. "We all got to help pull her over to the station on a sled."

There was no equipment with which to unload the unwieldy 3,800-pound piece of machinery. Laying a row of oil barrels, Jefford and his helpers cribbed it with four-by-four planks till it was flush with the plane floor. The generator was too heavy to slide so, pushing and hauling, they rolled it out the door on lengths of pipe. "I brought you some meat,"

Jefford told the crew. They unloaded it, and a pile of groceries. By the time the cargo was all out the fog was pouring in still lower across the sea. The big plane shook in the wind.

"You better stay the night, Jack," Otto challenged. "Maybe you could win back that fifty bucks."

Jefford grinned, glanced at the stormy sky, looked tempted.

"I tell you," he slowly replied, "I'll be back in a couple of weeks. I have some engineers waiting at Nome and there's a load of cable at McGrath to go into Farewell."

He leaned vaguely for a moment against his shuddering ship, the wind tugging at his open parka. Then, almost automatically, his hand reached for a pocket. He began to jingle coins. Pulling out a silver dollar, he flipped it onto his wrist. "Odd man for a dollar?" he asked. "Just one time?—"

No man, it is said, can do business with Jack Jefford until he has matched a dollar with him. One usually leads to more. Jefford is happy-go-lucky. His good humor never changes. Only a silver streak in his black hair suggests that he has known tension in flight. Slow-talking, slow-moving, he goes about his work easily, as if it were some kind of a game. He is careless of dress, forgetful of time, and he has, on the ground, an air of good-natured befuddlement. But few pilots work as hard or captain their ships as meticulously. Beyond this, Jefford is one of the most versatile flyers in America.

During the war one Army general in Alaska declared he would rather ride with Jefford with one engine out through a blizzard than with most other pilots on two engines in clear and unlimited weather. This, the general explained, was not only because Jefford is an accomplished "seat of the pants" flyer, knows Alaska and can "set a ship down on a dime." Jefford is a combination rare among airmen. Expert in bush flight, he is equally expert on instruments.

Time and again at the fog-drenched air base at Nome the ceiling would be less than 200 feet, visibility less than a quarter of a mile. Long rows of bombers and fighters would stand motionless along the runways. The airdrome, so far as the Army was concerned, would be closed. Suddenly there would be a thunder of engines aloft, traveling back and forth as the pilot executed an elaborate and carefully timed instrument approach in the narrow space between mountains and radio towers. Men of the Air Forces would shake their heads. "Must be crazy. Or else it's Jefford."

Jefford, in point of time, is not one of the veteran flyers of Alaska. He did not arrive in the North until 1937. But he belongs in the ranks of the pioneers in another sense. He was one of the first bush pilots to hold an instrument rating. Working for the C.A.A., he has used his twofold skill to help build air navigation aids so that all pilots, Army and civilian, may operate more safely. As northern flight has crossed new technological frontiers, Jefford has moved in the front line, eager for hard work because he, personally, has been keen for the kind of progress that is in the making.

Construction of Alaska's airports and airways, rushed for war emergency, was divided by the Army and the C.A.A. The Army built most of the facilities in the Aleutians, the C.A.A. most of those on the mainland. It was the most formidable job the C.A.A. had ever faced—building in this land of shifting, frozen soils and steep weather extremes, this land largely unmapped and offering almost no means of ground supply. To help lay out the airways the C.A.A. needed a pilot with firsthand knowledge of Alaskan conditions. To haul workers and supplies to remote station sites it needed a pilot of bush-freighting ability. To check the functioning of the new radio beams as they went on the air it needed a pilot adept on instruments. It was lucky to find this combination in Jefford.

Son of a building contractor, Jefford grew up at Broken Bow, Nebraska, and soloed at the age of nineteen. He organized a flying club and ran an air service throughout the state with his brother Bill. In 1935 he did his first scientific work, making high-altitude weather hops in Oklahoma. Those trips, comparable to Gillam's, gave him his first experience in blind flight. He spent many hours practicing under the hood and qualified that year for a C.A.A. non-scheduled instrument rating—one of the first in the United States.

When the weather contract expired he returned to Nebraska and managed the airport at Hastings. He also barnstormed, stunted and joy-hopped. In 1937 he received a wire from a chance acquaintance offering him a job with the

Mirow Flying Service at Nome. He and his brother took the next boat north. "We had heard that aviation was important in Alaska," he explains. "People depended on it and respected it. It wasn't just a stunt business."

Like many another distinguished Arctic airman, Jefford arrived in the North with less than a dollar in his pocket. He flew out of Nome bush style for three years. One winter day, heading across a mountain range, his Gullwing Stinson was sucked down into blowing snow at the rate of 2,000 feet a minute and smacked against a peak. Jefford was uninjured but the left wing tip and landing gear of the Stinson were damaged. A sixty-mile wind rocked the ship perilously at the edge of a precipice; he had no means of tying the plane down and no snowshoes to navigate the deep snowdrifts. He spent five days and nights huddled in the cockpit before the gale abated and Pilot "Smiling Jack" Herman came to his rescue.

In another winter storm Jefford's sister-in-law and her sixteen-month-old baby were forced down with Pilot Fred Chambers in the empty Nulato country. Chambers reported by radio that their supply of fuel and rations was nearly gone. He did not know his location. Five planes searched fruitlessly till Jefford, flying at night, sighted the flash of the party's campfire. He made another outstanding "mercy" flight when he hauled Frank Alba, a prospector with a fractured leg, to Fairbanks through a night snowstorm. He navigated "Gillam style," hovering along a river, and his landing at Fairbanks was one of the most sensational the town has ever known. The blizzard was so thick that it was necessary for Gillam's mechanic, judging by the sound of Jefford's engine, to "talk" him down by radio. Gillam was so struck by Jefford's performance that he offered him a job.

Sig Wien once declined to land on an extremely short Arctic clearing. "Who do you think I am" he asked. "Jack Jefford?" The new-comer swiftly earned a place of high prestige in the North's flying fraternity. During one of his first winters in Alaska Jefford was chartered by the federal government for its first complete survey of the Territory's reindeer herds. He flew an official, Charles Burdick, far and wide across the Arctic, following the ruffled animal tracks in all kinds of weather, setting him down as close as possible to the herds and corrals. The tri-motor Stinson in which they made the expedition was one of the largest ships that had ever operated on skis in the North. Despite this fact, Jefford at no time damaged the plane although he landed it in many difficult places, often through dusk so dim he could hardly see.

Once he flew Burdick to the Akolokotuk corral, where they had a rendezvous with a group of herders. There was no safe landing place in the deep, soft drifted snow nearby. Burdick suggested that they come down on a lake several miles away and hike back. Jefford circled over the hoof-beaten surface of the corral. He hesitated. "Hell," he finally said, "I can set her down right inside." He landed the tri-motor plane into an entrance little wider than the wing-spread, stopping just short of the far end of the corral enclosure.

"One of the ruggedest flyers I've ever seen," says Burdick, "also one of the cheeriest." When the two men landed at Unalakleet one dark night, a throng of pleased Eskimos surrounded Jefford and followed him from the air strip to the trading post. "Have you got my fiddle?" Jefford genially asked Charlie Traeger, the old-time storekeeper. "We thought we would play a while." A Laplander got his saxophone, several of the Eskimos fetched accordions and guitars. Jefford started fiddling and was soon leading them in a sentimental tune. The room was full of happy, dusky-faced spectators and others crowded in the snow outside. The harmony was good, Burdick says, although Jefford was self-taught and all the Eskimos were playing by ear. Jefford still keeps his fiddle at Unalakleet and says he would rather be grounded by weather there than anywhere else.*

In 1939 Jefford made a new kind of Alaskan air history. He was the first American pilot to guide a boat systematically for any distance through the ice pack.

In June, 1939, the Alaska Steamship Company's *Columbia*, first boat of the summer, headed from Seattle toward Nome. Most of her 486 passengers were miners eager to reach

---

* When Jefford was married in 1946, he flew his bride to Unalakleet for the ceremony.

Nome for the short placer season. The people of Nome, anticipating fresh supplies, were even more eager for the *Columbia's* arrival there. But the spring had been freakishly cold and the ice pack was heaviest in forty years. The steamer dropped her anchor forty-eight miles off the mouth of the Yukon River, unable to proceed. Icebergs choked the way ahead. The first mate, climbing the mast, said the white mass of floating chunks extended as far as he could see.

Four days and nights the *Columbia* stood motionless. "Every day added to the overdue period means so much loss in vitality, health and energy of the community," lamented the *Nugget*, Nome's newspaper. Aboard the ship the miners were fretful; the delay was costing each man $20 to $30 a day. Captain A.A. Anderson was unable to sleep or eat. A towering, bluff Norwegian, "Big Andy" had traveled his route for twenty-five years and never faced such a crisis. The *Columbia's* water supply dwindled so low that he was forced to ban baths. Food ran so short that he had to break into the produce consigned to Nome. Big Andy does not ordinarily have much use for airplanes. "The Aviation," he says with salty condescension, "will not run a steamer on the water. But there was a proper time and place for a plane to do something for a ship."

At first he pinned his hopes on a Coast Guard cutter which, equipped with an amphibian, was also heading north toward Nome. But fog and ice discouraged those aboard: the cutter returned south. An Alaska pilot was the only possibility. Big Andy wirelessed an emergency appeal to Nome.

The rescue could have been accomplished with relative safety in a float plane, but there was none at Nome. Jefford agreed to make the flight on wheels in a single-engine Lockheed Vega. The plane had no radio, but a local operator rigged up a homemade broadcasting set for communication with the steamer. Jefford took off as soon as it was ready—at ten in the evening—accompanied by his brother Bill, who rode behind in the cabin with the radio. They followed the land around to the mouth of the Yukon and struck out over the sea.

When they sought to contact the *Columbia*, they found that the radio was not working. It was, by Jefford's description, "definitely a bunch of junk"—scattered over the cabin floor with the antennae trailing out the window. His brother was unable to fix it so he decided to have a try. As the Vega rushed through the air 5,000 feet aloft, he leaned backward and pushed himself through the aperture between the pilot's compartment and the cabin, leaving the controls unattended till his brother could crawl up in front. He managed to repair the radio and they exchanged places again as the ship speeded on.

They were navigating through the dim summer night entirely by dead reckoning. Jefford had marked the *Columbia's* position on a marine map but even with radio contact it was no easy matter to find her in the vast, mottled sweep of sea and ice. Calling Captain Anderson, he requested that all her lights be turned on and that all possible smoke be made. It was not long before he sighted a twinkling, puffing speck and flew to it. Passengers waved and cheered as he dropped low over the steamer's decks and rocked the Vega's wings. Heading west, he looked in vain for a break in the ice jam. He flew as long as his fuel permitted. After five hours aloft the Vega landed back on the Nome field with less than half an hour's gas in the tanks.

The next day Jefford made another try; throttling his engine down to less than fifty per cent horsepower, he stretched the flying time to seven hours. He took along an experienced Coast Guard man, Kurt Springer, to help scout the ice. The two men, after considerable exploring, discovered a wide-open lead, beginning seven miles north of the *Columbia* and extending all the way to Nome. They believed that the steamer, by following a crooked course through the channels and shoving against the smaller icebergs, could fight her way through the first seven miles to open water. Jefford so advised Big Andy.

Then began a process of navigation unprecedented in United States marine and aviation history. It was difficult: the *Columbia*, an old single-screw vessel, was not very maneuverable. It was dangerous, for she was no icebreaker: her plate was only five-eighths of an inch thick. It was complicated: while the plane was equipped for voice broadcasting, the steamer was not and Big Andy's messages had to be tapped out in code. Making repeated low passes over the *Columbia*, Jefford headed each time in the direction he thought the boat should take. He flew two miles each time, long enough for the nautical compass, resting on the floor of the plane cabin, to steady down for a reading. Springer shouted out the indicated heading and Jefford relayed it over the air to the boat. In addition, he gave Big Andy frequent advice. The ship's operator dispatched anxious queries in dots and dashes.

"How should we hit this one?" he would ask.

"Easy to the left," Jefford would reply.

"How much longer is this lead?"

"Half a mile."

They continued by this method for some time but it did not prove satisfactory. The *Columbia* crawled ahead at low speed but even so she moved too fast for co-ordination with the "seeing eye" above. Jefford, making two-mile passes and flying wide circles for his return approaches, was not able to advise the steamer closely enough. The *Columbia* rammed into an iceberg and sprang a leak. This was too much for Big Andy. He declared he could not risk his passengers' lives by proceeding.

Jefford then devised a new scheme. Circling closely above the ship, he stayed with her, scanning the ice ahead and broadcasting minute-by-minute directions. Hour after hour she moved forward, "slow as an ant," he says. It was monotonous work for the flyer, nerve-racking work for the skipper. Tempers ran short.

"The captain says you have him running around in circles," complained a dispatch from the ship's bridge.

"You tell the old man," Jefford barked, "that I can get him through here and if he don't like it he can go home."

At eight in the evening, five hours after the *Columbia* first started into the ice, she steamed into open water.

"This is it!" Jefford announced. "Straight ahead to Nome!"

He flew over her masts and rocked his wings. The *Columbia* whistled in parting salute as he opened up the Vega's engine full throttle and headed for Nome. The boat arrived safely the following day.

"It was no particular feat of navigation," Jefford comments. "We could see for twenty miles."

Big Andy has more to say about the flight. He knows that even the pilots of Alaska fear over-water trips in single-engine planes. They shun the hop to St. Lawrence Island, a matter of only some one and a half hours. Jefford, throttling his engine to low power, cruised above the maze of jagged ice and sea for nearly four. "I took my chance," Big Andy says, "and he took his. I was surprised he could direct me as well as he did. The boy is tops."

Jefford had enjoyed it, as he enjoys all technical problems. With little formal schooling, he is a scientist. Earlier than most of Alaska's pilots, he mastered the surest way to beat the treachery of fog, dark and wind. Soon after his arrival at Nome, he installed a gyro and artificial horizon in one of Mirow's ships, draped a hood around the cockpit, and flew blind on his mail trips. "It's like playing a fiddle," he explained with a grin. "You must practice and practice." With Gillam he was a pioneer of instrument flight in Alaska. But he did not rely as long as Gillam on his own blind-flying techniques. While Gillam did not secure his instrument rating till 1943, Jefford made a trip to the States, took instruction and qualified five years earlier.

When he went to work for the C.A.A. in 1940 he put this training to full use. One of his first assignments was to survey the possibilities of a coastal airway from Seattle to Alaska. At the time there were no radio ranges for a distance of 575 miles—from Vancouver north to the Annette Island base. Accompanied by C.A.A. Regional Manager Marshall Hoppin, he made this long trip over water and wilds in a twin-engine Cessna. As they approached Alaska they flew into a storm, and fog closed in behind them. In the same storm two bush pilots hovering low along the shore ran out of visibility and crashed. Jefford, ascending blind to a non-icing level of 7,000 feet, was able to proceed two and a half hours on instruments and follow the Annette beam down to safe landing.

Early in 1941, when most of Alaska lay under snow, the Army asked the C.A.A. if it could construct eleven airfields for military use that year. The C.A.A. did. By October, despite all the obstacles, military landings were possible on all eleven. There were Army officers who privately doubted that this could be accomplished. Many men contributed tirelessly for this result; but it is unlikely that it could have been accomplished without the help of a pilot like Jefford. According to W.L. Seeley, who supervised the engineering work on the airfields, Jefford personally speeded progress by at least fifty per cent.

Jefford flew Seeley all over the Territory, surveying airports and airways. It was the roughest kind of pioneer work; the strategic pattern of the far-flung C.A.A. system bore little relation to that of existing Alaskan fields, and repeated landings must be made deep in the wilderness. It was also the hastiest, riskiest kind of emergency work. On one rush trip to Anchorage Jefford and Seeley were caught in a downpour. Their ship iced up. Jefford barely managed, by following the dim outline of a railroad track, to land on the Cordova field, which was covered with half an inch of water. The deluge continued but after twenty minutes he decided to make another try for his base. He climbed up over a mountain range and was flying blind when ice again weighted the wings. He dropped to a warmer level to shake it, found a break in the cloud and flew to the mouth of narrow Portage Pass.

The twisting canyon was plugged nearly to the bottom with fog but he flew in. As he rounded a right-angle turn the plane was enveloped in murk. Wind tossed it down till it was only thirty feet above the rough face of a glacier. A passenger, sitting with his seat belt unfastened, was thrown headlong against the cabin ceiling. "Jack admitted it was close," Seeley reports. "In fact, he said it was the worst few minutes he ever had in the air. If he hadn't known that pass like a book I wouldn't be here now."

Jefford was more than a pilot on the C.A.A. job. He helped select the airport sites: "We sifted out half the possibilities," Seeley says, "as we flew along." He threw himself into the work with remarkable energy and versatility, working as hard on the ground as in the air. He helped "walk" the proposed runways, shoveled snow, dug holes. "He pitched in where it was really none of his business." One cold night, fearing that a thawing boiler would freeze without attention, he stayed with it in an Eskimo tent. "He's hardy. He can keep up with the natives and anyone else."

To reach a remote range site he landed the Cessna on a river bar, pumped up a rubber boat, and steered Seeley down two miles of whirling rapids. "Jefford has almost no experience as a boatman. But he got me there." Landing at the Naknek Army field after a grueling eight-hour Aleutian flight, he sat down in the radio station and spent the whole night sending coded weather reports. "What lid's that on there?" a C.A.A. operator at Anchorage complained. Grinning savagely, Jefford continued to work the key. There was a shortage of radio operators at Naknek and a job to do. He was doing it the best he knew how.

Fascinated by the problem of frozen-ground construction, Jefford quizzed Seeley about them for hours on end. Before long, he was making practical suggestions. "He has a brilliant technical imagination. Whatever a job is, he can size up the best way to do it easily and well." Seeley, an expert with many years of experience in the States, South America, and Alaska, insists that Jefford has missed his calling. "That man," he maintains, "should be a construction engineer."

When a Diesel engine broke down Jefford insisted on tinkering with it till he had it running again. "He loves to fool with machinery." He enjoyed driving tractors through the snow. His curiosity and craving for action were also insatiable after work hours. Finding a gold mine near one of the sites, he crawled into a large bulldozer and operated that. He climbed into a locomotive on the Copper River Railroad and said he would return after the war and run it for a week. During rare Sundays of leisure at his Anchorage base he built a sixteen-foot boat. "Jefford doesn't know what rest is. He can run anything and build anything, and he always wants to try something new."

As the C.A.A. program expanded, officials decided to purchase a large plane for heavy freighting. It was a great day for Jefford, early in 1943, when he got the DC-3. At the time there was only one other ship of this size in the Territory. He gave the transport a nickname—*"King Chris"**—and he has had the title painted with a crown on the side of the nose. But he has made no attempt to dress up to his silver airliner. His favorite garment is a fur parka made of rare sik-sik-puk skins which he bought from Archie Ferguson. The headgear he likes most is a filthy railroad engineer's cap scribbled with numbers and names. The first time he wore this cap to work the C.A.A. mechanics laughed and the girls in the office kidded him. But it did not look out of place as he boarded his government transport. The ship, like the man, is a workhorse.

Freighting to remote C.A.A. sites, Jefford has flown his Douglas as another man would fly a Stinson. He has landed the plane, fully loaded, in unfavorable winds, on "runways" that would curl the hair of its Santa Monica engineers. Once he set *King Chris* down on top of a bluff at Tin City on an abandoned mine strip 950 feet long. Asked how much of this runway he used in take-off, he replied: "All of it. I do not plan to go back." He regularly used small strips like the one at Unalakleet—so rough and short and buffeted by crosswinds that after a reconnaissance plane nosed up on it the Army closed it to military aircraft. To serve a C.A.A. station on St. Lawrence Island he lands the airliner in early winter on the snow-covered "main street" of an Eskimo village. There are boat racks on one side, houses on the other, and the wings nearly graze them on both sides.

Jefford was soon discontented with his airliner because it was not equipped for heavy freighting. He persuaded the C.A.A. to let him fly it to Texas, where $27,000 was spent converting it into what he calls a "DC-3½-BD (Big Door)." A licensed C.A.A. mechanic, Jefford personally supervised the major structural alteration, first of its kind to be made on a DC-3. He had the door width nearly doubled to forty-eight inches and a heavy cargo floor installed. He also had the cabin equipped with a winch and pulleys to haul and secure heavy loads, and secured an A-frame with a hoist to be

---

* In honor of his friend Chris Lample, Assistant Superintendent of Airways in Washington, who supervised the Alaska program.

carried in the plane, so that he and his co-pilot could unload the weightiest equipment by themselves.

Impatient with delays on the DC-3½-BD job, Jefford donned coveralls and worked day and night welding and hammering alongside of the Texas mechanics. A C.A.A. official reminded him of the conventional dignity of the pilot. "What's more important?" the grease-smeared flyer asked, "for me to be dignified or to get this thing in the air again?" He continued until the work was done.

Although he holds a scheduled airline transport rating, Jefford has turned down commercial offers at twice his government pay. Seldom have a man and a job been so well suited. The C.A.A. pilots enjoy an unusual combination of modern equipment and frontier freedom. All Alaska is their province. Bush operators have traveled as far and wide but not as a matter of daily routine. "We have our own little airline," Jefford boasts. "We fly everywhere and we haul everything on it. If we ever have a uniform it's going to be the real thing. We'll have hats like MacArthur, boots like the Russians, and international-orange pants!"

In one month Jefford had flown *King Chris* a total of 93,000 passenger miles and 49,930,000 freight-pound miles. *King Chris* had carried a 10,000-pound paving machine, in two trips. It had hauled the eight-foot frame of a TD 18 tractor. It had hauled 6,500-pound Diesel engine and electric generator installations, TLC radio transmitters, each broken down into eighteen pieces, some seven feet long. Knocked-down houses, cement, jeeps, tractors, fuel oil, drills, pipe, beacons—almost everything for the airways had by one means or another been fitted into *King Chris* and carried through the sky—even a 3,000-foot coil of heavy cable. Jefford and the mechanics had to twist it into a figure eight to cram it inside the fuselage.

By 1945, with construction virtually complete, Jefford's job had changed. Flying king of the 8,000-mile airways system, he both ruled and served it. He was ever vigilant for range course displacements or other malfunctioning of the radio aids. He was ever vigilant, too, for human error in the C.A.A.'s far-flung organization of newly trained radio operators. Knowing intimately the needs of both bush and instrument flyers, he was ever on the watch to see that they were met. To keep the C.A.A. personnel on its toes, he called the stations from time to time asking flight advice. "Our chief gripe," he wrote in the C.A.A. paper *Mukluk Telegraph*, "is the time taken to give us a heading. As time goes on we will make the problems more difficult, with drift, etc. to be computed. We have not yet called on Anchorage, which, as we all know, is the nucleus of brains and master minds, but when we do it will be a good one, with double drift, loop orientation, and all the fixings."

There was less freight to be hauled, but Jefford had his hands full with a host of C.A.A. problems, large and small. When the captain of the *Waipio*, last summer boat to Barrow, hesitated to proceed north of Kotzebue because of floating ice, C.A.A. workers at Barrow were anxious; the ship carried all their winter supplies. Jefford flew the captain 900 miles over the Arctic Ocean and persuaded him it was safe to go on. When the C.A.A. faced an acute shortage of radio operators Jefford noted and reported the remarkable skill of Irving Inguruk, self-taught Eskimo at Gambell. He was hired. Each Christmas, Jefford flew some twenty-five hundred miles across Alaska with loads of turkey, cranberries and all the trimmings for Yuletide dinners at the remote C.A.A. stations. On Christmas Eve of 1944 he did more than this.

Returning to Anchorage after a turbulent six-hour flight, he was settling down to his first eggnog when the telephone rang. There was trouble, he learned, at the Farewell station. One of the operators had a stroke and another had caught his finger in an engine. Accompanied by a communications chief from headquarters, Jefford and co-pilot Bill Hanson drove back to the field and flew to Farewell through a snowstorm. As C.A.A. workers carried the sick man to the plane, one of them slipped and broke his leg. Jefford flew the three victims back to the Anchorage hospital and arrived home at 4:30 Christmas morning.

In Alaska's system of airways, maintained by the government, Jefford's was an important trouble-shooting job. But the pioneering was over—and he was restless. Intrigued by reports of an island lying north of Barrow, he wanted to fly out and find it. He talked for some time about crossing the polar sea to Europe. During a trip to the States he took a course in celestial navigation. "I want to fly the oceans," he explained.

Those who knew Jefford predicted that Alaska would not hold him long. He had flown the Territory as low as fifty feet, and his mind held a vision of its every jagged peak and twisting river. But he had another vision of Alaska: long, hard-surfaced runways lying handily near the top of the globe on the natural, short airline route between continents.

This was a vision that pilots of the North have had since the days of Ben Eielson. Jefford is one of the few former bush flyers who experienced it in fact, flying Alaska at the controls of huge, multimotored *Queen Mary's* of the air. He has flown the world as skillfully as he flew Alaska, as casually as he flips a silver dollar, as gaily as he leads the Eskimo musicians at Unalakleet.

Index